Europe as a Cultural Area

World Anthropology

General Editor

SOL TAX

Patrons

CLAUDE LÉVI-STRAUSS
MARGARET MEAD†
LAILA SHUKRY EL HAMAMSY
M. N. SRINIVAS

MOUTON PUBLISHERS · THE HAGUE · PARIS · NEW YORK

Europe as a Cultural Area

Editor

JEAN CUISENIER

MOUTON PUBLISHERS · THE HAGUE · PARIS · NEW YORK

ISBN 90–279 7790–9 (Mouton)
0–202–90086–X (Aldine)
Cover and jacket design by Jurriaan Schrofer
Jacket photo by Cas Oorthuys
Indexes by Society of Indexers, Great Britain
Phototypeset in V.I.P. Times by
Western Printing Services Ltd, Bristol
Printed in Great Britain

General Editor's Preface

If the continent of Europe is an area which particularly requires cooperation between historians and social scientists, then anthropologists are the obvious brokers. The present book states the conditions and provides the data for what will, hopefully, stimulate the rapid development of what the Editor calls "historical anthropology." This happy outcome appears to stem only from the scholarly tradition of Europe alone, since none of the authors in the book are Africans, Asians, or Latin Americans. In fact, however, it derives from the absorption, in our post-colonial world, of a worldwide comparative perspective. Indeed, the book is one of the products of a congress of scholars unusually representative of that new world.

Like most contemporary sciences, anthropology is a product of the European tradition. Some argue that it is a product of colonialism, with one small and self-interested part of the species dominating the study of the whole. If we are to understand the species, our science needs substantial input from scholars who represent a variety of the world's cultures. It was a deliberate purpose of the IXth International Congress of Anthropological and Ethnological Sciences to provide impetus in this direction. The *World Anthropology* volumes, therefore, offer a first glimpse of a human science in which members from all societies have played an active role. Each of the books is designed to be self-contained; each is an attempt to update its particular sector of scientific knowledge and is written by specialists from all parts of the world. Each volume should be read and reviewed individually as a separate volume on its own given subject. The set as a whole will indicate what changes are in store for anthropology as scholars from the developing countries join in studying the species of which we are all a part.

The IXth Congress was planned from the beginning not only to include as many of the scholars from every part of the world as possible, but also with a view toward the eventual publication of the papers in high-quality volumes. At previous Congresses scholars were invited to bring papers which were then read out loud. They were necessarily limited in length; many were only summarized; there was little time for discussion; and the sparse discussion could only be in one language. The IXth Congress was an experiment aimed at changing this. Papers were written with the intention of exchanging them before the Congress, particularly in extensive pre-Congress sessions; they were not intended to be read aloud at the Congress, that time being devoted to discussions — discussions which were simultaneously and professionally translated into five languages. The method for eliciting the papers was structured to make as representative a sample as was allowable when scholarly creativity — hence self-selection — was critically important. Scholars were asked both to propose papers of their own and to suggest topics for sessions of the Congress which they might edit into volumes. All were then informed of the suggestions and encouraged to re-think their own papers and the topics. The process, therefore, was a continuous one of feedback and exchange and it has continued to be so even after the Congress. The some two thousand papers comprising *World Anthropology* certainly then offer a substantial sample of world anthropology. It has been said that anthropology is at a turning point; if this is so, these volumes will be the historical direction-markers.

As might have been foreseen in the first post-colonial generation, the large majority of the Congress papers (82 percent) are the work of scholars identified with the industrialized world which fathered our traditional discipline and the institution of the Congress itself: Eastern Europe (15 percent); Western Europe (16 percent); North America (47 percent); Japan, South Africa, Australia, and New Zealand (4 percent). Only 18 percent of the papers are from developing areas: Africa (4 percent); Asia-Oceania (9 percent); Latin America (5 percent). Aside from the substantial representation from the U.S.S.R. and the nations of Eastern Europe, a significant difference between this corpus of written material and that of other Congresses is the addition of the large proportion of contributions from Africa, Asia, and Latin America. "Only 18 percent" is two to four times as great a proportion as that of other Congresses; moreover, 18 percent of 2,000 papers is 360 papers, 10 times the number of "Third World" papers presented at previous Congresses. In fact, these 360 papers are more than the total of *all* papers published after the last International Congress of Anthropological and Ethnological Sciences which was held in the United States (Philadelphia, 1956).

The significance of the increase is not simply quantitative. The input of scholars from areas which have until recently been no more than subject matter for anthropology represents both feedback and also long-awaited theoretical contributions from the perspectives of very different cultural, social, and historical traditions. Many who attended the IXth Congress were convinced that anthropology would not be the same in the future. The fact that the Xth Congress (India, 1978) was our first in the "Third World" may be symbolic of the change. Meanwhile, sober consideration of the present set of books will show how much, and just where and how, our discipline is being revolutionized.

Readers of the present volume will be especially interested in other books in the series treating problems of historical and cultural theory and the history of ideas, as well as those which provide comparative data on other continental areas.

Chicago, Illinois   SOL TAX
January 10, 1979

Table of Contents

Introduction

JEAN CUISENIER

During the IXth ICAES more than two hundred and forty communications whose theme, subject matter or field of investigation was Europe were issued. Was this to be interpreted as a revival of anthropologists' interest in an area more easily accessible than Africa, Asia, or the Middle East, which are gradually closing their doors to foreign ethnographical research? Or a significant symposium gathering of specialists in the European aspect of fields as different as folklore, archaeology, history and museology, linguistics and ethnology, who found there the opportunity for an interdisciplinary approach? Or else a new interest shared by an increasing number of intellectuals as regards the destiny of that part of the world, the motherland of anthropology?

Whatever the case it is true that after being deserted for the benefit of other parts of the world, Europe is gradually becoming a preferred place for anthropological research. But we would be mediocre anthropologists if we were content with stating that fact without trying to interpret it. In fact the growing interest for Europe is not really new. It is only a revival. During the Enlightenment the inquisitiveness of naturalists, men of letters, engineers, physicists, doctors, and jurists was as acute as regards Europe as regards other parts of the world. As a matter of fact, in Diderot and d'Alembert's *Encyclopédie*, the chapters devoted to *technique* were a compilation of the knowledge acquired mainly by European societies rather than by other civilizations. During the nineteenth century anthropological research as regards Europe was very active, and included the identification of monuments and ancient sites, archaeological excavations, investigations in dialectology, fauna and flora surveys, and compilation of customs, proverbs, common sayings, tales and legends. Nowadays we can see clearly how much all this was linked to the nationalist movement, and promoted by the desire to set up, region by region, the principles of a cultural identity. We better understand now how it provided with arguments those who, politicians and patriots, were fighting in order that the relations between the state and civil society be organized on a national basis. But at the end of the First World War this period of intense activity gave way to one of withdrawal and a general decrease in research. There were many reasons for this, and not least among them the heavy losses of people, from which the university communities were not spared, for most of the members of the French school of sociology died on the battlefield. Yet, no matter how heavy the loss, it does not account for the fact that between the wars most of the anthropologists in England, France, Scandinavia, and Italy preferred an exotic field of research to a European one. The colonial tradition, which was then triumphant, bears a great responsibility for that choice, even if later on anthropological research was to question it. Indeed colonialism, the violence of which was the counterpart outside Europe of the violence within, revealed to the anthropologists a difference between civilizations more important than the one they experienced in their own European society. Social anthropology appeared at that time and had no link with dialectology, folklore, and history such as they were used in and about Europe. Social anthropology and the other disciplines diverged from one another, becoming more and more alien to one another, being linked and backed by more and more different institutions: on the one hand the *Völkerkunde*, museums of ethnography, and departments of ethnology in universities, on the other hand the *Volkskunde*, museums of folk arts together with departments of folklore, dialectology, and regional history in universities.

Yet along with decolonization things changed once more. Countries which were formerly colonies rejected anthropology as being linked to colonial institutions. Others, anxious to avoid that anthropological studies carried out by foreign scientists be used for intelligence purposes, imposed upon their work limits incompatible with the usual standards of such a work. Others agreed to the presence of foreign anthropologists, sometimes even requesting their assistance, provided that their work of investigation was carried out in collaboration with colleagues of the country and was included in a program of economic development. Being more and more numerous, European anthropologists have recognized the fact that the non-European countries they are studying evaluate the methods used and the results reached according to political criteria. They have come to realize that the governments which are to deliver the certificates of registration and cooperation contracts are little interested in the general progress of knowledge, and much more attentive to the contribution that anthropology can make to the building of their nationalist states. Now, at the same time, the economic, social, and cultural bases of Europe and its nations changed more deeply than at any other former period. A vast range of countries emerged and the relations between the state authority and its ethnic components became less obvious and necessary. Consequently, the folklore, dialectology, and history studies which had justified the demand for frontiers but remained outside the general movement of social sciences acquired a new importance. Indeed, how can a European community or something alike be established without examining the supranationalism of its institutions, modifying the relations between the nation-states and giving a new definition of the relations between the central and regional authorities? How can we consider that situation without securing the elements for a detailed knowledge of regions, of their relations and the conflicts which oppose them, without analyzing the mechanisms at the root of their cultural identity and their basic principles? How can, what is called so rightly in the continental tradition, an "ethno-logy" be developed without the help of the hypotheses, instruments and techniques of the Anglo-Saxon social anthropology?

It is not then by mere chance that at the Congress such a large proportion of the contributions deals with Europe, and that those contributions belong to such different intellectual traditions. These differences provided the principle of the gathering of the contributions in this book. Since it was obviously impossible to publish all the texts, it was necessary to make a choice, and so three kinds of texts will be found in this volume, each being elaborated according to a specific intellectual tradition.

The first, written by William H. McNeill, deals with the main characteristics of European history. It was necessary to begin with a wide historical survey. It would be impossible to deal with European cultural differences as Kroeber did for North America — by favoring synchrony for lack of precise and abundant archaeological and historical data. The main point here is to take into account the length of the period. The anthropology of Europe, whether used by Japanese, Americans or Europeans, cannot be developed without a conceptual framework in accordance with the standards of European learning, or without the archivistic and archaeological documentation in accordance with the rules of the historical method. To what extent does McNeill's essay reach that aim? What does he teach ethnologists and historians? On what theoretical bases does he bring together social history according to Marc Bloch and Fernand Braudel and social anthropology according to Franz Boas and E. E. Evans-Pritchard?

The second series of texts is the result of Branimir Bratanić's work. In the first of his two contributions he sets forth the principles on which the European ethnographical atlas rests, and develops the obvious and specific problems which appear because of the unequal historical age of the cultures being treated. It is time now to examine the relevance of those ethnographical atlases which gather data belonging to the same ethnographical present-time. In fact they concern the old traditional folk culture. But that culture is disappearing everywhere, either more quickly here or more slowly there, so that the problem is always to compare what may be still alive somewhere with what disappeared some or even hundreds of years ago elsewhere. The question is whether this is legitimate. Yes, Bratanić asserts, if it is true:

... not only that history is a chronological sequence of events, a process (what it surely is), but also that what has happened, originated and remained as a result or product of the historical process and continues to live, to change, to 'move' at its own pace as a concrete pattern of cultural life (Bratanić, this volume, p. 106).

Bratanić's second contribution traces some of the similarities existing in peasant cultures thousands of miles apart, positing possible topographical reasons for their existence.

The third series of texts represents a significant sample of studies in anthropology, with papers by Matilde Callari-Galli and Gualtiero Harrison, Joel M. and Barbara K. Halpern, Claude Karnoouh, Mübeccel B. Kiray, Mihai Pop, Martine Segalen, and Paul-Henri Stahl. Each articulates in his own way the theoretical approach, the ethnographical description, and the historical inscription which are required for studies in European anthropology. Each develops his own method, which, whether right or wrong, I think will open later on to wider perspectives. For anthropology of the European field still remains on the whole a "task," whatever the intellectual tradition in which it is used. This volume will have achieved its aim if it could show that as regards European anthropology there is no need to sacrifice an intellectual tradition to another, but to study thoroughly each tradition by confronting one to another and building up what I would call a historical *anthropology*.

PART ONE

Time and Space

Patterns of European History

WILLIAM H. McNEILL

RÉSUMÉ: MODÈLES D'HISTOIRE EUROPEENNE

Notre concept de l' "Europe" est hérité des Grecs : divisée en une zone méditerranéenne et une zone atlantique et baltique, c'est la première qui, jusqu'en 1600, exerça une prééminence culturelle. Le pluralisme des sociétés et des cultures la mit sur la voie du modernisme. A partir des années 900, les centres économiques et culturels oscillèrent fréquemment, quand la Russie et l'Europe du Nord-Ouest, grâce à leurs voies navigables ainsi qu'aux progrès de la navigation maritime, participèrent au mouvement des marchandises et des hommes. L'Europe vit surgir soudain sur ses confins orientaux une puissance mongole, cependant que l'Espagne musulmane et Byzance déclinaient peu à peu et que l'Italie regroupait toutes les richesses, la puissance et les facultés créatrices du temps. Après une période d'apothéose, les empires ottoman, espagnol, et britannique entre autres manifestèrent leur suprématie par rapport à l'Italie, dont le rayonnement culturel s'exerça encore néanmoins pendant plus de 150 ans. Cependant, on peut considérer que 1500 constitue la charnière entre ce que l'on appelle traditionnellement le Moyen Age et les temps modernes.

Après cette date, de nouveaux modèles économiques et socio-culturells supplantèrent les anciens. L'invention de la poudre à canon bouleversa l'équilibre politique des puissances : les ottomans et espagnols reconquirent leur prééminence ; au nord-est, Ivan III et Basile III jetèrent les fondations d'un empire russe immense. En revanche, l'empire de Charles Quint, qui semblait former le noyau d'un territoire considérable, ne put résister à la concurrence des états voisins, militairement aussi bien équipés que lui-même, pour aboutir à une répartition des forces et à un état de guerre perpétuel entre les nations d'Europe occidentale, avec pour corollaire des divergences culturelles. Les contacts avec les Indes Occidentales et Orientales firent affluer biens, techniques et idées, entraînant un bouleversement des valeurs culturelles de tout le continent. Au terme d'une grave crise économique, au début du XVIIᵉ siècle, les pays méditerranéens, surpeuplés et pauvres en combustible, disparurent de la scène européenne jusqu'à la seconde moitié du XXᵉ siècle, quand l'électricité leur permit de sortir de l'impasse. En contrepoids à ce déclin, la Hollande, l'Angleterre et la France connurent un développement économique grâce à de nouvelles techniques agricoles, ainsi que par la mise en exploitation des mines de charbon, entraînant de profondes mutations sociales. Simultanément, la Russie et les nations de l'Europe de l'Est virent leur agriculture se développer. Parallèlement, cette époque connut un développement universel, artistique et intellectuel, ère des lumières en cours de laquelle les idées religieuses devaient être reconsidérées. La Révolution Française, qui succéda à la Révolution Américaine et dont les effects s'étendirent dans toute l'Europe, peut être mise sur le même plan, par ses conséquences, avec la révolution industrielle, les deux phénomènes concourant à parachever la suprématie définitive de l'Europe sur le reste du monde. Entre 1750 et 1850, les nouvelles ressources en produits alimentaires et en combustible, autant que la nouvelle mobilité sociale, constituèrent les fondements de cette révolution industrielle à l'échelle mondiale, et jusqu'en 1870, l'effervescence économique renforça le bouillonnement politique, aboutissant à un remaniement des structures sociales. Puis le processus d'industrialisation européen, plus particulièrement anglais, gagna l'Amérique où il s'emplifia grâce à une forte immigration d'Européens.

Vers 1914, les Allemands que avaient réalisé leur unification grâce à la guerre de 1870 s'attribuèrent la primauté dans le domaine industriel et dans celui de la recherche. La politique bismarckienne inquiétait l'Europe au point de susciter l'alliance de la France, de la Grande-Bretagne et de la Russie où deux élites rivales s'affrontaient pour s'emparer de la direction politique et économique du pays.

Au terme de la première guerre mondiale, les Etats-Unis étaient les protecteurs de la révolution nationaliste en Europe, trainant dans leur sillage la France et la Grande-Bretagne récalcitrantes, cependant que la Russie se plaçait à la tête de la lutte de classes.

Le XIXe siècle constitua un âge d'or, où les arts et les sciences connurent un développement tel que l'Europe accéda à la domination du monde par les sciences, la technologie et sur le plan intellectuel. Cette époque vit se constituer deux super-puissances à l'est et à l'ouest : la Russie et l'Amérique.

La deuxième guerre mondiale entraîna des migrations et des remaniements économiques d'une ampleur telle, que les frontières — obstacles majeurs au XIXe et au début du XXe siècle — perdirent leur rôle, resultat paradoxal et inattendu de toute la politique hitlérienne. Les progrès technologiques en matière d'armement, puis l'utilisation de l'atome, fruit d'une collaboration internationale, conduisirent après la fin de la deuxième guerre mondiale à modifier les rapports entre les inventions et le marché économique.

Le rôle prééminent de l'Europe se maintint dans le monde, en dépit de la perte de ses colonies d'Afrique et d'Asie, d'une part, et d'autre part de sa division en deux zones d'influence (l'Europe orientale fut soumise par la Russie à un régime semi-colonial cependant que l'occident était entraîné dans l'orbite américaine). Mais on peut se demander si l'avenir ne verra pas l'Europe reconquérir une indépendance effective fondée sur de nouvelles structures politiques transnationales, où Français, Anglais, Allemands et Italiens regroupés constitueraient une force nouvelle apte à jouer un rôle mondial.

The pages that follow were written for historians rather than for ethnologists and anthropologists and were aimed at an American rather than at a European audience. Experts with other backgrounds and concerns will probably find odd discrepancies and some glaring biases. The intellectual justification for this essay is that both the available models for understanding the history of Europe as a whole — the Marxian and the Liberal — show serious signs of wear. Not everyone will agree with this assertion and an effort to improve upon nineteenth-century theories will only be welcome insofar as men recognize inadequacies in the older views. Defenders of the Liberal version of European history (which, in its pure form, declared that what mattered in the tangled record of the past was the growth of limited and representative government) would be hard to find today. Marxism, on the other hand, commands a considerable following, both in socialist countries, where the government officially supports Marxian doctrine, and in lands where no single political orthodoxy exists. Yet Marxism has come to mean many different things, so that some of the generalizations advanced in the pages that follow will seem familiar and acceptable enough to some Marxists, even if the notion of a plurality of cultural styles and civilizational centers is alien and unacceptable.

The organizing concepts behind my remarks on the shape of European history derive mainly from an almost casual undergraduate encounter with cultural anthropology as taught by Robert Redfield. The immediate occasion for writing this essay, however, was a clarification of my view of Europe's past that took shape as I worked on a history of Venetian relations with Orthodox and Ottoman Europe between the eleventh and the eighteenth centuries. Hence a modest kind of disciplinary cross-fertilization lies behind this work, though my acquaintance with anthropology and ethnology remains fragmentary and largely accidental. Whether such an essay will survive professional criticism from anthropologists and ethnologists specializing in European studies remains to be seen, and whether such a hasty overview of Europe's past is of any use to students of these subjects is even more problematical. But an international congress seems an ideal place to find answers to both questions.

EUROPE TO A.D. 900

Like so much else, our concept of "Europe" as contrasted with Asia and Africa descends from ancient Greece. Early Hellenic seamen located Asia on the eastern side of one of the most easily traveled seas of the earth — the Aegean — and located Africa to the south of an only slightly more difficult traverse between Crete and Egypt-Libya. Yet the terms stuck, largely because the cultural configurations of the time gave "Asia" and "Africa", thus defined, a palpable reality, capable of challenging Greek autonomy, as the invasion of Xerxes' armies, and Herodotus' awe at the attainments of the sophisticated Egyptians clearly showed. The effort to use the Urals and Caucasus as boundary lines came much later, though still within classical times, as a way of lending precision to what by

then had become a fixed habit of thought among Greeks and those influenced by them.

This evolution of geographical terms points to an important fact of
human geography. Distant and culturally alien lands like "Asia" and
"Africa" were named by Greek seamen because their ships took them
there. Travel overland was far more difficult, and when it came to
carrying goods, costly, since pack animals had to be fed, whereas a sailing
ship, once put together, derived its movement from the boundless air. As
a result, under the conditions of transport prevailing until the mid-
nineteenth century, when railroads began to change things, water transport was so much superior to transport overland that large concentrations
of men who did not produce their own food by their own muscular effort
could only flourish close to navigable water. Cities that could not be
reached by shipping remained small and comparatively unimportant.
Waterways, therefore, remained until very recently the major determinants of where cities and civilizations arose.

Europe's configuration divides the continent into a southern or
Mediterranean zone and a northern or Atlantic and Baltic zone, depending on which way navigable streams run. Despite several important
military incursions from the north, until about 1600 the Mediterranean
zone of Europe remained culturally dominant; since that date the Atlantic zone has surpassed the more ancient centers of the south in most
respects. This is probably the most important watershed in European
history, though four hundred years of Atlantic dominance is a small
segment of time to set against the four thousand years during which the
Mediterranean zone of Europe was culturally ahead of the north.

Mediterranean primacy rested partly on historical circumstance. The
earliest European civilized societies were domiciled around the shores of
the Aegean. Subsequent ages inherited skills and techniques which,
elaborated over time, sustained comparatively vast concentrations of
wealth and population at varying key locations within the Mediterranean
zone, from the beginnings of Minoan civilization in Crete (circa 2100
B.C.) until the present. On this basis, a long series of civilizations arose and
flourished within Europe's Mediterranean zone. No other part of the
continent enjoyed such an inheritance, and to overtake and surpass the
achievements of the men of the south was not easy, given the severer
climate and initial technical handicaps under which northern peoples
labored.

These technical differentials between north and south constituted a
second basis for Mediterranean primacy. They were fundamentally twofold: agricultural in the first place, nautical in the second. The agricultural
superiority of Mediterranean lands over northerly ones lasted only until
A.D. 900 or thereabouts; hence this section breaks off at the time when
one of the important bases of Mediterranean primacy disappeared. The

nautical superiority of the Mediterranean lasted longer, for it was only shortly before 1500 that improvements in ship design and navigation began to make travel on the stormy and tide-troubled Atlantic waters almost as safe as seafaring within the Mediterranean. As this was achieved, northern-built ships came to enjoy a clear superiority to less stoutly constructed Mediterranean vessels, and the second technical basis of Mediterranean cultural primacy dissolved. Within about a century, Atlantic Europe was in a position to overcome its age-old deficiencies *vis-à-vis* the south, and in due season, soon after 1600, for the first time took over cultural leadership of the continent as a whole.

Throughout pre-modern times, the steppes of the Ukraine, Rumania, and Hungary constituted a different kind of sea — a sea of grass — across which horse nomads traveled with an ease and speed rivaling that of seamen. Nomads ordinarily could not conveniently carry large, bulky goods; they often preferred rapine and raiding to more peaceful encounters, since their superior mobility gave them persistent advantages in military confrontations with settled, agricultural folk. On occasion, however, civilized defenses made raiding costly, inducing nomads to fall back on more peaceful trading. Their abundant animals made it comparatively easy for them to organize pack trains capable of carrying goods of high value in proportion to their bulk for very long distances.

The nomads of the steppes checked agricultural exploitation of the fertile Ukrainian grasslands for many centuries. Not until after 1600, when handguns transformed the age-old military balance between agricultural and nomad communities, did the steppes of southeastern Europe really open up for pioneer settlement, although in earlier ages there had been several periods during which relatively peaceful conditions permitted cultivators to extend their fields into the grasslands on a significant, though never on a decisive, scale. Such advances of agriculture were subsequently rolled back when new and more ruthless raiders arrived from the east, ravaging farmsteads, slaughtering or enslaving whomever they could catch, and driving survivors to take refuge in the forests of the north or in the Carpathian and other mountain zones lying south and west.

The soil and climate of the forested zone of eastern Europe made agriculture a less rewarding occupation than it was in more westerly parts of the continent, where in most years a longer growing season and richer soils allowed a better return on seed than was to be expected in the northeast. The marginal character of cereal cultivation in Sweden, Poland, and Russia,[1] combined with the exposure of the more fertile parts

---

[1]   Seed to harvest ratios of 1:2 and 1:3 were more or less normal; in a bad year total loss, or a harvest only a little larger than the seed that had been planted, was to be expected. By contrast, seed to harvest ratios of 1:10 were possible and 1:4 or 1:5 were common in western Europe. See the very instructive data gathered in Slicher van Bath (1963).

of the two latter lands to nomad raiding from the steppes, meant that only small populations, dependent in part on hunting and gathering from the forests, could survive in most of these regions, at least as long as the steppe nomads remained a threat.

Yet the vast reaches of Russian rivers, easily navigable for hundreds or even thousands of miles, made it possible to gather trade goods — furs, wax, honey, slaves, amber — across comparatively long distances. Beginning in the tenth century, the same arterial system allowed state building on a territorially vast scale despite the sparse and impoverished condition of the population. Rivers, in short, did for northeastern Europe what seas did for the south — provided a means of easy transport across long distances. Northwestern Europe had the best of both worlds, enjoying access to a fine natural network of navigable waterways debouching into a number of narrow and at least relatively protected seas: the Baltic, the North Sea, and the English Channel. Yet this advantage remained only potential until techniques of ship-building and navigation reduced movement by sea to routine regularity. In a similar fashion, the full potential of the Russian river system could not develop without free movement across the sea of grass lying to the south. The struggle of Russian agriculturalists and rivermen to stave off or overcome the horsemen of the steppes was analogous to the problem northwestern Europeans faced in trying to tame the tides and storms of the Atlantic waters. The one called for military, and the other for naval, organization and technique; the one confronted a human opponent, the other struggled against natural forces. Both aimed at breaking through a persistent barrier to movement of men and goods; and neither succeeded in more than sporadic and temporary fashion until after A.D. 900.

The Mediterranean zone lacked large navigable rivers, with the conspicuous exception of the Nile , the Po, and the rivers debouching into the Black Sea. As long as their horses sustained their military dominance, the nomads of the steppes deprived the Black Sea rivers of most of their potential significance. But the Nile from deep antiquity and the Po from A.D. 900 provided a basis for local and markedly individualized styles of civilization that stand somewhat apart from the cultural history of the rest of the Mediterranean. That history turned on movement across open water, whether the Mediterranean proper or its connecting seas — the Black, the Aegean, and the Adriatic. Navigation in these waters required far less skill than was needed amid the storms and tides of the Atlantic and its connecting seas. Yet the storms which do afflict the Mediterranean during winter months were more than ships and mariners of Greek and Roman times cared to confront, and with good reason, as the Bible story of Saint Paul's shipwreck may remind us. Indeed, in ancient times, it was customary to haul ships ashore in winter and to sail only during the season of the year when the trades, blowing steadily from the northeast under constantly clear skies, made navigation easy. Since grain harvest fell in May or in June, and good sailing weather lasted until about October, this allowed enough time to carry grain supplies to whatever capital city or cities dominated Mediterranean shores. This essential attended to, movements of other goods and of men could and did accommodate the seasonal pattern of Mediterranean shipping without much difficulty.

Capacity to concentrate enough food to support scores of thousands of city folk who did not raise their own food was an important prerequisite for developing the kind of culture in the Mediterranean zone that was capable of commanding admiration and inspiring imitation elsewhere in Europe. This required not only ships and sailors, but a hinterland whose inhabitants were either compelled or induced to produce and part with a surplus of grain and other commodities. This sleight of hand, prerequisite for all pre-modern civilizations, was achieved sometimes by force, sometimes by offering goods produced in civilized workshops in exchange. In most situations both elements were present; and both trade and compulsion often achieved a customary definition that softened and disguised the collision of interests involved in such exchanges.

Characteristically, rents and taxes were collected by force or threat of force. Local magnates usually collected small surpluses locally, playing the role of landlord, and then exchanged part of what they had thus accumulated for luxury goods brought from afar. Such civilized luxuries were offered for sale by seafaring merchants whose numerical weakness *vis-à-vis* local populations made forcible seizure of desired local commodities — grain, metals, lumber — impracticable. This sort of symbiosis between a local landlord class and civilized merchants and traders allowed relatively smooth concentration of food and other raw materials at the center. Local landlords, glimpsing the refinements and luxuries of civilized life, became barbarians *par excellence*: they were aware of what was possible, and aware also of their own inability to rival locally the products and skills of full-blown urban civilization.

In ancient times the Mediterranean urban centers had more than fine cloth and trinkets with which to charm the barbarians of the European hinterland. Olive oil and wine served as civilized staple exports. These were commodities requiring some capital, for a first crop could only be produced after several years of waiting for the trees and vines to begin to bear fruit. In addition, olive trees will not survive severe or prolonged frost. This set sharp limits on their habitat even within Mediterranean lands. Some skill and fairly elaborate machinery are also needed to produce wine and oil from the fruit as it comes from the vines and trees. Yet once the uses of wine and of oil became familiar, landlords and chieftains of the backwoods areas of the ancient Mediterranean, wherever they lived, were willing, indeed eager, to exchange grain and other products of their fields and forests for wine and oil.

Terms of this trade favored the civilized center. The produce of an acre of land in vines or olive trees could usually be exchanged for a quantity of grain that required far more ground. This made it practicable to concentrate relatively large amounts of food and raw materials in places where wine and oil were available for export. In effect, the pattern of trade enlisted the active cooperation of thousands of distant landlords in the delicate and difficult task of squeezing unrequited goods and services from the peasantry. Only after local magnates had collected a quantity of goods in demand at the civilized center could they hope to exchange such goods for the wine and oil they had come to prize so highly.

In the earlier stages of Mediterranean civilized history this pattern of exchange was of central importance. Crete appears to have been the first great center of both wine and oil export; the wealth of Minoan palaces probably depended upon exchange of these two commodities for metals, grain, and whatever else the lords of Knossos required or took delight in bringing to their courts. Similar exchanges may also have helped sustain the might of Mycenae, although there can be no doubt that direct resort to force — the plundering of distant coasts and sacking of cities as celebrated by Homer — played a much larger role in Mycenaean economics than had been the case in Minoan times.

We are much better informed about classical Greece, where first Ionia and then Attica rose to prosperity and mercantile preeminence with the help of massive oil and wine exports. To be sure, Athens in its most glorious days supplemented income from trade with tribute monies collected from subject cities all round the Aegean; but many if not most of these tribute-paying communities in turn derived the means wherewith to pay the assessed tribute by exporting wine and oil.

In the fifth century B.C. market production of wine and oil was still quite new, and was restricted to the Aegean area for the most part. Yet Greek vessels made these products available throughout the Mediterranean coastlands. Response among Scyths, Thracians, Macedonians, Illyrians, Italians, and other barbarians was tremendous. In later times terms of trade within the Mediterranean regions never favored oil and wine producers so strongly. It was never afterwards possible to concentrate such a preponderance as Athens enjoyed from 479 to 431 B.C. without resort to taxes, rents, and tributes on a far larger scale than anything of which Pericles or even Cleon conceived.

The special quality of Athenian culture in its golden age, when custom lost its hold and everything had to be examined and considered afresh, was deeply tinctured by this unique geo-economic balance between an oil-wine export metropolis and a hinterland eager to accept all that the Athenians and their fellow Greeks cared to spare from their own consumption of these commodities. In particular the equal participation of citizen farmers in the affairs of the Athenian polis was sustained by the active role these same farmers had in the production and marketing of the wine and oil whose export, more than anything else, sustained the entire Athenian economy. City folk could not afford to scorn and deride those whose land and labor provided such a vital link in the city's prosperity; still less could they neglect the armed and organized might of these same stalwart farmers, concentrated in the city's phalanx. In this fashion a firm bond between urban and rural segments of the Athenian citizenry could be maintained. The agricultural producers of Attica, instead of sinking to the level of an excluded and oppressed peasantry (as seemed to be happening before Peisistratus, who ruled from 554 to 527 B.C., organized production of wine and oil for export), instead came to embody the very essence of the civilized ideal. The Athenian farmers were free men, each the master of himself and his land, head of his family and household, and an autonomous participant in public affairs, with the right to vote on all important matters of policy.

Lest we idealize Greek democracy unduly, it is worth reminding ourselves that foreigners and slaves resident in Attica did not participate in public life, and by the time Athens' power crested in the latter part of the fifth century B.C., slaves and foreigners had become almost as numerous as citizens. Moreover, the freedom and civil equality that prevailed among the Athenian citizenry depended upon the labors of distant cultivators who raised the grain the Athenians consumed. Like excluded peasantries the world around, these distant populations did not share directly or indirectly in the high culture generated by the city their labors helped to sustain.

Collective exploitation of distant communities is not necessarily less oppressive than similar exploitation by individual landlords or industrial entrepreneurs. Indeed it is arguable that when the exploiting collective is large enough its members may be insulated from any lively fellow-feeling with their victims by the sustaining force of their own in-group norms and standards; whereas a landlord, living in semi-isolation from his peers and close beside those whom he exploits, may lack the practical means and psychological insulation required to carry exploitation to its greatest practicable extent.

Yet viewed from within the exploitative community, the phenomenon was entirely different. Instead of being surrounded by "inferiors," members of the privileged community were surrounded by "equals." Possibilities of open-ended and open-minded encounter within such a community were enormously enhanced. In the city's golden age the citizens of Athens lived modestly, but all had enough to eat without working very hard. Vineyards and olive groves of the modest size ordinary Athenians possessed required some sixty to eighty days' work per annum; the rest of the time men could devote safely enough to noneconomic concerns.

Indeed, the real measure of the city's wealth was the leisure its citizens enjoyed without starving.

A leisured mass of citizens several thousand strong constituted the best possible audience for anyone who had something special to say, whether about practical or theoretical questions. As a result, literary, intellectual, and artistic creativity have never been so intensely concentrated before or since; and the subsequent influence of classical Greek culture upon European (and Islamic) civilizations enhances the significance of what was then achieved.

Being first to elaborate a literary and learned tradition that has lasted uninterruptedly to the present mattered a great deal. Assumptions and biases that have been taken for granted ever since among European men of letters could establish themselves easily merely because there were no competing notions about to dispute the ground. An example: no logical necessity supports the assumption that the most important human association beyond the nuclear family is the territorial state. Yet this notion pervaded Greek and subsequent European life all the more forcefully because it was so often taken for granted. Even more remarkable is the implausibly bold speculation that just as human affairs could be regulated by law, agreed to and recognized in public assembly of the citizens, so also the behavior of natural objects and forces might conform to laws, if only men were clever and observant enough to discover what they were. European natural science, whose importance in recent centuries has been enormous, would be inconceivable without this assumption. Yet there is remarkably little in the behavior of earth, wind, and water, as observable to ordinary men engaged in ordinary occupations, to justify such a wild assumption.

Even the movements of the heavenly bodies, when considered closely, offered stubborn resistances to being reduced to definite "laws," although persistence in what an outsider would surely have regarded as a vain pursuit did pay off after centuries of effort in the form of Ptolemy's *Almagest*, and a mechanical model of the universe that accounted for almost everything — except for such conspicuous motions as those of comets and shooting stars!

Being first enhanced Athens' historical significance enormously. Moreover I find it impossible to deny that the Athenian model of high culture had a kind of intrinsic excellence that sets it apart from all other great civilizations. Such a judgment smacks of ethnocentrism. And it is true that the early Pharaohs, for instance, built their pyramids and other monuments with a perfection unequaled later. Yet the range of the Pharaonic culture and its capacity for later growth was far less than that which inhered in Greek civilization. Other early classic formulations of great cultures — Confucian, Buddhist, Judaic, Islamic — that have endured to the present seem somehow narrower, perhaps because what has survived to our times from these ancient fonts of inspiration has been encapsulated into organized religions. In the process discordancies were largely edited out. No single hand ever edited the diverse literature of ancient Greece, though the taste of generations and accidents of copy-making and survival have certainly left deep marks on our classical inheritance and may, for instance, exaggerate the primacy of Athens by combing out texts that originated elsewhere.

Yet when all appropriate reservations have been made, there remains a special awe and reverence for what the Athenians and a few other Greeks accomplished. Who can compare with Herodotus and Thucydides among early writers of history? Or who can match Plato and Aristotle among philosophers? What literature excels Homer, Aeschylus, Sophocles, and Euripides? And classical Greek art, with its idealized naturalism and technical mastery, can surely bear comparison with any other art tradition of the earth, though the unique value nineteenth-century art critics once assigned to it is perhaps unacceptable in an age when contemporary artists have so emphatically repudiated the entire classical inheritance.

In such matters there is great danger of naïveté. One praises the familiar and may be tempted to reject strange ideas and disregard alien traditions of art simply because they arouse no echoes from prior personal experience. It may therefore be a confession of my own culture-boundedness to say that the classical Greek style of civilization seems to excel all its contemporaries. Yet there is this tangible basis for such an assertion: men in Macedon, Asia Minor, Scythia and central Europe, Italy, Carthage, Syria, Parthia, Egypt, and even Judea, all found Greek accomplishments impressive. They proved this by borrowing aspects of Greek civilization when Alexander's conquests (334–322 B.C.) and subsequent churnings of peoples and armies throughout Mediterranean and Near Eastern lands brought the achievements of classical Greece — warlike as well as peaceful — vividly to their attention. Elements of Greek art and thought seeped even into distant India and China, modified and transformed in the process of transmission all the way from one side of Asia to the other, yet recognizably continuous throughout. For more than half a millennium everybody who could borrowed from the Greeks. Some, like the Romans, took so much that their own traditions were almost overwhelmed. But borrowing ran both ways. Thus the spread of mystery religions of salvation among Hellenized populations of the Mediterranean brought what had begun as a Middle Eastern religious tradition into the heart of the Greek world. But prior to about A.D. 100 such movements made only slight inroads among the upper classes of the Mediterranean world. They found almost everything they wanted in refined and variously watered-down versions of classical Greek culture.

Throughout the fifth century B.C., the Aegean metropolitan center of classical Greek civilization remained sharply defined. It embraced some fifty to sixty city-states located on both sides of the Aegean, where vines and olives abounded. Greek craft skills — shipbuilding, weapons manufacture, pottery production, mining, monumental stone construction, and the like — did not differ much from professionalized levels of skill long familiar on the Syrian coast and in Asia Minor. On the other hand, the polis or city-state was distinctively Greek. In order to flourish, a polis had to command the services of a richly leisured citizenry. Otherwise the long hours spent in public business — training for the phalanx, campaigning, deliberating, administering justice, conducting diplomacy, not to mention participating in festivals and discussing matters of common concern in private gatherings of every kind — could not have been spared from the tasks of finding food enough to eat. Mass leisure was secured through the favorable terms of trade wine and oil exporters enjoyed.

No less vital to the success of the Greek city-states were sentiments of solidarity binding all citizens together. Such feelings were built up in all young men by prolonged drill exercises, preparatory to and climaxing in the experience of battle, when each man's life depended on his neighbor's readiness to keep his place in the ranks of the phalanx. The concept of law, above and beyond any merely human will or preference, applicable to everyone and accepted knowingly by all citizens, gave intellectual form and definition to such sentiments and sustained remarkably effective cooperation among the entire body of citizens.

All these elements had to be present for classical civilization to flourish. Regions where the agricultural-commercial-industrial complex failed to take root because of climatic or other obstacles remained incapable of constructing strong and effective city-states, lacking a sufficiently leisured citizenry. Thus Thessaly and Arcadia, although inhabited by Greeks who were continuously in touch with the centers of classical civilization, nonetheless remained rural, marginal, and unimportant, because in these landlocked areas the requisite number of leisured citizens could not be found. Sparta was a special case. Spartan citizens won the requisite leisure for constructing a formidable city-state by enslaving the entire population of neighboring Messenia. The Athenian pattern of trade required grain-growing landlords to exploit local peasantries living in the coastlands of the Black Sea and in Sicily and southern Italy; the Spartans exported only threats to Messenia whence came the grain and other food supplies that the Spartan citizens needed so that they could devote all their adult years to military training and campaigning. But the immediacy of the threat of revolt in Messenia required the Spartans to concentrate their leisure narrowly on military preparedness; the cushion — both geographical and sociological — between the Athenians and the excluded oppressed peasantry who fed them allowed scope for a far wider range of leisured activity. Though their means of support differed in detail, the upshot was similar. In both Sparta and Athens a sufficient body of leisured citizenry with intensely shared common sentiments provided the human material from which emerged the fine flower of classical Greek civilization.

In subsequent centuries the enormous geographical spread of aspects of Greek classical civilization involved radical transformation of the socioeconomic structures that sustained its initial flowering. Leisure remained critical always: men who had to work every day just to find enough to eat were never sharers in classical civilization. But the basis of leisure shifted from the sort of collective exploitation of others that had raised Athens and Sparta to greatness. Instead, a more dispersed pattern of exploitation took over. Local landlords and tax collectors with their hangers-on gathered into small towns and cities and there set up plausible simulacra of the city-states of classical Greece — with one important difference: military power and political sovereignty were, from the age of Alexander of Macedon, snatched away from mere city-states and transferred to new-sprung military monarchies, of which the last and greatest became the empire of Rome.

This vast political upheaval was matched by a dispersal of economic activity as well. The great advantages of wine and oil production meant that vineyards and olive groves tended to spread to new ground, wherever soil and climate allowed. As new sources of wine and oil came into production the older centers sometimes lost markets, and it is likely (though data are lacking, to be sure) that the relative price of oil and wine as against grain declined over the centuries from what it had been in Athens' glorious days. The small farmers in the original Aegean heartland lost out in the course of the fourth and third centuries to rival producers located mainly in Italy and Asia Minor. Italian producers, in turn, confronted disastrous market conditions in the first century A.D., when Spanish and North African oil and wines usurped western Mediterranean markets, and vines were successfully acclimated through most of Gaul all the way to the Rhine. Accordingly, from the time of Domitian (reigned A.D. 81–96), Italy lost export markets that had been vital to the prosperity of the slave-staffed latifundia that had sprung up in the southern part of the peninsula after the Second Punic War (218–202 B.C.).

Wherever wine and oil for export commanded a substantial market a region of relatively high prosperity was always to be found. As such regions multiplied and dispersed toward the geographical limits of the Mediterranean world, various provinces of the Roman Empire achieved a level of wealth that permitted a far-reaching reception of Greco-Roman culture, at least among the leisured, landowning class that dominated Roman provincial society almost everywhere. But no single metropolitan center could arise and sustain itself on a commercial basis once the original Aegean heartland had lost its initial near-monopoly of such exports. Instead wealth and food supplies were concentrated at political headquarters — Pella, Pergamum, Antioch, Alexandria, Rome — by a combination of predation and taxation (the difference between the two was not always very obvious to any of the parties concerned). The great city of Alexandria by Egypt, for example, where Hellenistic high culture had a particularly full development, lived largely on tribute paid by the Egyptian natives, from whom Ptolemy's agents extracted everything not required for mere survival. Industry and trade soon brought additional wealth to supplement this hard core of tax income, so that even after the Romans intervened and siphoned off for their own uses the major part of Egypt's tax yield (30 B.C.), Alexandria remained an important city and, as a matter of fact, developed a new commercial hinterland of some importance in distant India.

In the western Mediterranean, however, commercial-industrial development never got very far in ancient times. As the Romans extended their power throughout the Mediterranean the city of Rome became a vast parasite. By the second century B.C., almost all of Rome's inhabitants lived directly or indirectly on plunder and taxes. After the time of Augustus, however, the Roman armies were stationed permanently along the frontiers of the empire. Among other things this meant that a major disbursement of tax income was shifted away from the city of Rome to the garrisoned provinces. This powerfully reinforced the tendency for economic prosperity to disperse toward the fringes of the Mediterranean world as a result of the simultaneous diffusion of grape and olive cultivation.

The result, therefore, was that the peculiar circumstances that had provoked and sustained the brilliant cultural innovations of the fifth century never recurred. The bearers of the Greek and Roman cultural tradition became a privileged class dispersed widely throughout the Mediterranean lands, dependent in large measure on rents and taxes for their income, and surrounded by comparatively vast numbers of social inferiors, with whom they shared relatively little in the way of common sentiments, ideas, or way of life. Such a milieu was not conducive to bold and restless innovation of any kind. Moreover, the easy availability of superbly attractive models of art, literature, thought, not to mention the delights of elegant eating, drinking, and sex, as worked out by Greeks of the fifth and fourth centuries B.C., inhibited innovation still further.

There were changes, of course, and for a generation or two when Rome was rising to political preeminence, a handful of Roman writers and sculptors reacted to the collapse of customary Roman ways by using Greek patterns of thought and art to express deeply felt and profoundly serious concerns. Vergil, Cicero, Lucretius, and the artists who carved the Ara Pacis belong in this select company. They created, with others of lesser rank, a truncated version of the Athenian golden age all over again. But the Roman efflorescence did not last very long and died away without attaining richness and variety to equal the Athenian inheritance. Roman drama, for instance, remained trifling; and the historical insight and range of Livy and Tacitus fall far short of their Greek predecessors, Herodotus and Thucydides. Still, the age of Cicero and Vergil made Latin into a vehicle capable of rivaling Greek as a literary and intellectual language; and the use of Latin for administrative and legal purposes guaranteed the spread of Roman speech widely throughout the western provinces. On the other hand most of the east continued to use Greek as a *lingua franca*, even where older local mother tongues continued to survive, as in Egypt and Syria.

The division of the Mediterranean lands between two major linguistic provinces, one Latin, one Greek, became a lasting demarcation, reinforced and institutionalized after the third century A.D. when reforming emperors divided the empire into eastern and western halves for convenience of administration. Christian administrative lines of demarcation also developed in conformity to the language demarcation, so that a Latin Christendom in the western provinces emerged from the ruins of the Roman state in juxtaposition to Greek or, as it is often called, Orthodox Christendom of the eastern Mediterranean.

Because Christianity attracted the urban poor and oppressed in its initial period of growth, the church became a channel for expressing Syrian and Egyptian restlessness against, and repudiation of, the Greek cultural traditions which had so thoroughly seduced the upper classes since Alexander's time. When the church became powerful and attained legal rights and privileges these sentiments found expression through divergent theological formulations and led to schisms by which Syriac and Coptic (Egyptian) churches broke away from Greek Orthodoxy. In a similar way Donatism in North Africa expressed a rising sense of cultural separatism — in this case aimed against a Latin rather than a Greek upper class — on the part of the Berber populations. These cultural and religious movements in turn harmonized well with the economic dispersals that had been weakening the Roman and Italian center of the empire from the time of the emperor Domitian (died A.D. 96), if not before.

Greco-Roman pagan culture had, therefore, become a brittle thing by the third and fourth centuries A.D. By then the lower classes of the cities had found new cultural institutions and ideals — the mystery religions in general, Christianity in particular — and felt little attraction toward any of the norms and ideals their betters had accepted — often tepidly enough — as their heritage from the already ancient Greeks. Moreover, the bearers of this attenuated tradition were no longer in any position to defend themselves against armed assault. For nearly two centuries, professionalized soldiery, stationed far away on the frontier, made local self-defense unnecessary. Then, when more formidable assaults from beyond the frontiers required strenuous countermeasures and far-reaching military reform, as happened from the middle of the third century onwards, the landowning classes of the Roman provinces were unable and unwilling to do anything personally. The emperors, seeking more and more desperately for additional resources wherewith to support their greedy and unruly soldiery, resorted to confiscatory taxation. An entire class of landlords was speedily squeezed out of existence. This meant that the class which had been the main bearers of the classical tradition also disappeared. New landlords came along, to be sure, but they owed their position to bureaucratic and military office and stemmed, usually, from a rude and crude soldier tradition. Repeatedly, individuals born as simple peasant boys rose to the purple through the ranks of the army. Such self-made men carried with them a multitude of similarly rough and ready colleagues and assistants, for whom the nuances of ancient Greek and Latin philosophy, art, or literature meant little or nothing.

Two important external factors assured the ultimate breakup of the Roman Empire and the disruption of classical culture. First, various epidemic diseases ravaged the Mediterranean lands between the first and sixth centuries A.D., leading to widespread depopulation. Early in the Christian centuries, malaria arrived from West Africa when anopheles mosquitoes succeeded in making it across the Sahara in the shelter of someone's packtrain baggage. Many of what in later ages became ordinary childhood infections — smallpox, measles, mumps, chicken pox, and so on — probably first impinged upon Mediterranean populations in this same period. These diseases, too, presumably penetrated the Roman world when regular and more rapid transport connected the Mediterranean with diverse, previously isolated disease pools. Other factors may have affected population, too, but the crippling and pervasive decay of population that afflicted the Roman Empire after the second century A.D. was probably mainly a result of the devastating arrival of new diseases for which no previous immunities existed among the population.

Urban dwellers were, of course, more frequently exposed to such infections; rural and isolated communities were best situated to survive. Individuals engaging in commerce or any other activity that required encounter with strangers and movements across country were more exposed than others. As mortality mounted, we may well believe that these aspects of ancient Mediterranean society were the ones that withered fastest. Decay and retreat of market relations made effective administrative control of the state increasingly difficult. Without a ready supply of tax monies, central authorities had to fall back on levying taxes in kind. But control from afar of what came into and went out of public granaries was practically impossible. The compromise of dividing the empire into a number of parts, each subject to a different sovereign master, proved only a way station toward a final breakup of the imperial fabric, a breakup published to the world by the Germanic invasions of the late fourth and fifth centuries.

The increased formidability of the Germans and of other barbarians beyond Roman frontiers was the other external factor contributing to the fall of Rome. Exact details are quite unknown, having, for the most part, never been recorded, and archaeological investigation can only tell part of the story. Still, two major developments seem well attested, and both increased the power of barbarian assault against the Roman limits. The first of these two was the development of a technically improved style of agriculture on the German side of the Rhine frontier; the second was the increased formidability of steppe nomads along the middle and lower Danube frontier.

Where trackless forests had prevailed in the time of Augustus, settlements of west German agricultural pioneers slowly proliferated during the first Christian centuries. As fields multiplied, population grew until by the third century or so it equaled or perhaps even surpassed the density of settlement existing within Roman frontiers. The best evidence of this shift in population equilibrium was the ready availability of German manpower for military service in Roman armies, accompanied often by the settlement of Germanic populations on the Roman side of the frontier.

It is worth asking why German farmers multiplied when agriculturalists on the Roman side of the frontier were shrinking in numbers. For many centuries German agriculture aimed only at providing subsistence to the cultivator and his family. Hence neither taxes nor trade mattered much. This in turn implied that disease-carrying strangers were fewer among Germans than in Gaul and Britain, where maintenance of Rome's administrative and commercial framework required considerable coming and going. Secondly, on the Roman side of the frontier cultivators had to part with a substantial share of their crop to tax and rent collectors. This meant less for their own support, and in a year of bad harvests, famine compounded by lack of sufficient seed for the following year's planting presumably would have more devastating demographic effects among Roman subjects than among the free Germans. Obviously, precise reasons cannot be recovered, but the fact of sharply differential population patterns on opposite banks of the Rhine seems certain.

The spread of agriculture among the Germans was connected with the development of an improved kind of plow, capable of turning a furrow (as Mediterranean scratch plows had not done) and able to create an artificial drainage pattern on naturally flat land. By the fifth century A.D., when Saxon settlers crossed the North Sea to Britain, they brought with them this new type of moldboard plow. It enabled them to till the heavy clay soils of Norfolk and Suffolk where British and Roman cultivators had been entirely unable to raise a crop. Similar techniques allowed German farmers of the lower Rhine and Weser valleys to reclaim increasing areas of what had before been waterlogged plains, naturally covered by dense and, to the Romans, all but impenetrable forests.

The importance of this technical breakthrough was enormous. Wheat and barley, the staples of Mediterranean and Middle Eastern cultivation, were naturally adapted to semiarid conditions. In the much wetter climate of northwestern Europe, Mediterranean methods of tillage had only been able to make grain flourish on specially well-drained soils — chalk downs, loessland, and hilltops. The potentially rich, flat plains of northwestern Europe could not grow successfully without the artificial drainage created by the action of the moldboard plow. Hence the invention of such a plow, and the discovery of how effective it could be, opened broad new zones of Europe to agriculture.

Multiplication of nearly self-sufficient farmsteads among the west Germans did not of itself create the complexities of civilization beyond the Rhine frontier. Yet population growth probably did lead to some quickening of transport by sea. The Anglo-Saxon migration to England in the fifth century A.D. proves that several thousand people were able to cross the North Sea, arriving on a shore that had been familiar to Saxon and Frisian pirates for some two hundred years. The swarming of the Saxons in the fifth and sixth centuries was followed in the eighth and ninth centuries by a similar swarming of Scandinavian sea rovers and emigrants. By the time the Vikings made themselves the scourge of northern Europe, northern ship design and seamanship had produced an Atlantic nautical tradition equivalent to, though divergent from, the far older skills of Mediterranean seamanship. Thus by A.D. 900 or thereabouts, ships and sailors of the Atlantic seas were able to move goods and men almost as easily and nearly as safely as had been the case within Mediterranean waters since 900 B.C. The north was catching up.

After about A.D. 500, therefore, the new sort of moldboard plow on the one hand, and increasingly seaworthy ships on the other, provided a new technical basis for the eventual flowering of high culture in northwestern Europe. But before that result could be achieved, drastic social differentiation had to occur. The free barbarian husbandman had to become a peasant paying dues and services to his social superiors. The principal impulse pushing in this direction was the need for more effective defense against raiding parties, whether coming by land on horseback, as did the Huns (and many other steppe nomad people), or by sea and river as the Vikings did.

Before considering how Europe's cultural shape altered under these circumstances, we must backtrack briefly to consider the changes in nomad life that made the Huns and similar peoples so formidable. Two important improvements in cavalry equipment favored mounted soldiers as against foot soldiers during the first Christian centuries, though all details of when and where these improvements originated remain unsure.

One was the use of stirrups to give the rider a firmer seat on his horse. This simple invention benefited both bowmen and lancers. By rising out of the saddle and assuming a crouching position a practiced rider could compensate for the vertical motion of his galloping horse. This allowed archers to shoot far more accurately from the comparative safety of a rapidly moving horse than had been possible without stirrups, when riders, however skilled, bounced up and down with every gallop. The advantage for lancers was even more dramatic. By leaning far forward and bracing his body against the stirrups at the moment of impact, a lancer could put the vast momentum of horse and rider behind his lance head, thereby, as Europe's medieval knights repeatedly demonstrated, achieving an all but irresistible force. Unfortunately details of the origin, spread, and exploitation of the military value of stirrups are mostly unclear but in the first century A.D. this seemingly simple and obvious invention was still new among horsemen of the steppes and in civilized lands as well. In succeeding centuries, as nomads learned to exploit the possibilities of stirrups fully, the older balance of forces between infantry and cavalry was everywhere upset.

The second improvement in cavalry techniques was the introduction of a larger and stronger horse that could carry armor and an armored man without too much difficulty. This seems to have developed among Iranians in the first century B.C., perhaps when they found out that by cultivating alfalfa they could produce suitable and sufficient winter fodder to keep even large and hungry horses in shape. Such beasts remained exceedingly expensive to maintain, however, and on the open steppe the small, tough pony, capable of scraping a living even in winter from beneath the snow, remained the normal nomad mount. The big horse suited the shock tactics of the lance better than any smaller mount could do, and its importance was confined to places where these tactics prevailed over archery. On the steppe itself the bow remained supreme as it had been even before stirrups increased the accuracy of archery from horseback.

Technical changes of this magnitude accompanied and presumably provoked or at least permitted large-scale migrations and conquests to sweep the European steppe. Before the Huns appeared on the scene in A.D. 370 from somewhere farther east, the penetration of Germanic-speaking Goths from the north, beginning in the second century A.D., created considerable upheaval. Warfare and plundering associated with this change of sovereignty may have damaged agricultural communities on and adjacent to the steppes, but the Huns ruthlessly carried harassment and extermination to a new height. The Hunnic Empire lasted a mere eighty-five years, to be sure, but the Huns were succeeded by a seemingly unending flow of Avars, Bulgars, Khazars, Pechenegs, and Magyars. Each nomadic wave pushed back the limits of agricultural settlement further, so that during the more than 600 years, from 370, when the Huns crossed the Don, until 896, when the Magyars crossed the Carpathians, the natural grasslands of eastern Europe were reclaimed for nomadry. Even in naturally forested lands many places where cultivation once had flourished were abandoned and went back to woods.

If we try for a synoptic view, therefore, we may say that the regions north of the Roman frontiers entered upon a sort of enormous seesaw during the first millennium of the Christian era. A substantial development of agriculture took place in the west, and barriers to cultivation that had prevented dense occupation of the plains of northwestern Europe were permanently broken through. In the east an opposite trend prevailed. The increased formidability of horse nomad peoples tended to drive agriculture from the grasslands, where it had never made more than modest lodgement, and created a zone adjacent to the regions of open grass where agricultural settlement remained thin and precarious.

Within the Mediterranean lands, too, a sort of east-west seesaw occurred during the same centuries, but in an opposite sense, for within the Mediterranean it was the east that reasserted itself while the wealth and power of western Mediterranean regions diminished. Exactly why Italy, Gaul, and Spain should have failed to keep pace with the Aegean and Asia Minor coastlands, not to mention Egypt and Syria, is hard to say. After the prolonged military upheavals of the third century (A.D. 235–285), the city of Rome ceased to be a major center of government. Italy as a whole ceased to receive significant tribute income from the provinces, so that the concentration of wealth which had supported the brief efflorescence of Roman culture dissipated long before the imperial structure decayed. The emperors of the third and fourth centuries, having abandoned Rome, set up headquarters nearer threatened frontiers, where local food resources were available to feed a substantial body of troops, or where lines of communication made it relatively easy to concentrate supplies from a distance.

By far the best such location was on the Bosporus, where Constantine the Great renamed the ancient Greek city of Byzantium after himself, when he made it his capital in A.D. 330. The Aegean and Black Sea waterways converged at Constantinople, making it possible to move both goods and armies to and fro, even across long distances, with comparative ease. This in turn meant that a reasonably effective central power could be maintained from such a headquarters. Taxes (whether in goods or money) could be concentrated in the capital and used to support an army and navy strong enough to overawe most rivals. Such a force as it turned out, was capable of defending the walls of Constantinople against all comers for nearly a thousand years. When one part of the city's hinterland had been ravaged and depopulated, whether by nomad raiders or through some other form of disaster, other sections of the accessible coastlands could be counted on to escape damage and be available, therefore, to feed the capital and sustain the imperial administrative and military machinery until 'such time as local recovery allowed the devastated regions once again to contribute their share to the support of the central power. Similarly, even if command of the Aegean might be lost for a while, as it was in the ninth century to Moslem seafarers from the south, command of the Black Sea and its connecting waters offered the empire a viable, if reduced, means for concentrating resources. Similarly, loss of control of the Black Sea to Varangian raiding parties could be countered by means of resources concentrated from Aegean coastlands.

The unique geopolitical advantages of such a capital (reinforced by formidable walls and a good natural harbor) do much to account for the survival of the Roman Empire in the east long after imperial administration had vanished from the west, where no remotely comparable location for an imperial headquarters existed. Moreover, the survival of an effective imperial administration in the east generated commerce and industry, as the goods and tax monies brought together in the capital never of themselves sufficed to equip the soldiers, ships, and courtiers with exactly the assortment of things needed and desired. Imperial and private workshops were required to turn raw materials into suitable end products. Similarly, tax monies filtered back to the provinces whence they had come when officials and soldiers used cash to buy needed commodities produced in the provinces. Industry and commerce in turn sustained town life and the relatively complex social stratification that urbanism implied.

On this basis a relatively high state of civilization could be and was maintained in Constantinople and a few other major cities of the eastern Mediterranean. The sociopolitical regime was more like that of ancient Near Eastern empires — Persia, Assyria, Babylonia — than like that of classical Greece, and there is perhaps more than symbolic significance in the fact that from the time of Diocletian (reigned A.D. 285–305) the Roman emperors used insignia of office borrowed from Persian kings. Similarly the dominant place held by the Christian church after Constantine's time in all matters intellectual and for the patronage of art gave the high culture of the East Roman or Byzantine Empire a strong oriental flavor.

Yet it would be unfair to emphasize the derivative character of Byzantine civilization unduly. The originality and power of Byzantine high culture survives for us mainly through art. In thought and letters there is less to admire. Learned Byzantines decried innovation, for innovation implied some inadequacy in the inherited traditions of the past, and the revealed truths of Christianity could not, by definition, lack anything essential. Such stoutly conservative views gained urgency due to the bitter doctrinal controversies of the fourth to the sixth century that subsided only when dissident Syriac and Coptic Christians, not to mention Donatists of North Africa and Arians in Spain, passed under Moslem political control between 636 and 711. Thereafter a rigid definition of Orthodoxy defied alteration, even when the emperors themselves (perhaps deferring to Moslem reproaches of idolatry) attempted to banish sacred images from the churches.

Yet in spite of the professed conservatism of Byzantine thought and the pervasive ritualism of their practice, it seems just to concur with the long-standing historiographical tradition that recognizes both Byzantines and Moslems as bearers of new civilizations, different in so many ways from any that had gone before as to deserve to be called by a distinctive name. Greco-Roman and ancient Near Eastern (mainly Hebraic) elements intermingled to shape both Byzantine and Moslem cultures. Despite the obvious and deeply felt doctrinal differences that divided them, there was much they shared. Convention, however, does not treat Moslem history and civilization as part of the history of Europe, and for the purposes of this essay it seems wise to conform to this view as well, and to acquiesce in breaking up the cultural unity of the Mediterranean that had prevailed in Roman times.

Leaving Islam to one side therefore, it remains to consider the state of Europe of about A.D. 900, when the two vast seesaw movements mentioned above had had time to work themselves out.

First and most important: the Byzantine center far exceeded anything existing elsewhere in Europe at the time. Byzantine art, ceremonial, artisan skills, administration, diplomacy, and literary sophistication all surpassed their analogues in any other part of Europe, and were rivaled or exceeded only in the great centers of Islam — Baghdad, Damascus, Cairo. Yet the centrality of dogmatic religion in Byzantine civilization meant that those who rejected the Orthodox definition of Christian truth were also prone to reject Byzantine culture as a whole. Such attitudes, reciprocated from each side, insulated Moslems from Christians far more effectively than their propinquity and shared cultural ancestry would suggest and within Christendom a similar though less pronounced barrier divided Greek from Latin Christians. Memories of the Roman past, when the west had dominated the east, remained alive, especially in Latin ecclesiastical circles. Among laymen, barbarian pride in personal prowess made it possible for crude warriors to sneer at the effete, urban, and (at least sometimes) urbane Greeks who governed the Byzantine state and society. Among Slavs of the Balkans and Russia, however, competing models of civilization were too distant to matter, with the exception of Islam, which soon became identified with the nomad raiders of the steppe — the Slavs' perpetual and dangerous enemies. Hence the major field of cultural expansion for Byzantines lay northward into Russia and inland from the Aegean coasts toward the Balkan interior. In A.D. 900

penetration of Byzantine culture along the Russian rivers and into the Balkans was still in its initial stages but the pattern of acculturation was relatively straightforward, with Constantinople (and the Mount Athos monasteries) acting as metropolitan centers while lesser courts and capitals and their associated monasteries did all they could to imitate the imperial model.

In western Europe the situation was less clearly defined. The popes of Rome aspired to exert an imperial sway in matters ecclesiastical and did indeed organize successful missionary efforts in England and much of Germany. There were, however, other aspirants to imperial rank in western Europe, namely the Frankish kings. Their power centered on the middle and lower Rhine, but extended widely into Gaul, Germany, and northern Italy. The greatest of these kings, Charlemagne (reigned 768–814), took the imperial title on Christmas Day, 800. Later he was able to persuade officials in Byzantium to recognize his legitimacy as an heir of the Roman emperors. But the Carolingian Empire lacked a capital capable of playing the role Constantinople played in the Byzantine state. Indeed, Charlemagne, like his predecessors, had to move around continually in order to feed himself and his court — it being easier to move a few hundred persons to and fro than it was to concentrate sufficient food and other supplies at one place to maintain the court throughout the year. A military campaign practically every summer went along with this itinerant style of life and the numerous, hardy foot soldiers who regularly went to war under Charlemagne's command gave the Franks numerical advantage over most foes. When the striking power of a few heavy cavalrymen, specially equipped with armor and lances, was added to the Frankish host (an innovation attributable to Charlemagne's grandfather, Charles Martel), a formidable force capable of routing almost any foe within reach came into existence. The enormous size of Charlemagne's empire was the result.

Yet against enemies who could move rapidly, whether by land like the Magyars on their light steppe ponies, or by sea like the Vikings who began to harass Carolingian coasts during Charlemagne's own lifetime, the Frankish host was ineffective. It took too long to assemble and moved no faster than a man could walk. Mobile raiders could easily outstrip such a force, plundering at will. The vast bulk of the Carolingian state therefore proved easily vulnerable and swiftly disintegrated in all but name in the century after Charlemagne's death.

Papal aspirations were vulnerable to a similar defect. As long as local bishops and abbots deferred to the pope, ecclesiastical unity seemed real; but when differences of opinion arose the papacy entirely lacked means of enforcing its will. As long as Carolingian and other German kings wished to maintain good relations with the pope the lay power supported ecclesiastical centralization. In return German rulers could expect the sanction of religion for their rather fumbling efforts at extending royal jurisdiction to include more than the functions of war leader which they had inherited from the barbarian and pagan past. But in proportion as such rulers lost power, being unable even to fulfill their traditional role of war captain successfully against Magyar and Viking attack (supplemented in the Mediterranean by Moslem pirates), the church, too, lost even the appearance of order and discipline. The pope, like many another bishop, became a pawn in the hands of local armed cliques, seeking whatever advantage was to be gained from putting one of its partisans in episcopal office. Therefore neither the Germanic Rhinelands nor papal Rome succeeded before A.D. 900 in organizing itself into a genuinely effective metropolitan center for western Europe as a whole. Communications were too slow, local self-sufficiency too prevalent, to permit any other result.

On the extreme periphery of the continent, first Ireland and then Scandinavia began to create distinctive local styles of civilization which, under other circumstances, might have grown into effective rivals to Rome and the Rhinelands. But the Irish monasteries were destroyed by Viking raids, and the vigor and attractiveness of Celtic Christian culture (demonstrated by some remarkable missionary careers in Great Britain and on the continent) soon faded away thereafter. As for the Vikings themselves, their roving brought them into touch with all of Europe's varying styles of high culture, whether Byzantine or Roman, English, Irish, or Frankish. Their indigenous paganism was unable to resist Christianity for very long, particularly when aspiring kings, needing religious sanction for their efforts at state building, found it convenient to make acceptance of Christian baptism equivalent to a loyalty oath, and equated paganism with rebellion.

For completeness, a word about Spain: conquered by Moslems from North Africa in the years after 711, the Iberian peninsula became politically separated from the rest of Islam after 755 when a scion of the dispossessed Umayyad dynasty made good his claim to sovereignty. The dynasty lasted until 1031, and during much of that time maintained a brilliant court at Cordoba. Umayyad sovereigns strove, as a matter of policy, to make their court a worthy rival to the Abassid capital of Baghdad. They often came close; but the Christians of Spain and *a fortiori* Christians beyond the Pyrenees paid little attention. Save for a few trifles which Christians later did borrow from Spanish Islam, Spain's cultural hinterland lay across the Straits of Gibraltar, in Morocco and adjacent parts of Africa. As such, this far western Moslem presence in Europe, though it endured more than 600 years in all, perhaps deserves to be omitted from the ambit of European history, as is conventionally done in (largely unwitting) deference to later Spanish religious and national prejudices against the Moors.

In sum: this section has tried to sketch a great pulsation in European history. The story begins about 900 B.C. when the disorders and dispersals incident to the Dorian invasions of Greece began to subside and classical civilization started to take shape. It ends with a similar movement of peoples accompanying the collapse of Roman administration in the western provinces of the empire. In between, classical Greek civilization came sharply and marvelously into focus in the Aegean basin between, say, 490 and 322 B.C. Thereafter the Greek model carried everything before it. With the political unification of all Mediterranean lands by the Romans, a relatively coherent pattern emerged, whereby civilized styles of life spread thinly throughout the Mediterranean lands, while beyond the Rhine and Danube frontiers barbarian freedom and simplicity shaded off into the desperate poverty of hunters and gatherers of the far north. Economic decentralization within the Mediterranean zone was soon followed by the political breakup of the Roman state. This inaugurated a more complicated pattern, whereby a revived and somewhat displaced Greek metropolitan center arose around Constantinople in the east, whereas elsewhere in Europe a number of competing — or at least divergent — styles of life came into existence without organizing themselves clearly around any articulated metropolitan center, save insofar as Byzantium played that role for all of Christian Europe. After A.D. 900, however, a more distinct and powerful style of life emerged in the northwest and with that development Europe attained what we may perhaps appropriately call its medieval configuration. The next section will explore its major lineaments.

EUROPE, 900–1500

In A.D. 900, Europe was thinly settled. Communications were erratic, piracy rife. Most men lived and died close to home; a few went raiding, sometimes across great distances. Since raiding never turned up exactly the sorts of goods a war band needed to keep going, even the fiercest raiders had to supplement their rapine with more peaceful commerce by seeking out spots where weapons, sails and oars, food, horses, falcons, jewelry, and other necessary or desirable commodities could be had from suppliers who themselves hovered perpetually between haggling over a price and resorting to armed force as a way of making a living. In Byzantium and at a few other locations along the Aegean–Black Sea coasts, cities supported artisans, merchants, soldiers, tax collectors, rentiers, and other specialists; the same was true of Moslem Spain. Elsewhere in Europe, itinerant royal courts, monasteries, or a bishop's seat, served the functions cities performed in the two more civilized parts of the continent. Such places often acted as cities only during a few days of the year when a fair brought local people and a sprinkling of strangers together to do business for a limited period of time.

By 1500 a great change had taken place. Cities had spread widely through the continent; ships traveled regularly to and fro between the northern and Mediterranean seas; peaceful commerce had far out-stripped piracy and raiding as a way of making a living. Population had grown. Except on the tundra of the far north, where Lapps roamed freely with their reindeer, states, administered from a fixed center, had estab-lished their power throughout the continent. Civilization, in a word, had spread northward from the Spanish and Byzantine bridgeheads of 900, engulfing almost the whole of Europe. Geographical and climatic bound-aries that had checked the diffusion of classical civilization had been triumphantly broken through. The east–west axis of classical times, in which the Mediterranean seaways had always played the leading role, was supplemented by a north–south axis that balanced the Mediterranean lands against those of the Atlantic seaways in the west and of the Russian rivers in the east. Yet until a century or more after 1500, the primacy of the Mediterranean lands remained, in most respects, unshaken, despite increasingly vigorous currents of cultural creativity manifested in the northern lands.

By A.D. 900 the Viking raids, which had been so destructive to Irish, English, and Frankish societies, were changing character. Instead of returning to the winter twilight of the Scandinavian north, Viking crews began to spend the winter in softer, more southerly climes, at river mouths or some other convenient location. Liaisons with local women soon called a new generation of formidable warriors into existence, who more often than not spoke the language of their mothers — Flemish, French, Russian, English, or Gaelic, as the case might be. Simul-taneously, the increased wealth and sophistication that successful raids brought to the northlands stimulated efforts at state building in Denmark, Norway, and Sweden. As had happened in preceding centuries among the Germans, the aspiring monarchs of the Scandinavian north found a very useful ally in the Christian church. The pomp and mystery of Christian services plus the hope of salvation attracted barbarians of all ranks to Christianity. But what made the religion especially dear to would-be kings was Christian teaching about government, which accorded rulers the rights and majesty ancient Near Eastern kings and Roman emperors had in fact received. Such an ideal of kingship constituted an irresistibly attractive agenda for barbarian war captains seeking to make their power secure, hereditary, and effective in peace as well as on the battlefield.

For a while it looked as though the Scandinavian thrust toward monar-chy and centralization might succeed in building two impressive and extensive imperial structures: a Danish empire of the northern seas, and a Varangian empire of the Russian rivers, headquartered at Kiev. But the

Danish sea empire collapsed after the death of Canute the Great in 1025, and the empire of the Russian rivers disintegrated after the death of Yaroslav the Wise in 1054. Before their breakup both state structures attained impressive size. Canute controlled all the shores of the North Sea, including parts of Denmark, England, Scotland, and Norway; Yaroslav's empire extended from Novgorod in the north to the lower Volga and lower Danube in the south. Both, needless to say, depended on movement of men and goods by ship and were held together by very elementary administrative structures. To command such an empire the monarch had to be, like Agamemnon of old, a hero in his own person. Only a king who embodied the warrior ideal of reckless courage, boundless generosity and unwavering loyalty could attract and hold a corps of fellow heroes, whose valor and faithfulness to him was the critical factor making the central power as formidable as it was. But the heroic style of life was incompatible with niggling attention to routine administration; still less was it consonant with money-grubbing efforts to collect taxes and concentrate them in a central treasury. As a result, when a great captain such as Canute or Yaroslav died, his state vanished with him overnight, leaving only quarreling fragments behind.

External forces also had something to do with the failure of these imperial states. In the west a vastly improved system of local self-defense — the feudal system — made raiding unprofitable, and thereby deprived sea kings of easy access to booty income that was important, perhaps essential, for maintaining their following of fellow heroes. In the east, new hordes of steppe nomads, fresh from central Asia, intruded upon the river-based empire of the Varangians by taking over its southern portion. Yaroslav's heirs were unable to repel them successfully since the mounted archers were on the whole more mobile and self-sufficient than the swordsmen who had to move mainly by river, and who lacked the skill with the bow that made the warriors of the steppe so formidable at a distance.

Internal fragility and external pressures therefore wiped away most traces of both these northern empires rather quickly. Their only lasting mark upon the face of Europe resulted from the royal policy of alliance with and patronage of the Christian church. Newly founded monasteries and cathedrals acted as foyers for the propagation of literacy and the intellectual and artistic tradition of Christianity as defined and perfected in such great centers as Byzantium, Mount Athos, Canterbury, and Rome. Landmark dates were the establishment of Christianity as the official faith in Kiev (989) and Norway (by 1000). The intrinsic attractions of Christian faith and culture, consistently supported by princely policy, made such advances permanent. Older paganisms simply were not able to compete with the organized power of Christianity and of the latent seeds of civilization it carried within it.

During the same period of time, parallel changes cushioned central and western Europe from the risk of nomad raiding from the steppes. State building among Bulgars, then among Magyars led, as was happening in Scandinavia too, to the introduction of Christianity under royal auspices. The effect was to bring the lower and middle Danube plains within the circle of Christian culture by 1001, when Saint Stephen of Hungary's coronation was solemnized with a crown provided for the purpose by the pope in Rome. External checks to the sorts of raids that had been successful earlier contributed to the internal consolidation of both Bulgar and Magyar states. Collision with a revivified Byzantine military machine convinced the Bulgar khans that they should apprentice themselves as vigorously as possible to Byzantine civilization. In 1018 the apprenticeship terminated with the conquest of the Bulgarian Empire and its full incorporation into the Byzantine domain. For the Magyars, the defeat they suffered at the hands of German forces in 955 (Battle of the Lechfeld) had an analogous effect, convincing the Magyar court that Christian civilization in the German mold offered a model to be imitated insofar as possible.

North of the Danube and eastward across the Ukrainian steppes, however, no comparable political-cultural transformation occurred. The arrival of new Turkish tribes from the east — Patzinaks, Cumans — reinforced pagan, nomadic traditions just as the Magyars and Scandinavians decided to apprentice themselves to Christian patterns of culture. When they felt the need of civilization — as was scarcely the case as long as age-old patterns of nomadry continued to maintain military superiority over neighboring agricultural populations and provided a satisfactory if arduous style of life for the nomads themselves — the Turks turned toward Islam rather than toward Christianity. Affinities derived from central Asia where Turks and Moslems had extensive contacts contributed to this pattern of preference; the activity of Moslem merchant-missionaries in the steppes, and affinities with nomadic life deriving from the Arabian background of Islam itself also played a part.

In effect, therefore, what we see happening by 1000 or thereabouts is that three distinct southern centers of high culture began to stake out definite provinces in the north: Rome and the papacy exerted vague but real influence among the Latin and Germanic peoples, flanked by Celts on one fringe and Magyars on the other fringe of the realm of Latin Christendom; Byzantium developed a considerably stronger influence upon the Slavs and Rumanians of the Balkan interior as well as north of the Black Sea in Russia; and Baghdad developed its own, weaker field of force among the Turkish-speaking nomads of the Ukrainian steppes.

The remaining center of high culture within Europe, Moslem Spain, continued to influence a vast hinterland extending across North Africa and seeping into West Africa; but until the thirteenth century, so far as I know, Moslem Spanish civilization exerted almost no overt attraction among the rude frontier fighters of the Christian north, who, like Turkish nomads of the Ukraine, armored themselves against the seductions of civilization in the form most accessible to them by a nominal, but belligerent, adherence to a rival form of religion. By espousing Christianity or Islam, as the case might be, border raids became holy wars, taking booty was sanctified, and a predatory way of life acquired the support of organized religion. Fanatic barbarism therefore survived across both the Spanish and Ukrainian frontiers longer than elsewhere in Europe.[2]

In the three centuries that followed this redefinition of Europe's cultural patterns, between 1000 and 1300, two great changes occurred. In the Mediterranean area, both the Byzantine and the Spanish Moslem centers of civilization underwent drastic disruption. By way of compensation, however, in the middle of the Mediterranean, Italy gathered to itself enhanced wealth, power, and cultural influence, becoming, indeed, the metropolitan center *par excellence* of all Europe.

This shift toward the center in the Mediterranean coincided with a contrasting trans-Alpine pattern. In the northwest, a newly defined style of civilization and society achieved remarkable success and drew the allegiance of a very considerable part of all Europe, outstripping Italy itself in some important respects, especially in the thirteenth century. In the same century, the basin of the middle and lower Volga became the seat of a Mongol-Turkish style of life that dominated almost all of Russia in matters military and economic, although Christianity continued to set the Russian population apart from their new (presently Moslem) masters.

Of these great fluctuations, the most familiar and that which mattered most for the long-term future was the rise of new civilized forms of life in northwestern Europe. The technical basis for the remarkable upthrust which occurred between 1000 and 1300 in the region between the Loire and the Rhine (with the southeastern part of Great Britain as a not unimportant outpost across the English Channel) had been laid in the previous era. These were the spread of moldboard agriculture, the development of shipping, and the propagation of the cavalry shock tactics that made Frankish knights so terrible in battle. Minor improvements continued to be made after 1000, but the real difference was the vast enhancement of the scale upon which these new technologies were applied.

Intrinsic advantages no doubt explain the spread of each improvement. But the pace of change was enormously accelerated by the disasters and upheavals of the Viking age. Devastating raids on ex-Roman villas in the region between the Rhine and the Loire erased barriers to use of the

---

[2]   The frontier between the Scottish Highlands and Lowlands shows, however, that religious sanctification was not necessary for survival of a barbarous style of life into the eighteenth century.

moldboard plow which had checked its spread for centuries. Desperate survivors after such a raid had no incentive to maintain old obstructive field boundaries and property lines; on the contrary, they had every inducement to pool resources for tillage, as the moldboard plow required, because the four to six oxen needed to drive it through the soil were more than any ordinary cultivator could supply by himself.[3]

Similarly the essentials of knightly cavalry tactics were developed at the court of Charles Martel by 732, but for a long time the heavy expense of equipping and maintaining an armored horse and man made such warriors rare. When, however, local defense against Viking or Magyar attack became critical, German freemen as much as ex-Roman *coloni* agreed that even heavy payment for the support of a knight perpetually in residence and on call was better than periodic exposure to devastating raids. As this became clear to all concerned, the feudal system burgeoned. Counts and other administrators enfeoffed knights who promised military service in return for rights to collect income from one or more villages.

From the peasant point of view, the enhanced efficiency of moldboard cultivation and the possibility of putting new forest lands into cultivation as rapidly as available man and ox power permitted made support of a knight comparatively easy to bear. As a result, knights soon became numerous enough to form a formidable defense against raiders. Even a dozen knights, assembled on short notice from a radius of two or three miles, could take on a raiding ship's crew and expect victory, since in hand-to-hand combat the mounted and armored man had an enormous advantage over foot soldiers, however brave or numerous. The knights' superiority over Magyar horse archers was far less, as it was difficult for the knights' heavy horses to close with the Magyars' ponies. Consequently, the spread of knighthood and of the social structure required to support a numerous class of knights was slower in central and eastern Germany than it was in the regions exposed to Viking harassment. Older forms of social organization — the stem or tribal duchies — persisted longer, and the importance of the knightly class, with its heroic and chivalric ideals, was never as great as in the northwesternmost parts of continental Europe.

---

[3]   Scratch plow cultivation required cross-plowing, i.e. dragging the share in one direction through the field and then across at right angles to break up the soil more efficiently. This was best done in square or nearly square fields. The moldboard plow, on the contrary, turned a furrow which could not be disturbed without spoiling the drainage pattern parallel furrows created in the field. But the plow and its team was awkward to turn. Hence long (220 yards by convention) and narrow field slopes alone suited the moldboard plow. Only by abandoning old field boundaries and property lines could an established agricultural community shift from one to the other technique of cultivation, and in normal times resistance to such a step was obviously enormous. By breaking normal resistance to such innovation, Viking ravagers greatly accelerated the spread of moldboard cultivation which, once established as the norm, made almost all the forest land of northwest Europe into potentially fertile fields.

Effective defense on a local basis implied decay and all but disappearance of larger political units throughout the North Sea and Channel coastlands. In the interior of Germany, however, tribal and ecclesiastical authority mattered more, locally supported knights amounted to less, and from 962, Otto the Great's revived imperial title carried with it the claim to primacy in all of Latin Christendom, like Charlemagne if not exactly like Caesar.

As raiding became unrewarding and dangerous in more and more localities, the alternative of peaceful trade recommended itself more and more often to the ships' crews that continued to sail the northern seas in search of anything they could find to supplement the short rations available at home — whether home was in Scandinavia or in some overcrowded port of the southern lands. The knightly class, with a claim to rents and services from peasant cultivators attached to each fief by law and custom, was in an excellent position to accumulate surplus food and other commodities; and as trade developed, even the most heroic warriors soon learned that such surpluses could be exchanged for fine clothes and luxuries as well as for items they needed for success in battle — armor, weapons, war-horses.

Presently traders settled in places where communication lines met, built walls for their protection and organized a town government to make sure that all who benefited from such local improvements helped to pay for them. Artisans in turn quickly clustered within town walls. Other kinds of experts soon appeared: teachers, preachers, doctors, lawyers, and the like. The panoply of civilization thus rapidly developed in northwestern Europe, sustained and fed by a rapidly expanding agriculture, biting into the vast virgin forests that initially surrounded the cleared fields of each village. The expansion of tillage permitted and was in turn promoted by very rapid population growth, which spilled over from the countryside into the numerous towns which soon dotted the landscape.

Boom times continued until about 1270. By then nearly all suitable land between the Elbe and the Loire had been brought under cultivation. Any further clearance cut into woodlands which were needed to supply fuel and for other uses. In other words, after some three centuries of extraordinary expansion, in the regions where the new balance between man and nature based upon moldboard agriculture had first been developed, natural limits were reached. After about 1270, the disappearance of adequate woodlands — something that would have seemed inconceivable in 900 when forests were everywhere — began to put a powerful check on the maintenance, to say nothing of further expansion, of the economy of northwestern Europe.

This check was postponed and its impact reduced by emigration. Pioneer settlers confronted a broad belt of woodlands to the east. Clearance of land beyond the Elbe went steadily forward until the fifteenth century, with help from immigrants from the densely occupied core area on either side of the lower Rhine. But as farmers moved eastward, conditions of soil and climate became less propitious. Even when cultivators used exactly the same tools and methods as those familiar on the fertile lands of the northwest, they got poorer harvests and could therefore support fewer professionalized fighting men, clergymen, townsmen and other sorts of social superiors.

In Croatia, Bohemia, and parts of Poland, Slavs took up the moldboard plow; elsewhere the frontier of this sort of cultivation coincided quite exactly with the limits of German settlement. Farther east, farmers did not take to the heavy plow, partly because it required changes in habits of work, but mainly because it cost more to build and operate and did not increase yields sufficiently under eastern European conditions to make the extra costs worthwhile. Instead a shifting style of cultivation, using a light scratch plow like that long familiar in Mediterranean lands sufficed in the generally dryer conditions of eastern Europe. The boundary line between the long acre fields required by the moldboard plow and the squarish, irregularly shaped fields appropriate to scratch plow cultivation still runs through Europe and provides a tangible indication of exactly where pioneer settlers from the west reached the effective limit of their expansion.[4]

Simultaneously, a different kind of emigration spread the fame of western or "Frankish" knighthood far and wide across Europe and into the heartland of Islam itself. Having everywhere turned back barbarian invaders, knights took the offensive across every frontier of Latin Christendom in the eleventh century. Younger sons and other restless professionalized fighting men of western Europe rallied behind enterprising adventurers who led bands of a few hundred or a few thousand knights in a remarkable series of conquests. Normans, i.e. the Frenchified heirs of northmen settled around the mouth of the Seine, played a particularly distinguished role in this expansion, beginning with Duke William's conquest of England in 1066 and Robert Guiscard's no less remarkable conquest of southern Italy (and his brother's conquest of Sicily) between 1057 and 1091. Normans and Flemings played a leading part in the even

---

[4]   This vast eastward movement revived from time to time in later centuries, especially in the eighteenth, when the Austrian and Russian bureaucracies systematically recruited German settlers from Swabia and elsewhere in the west to occupy land in the Danube, Dniepr, and Volga valleys which had been newly won from nomad Turkish control. These settlers brought their plows and field shapes with them, creating islands of long acre cultivation amid the scratch plow, shifting agriculture that continued to dominate east European landscapes until the twentieth century. Successful eighteenth-century colonization was, however, limited to unusually fertile soils and usually required (or at least enjoyed) partial exemption from rent and/or tax payments assessed on other communities. By and large, it therefore appears that by 1500 or earlier, moldboard agriculture had in fact reached the geographic limits within which it was economically more efficient than scratch plow cultivation.

more spectacular First Crusade (1097–1099) which penetrated all the way to Jerusalem and established a string of Christian states along the Syrian and Palestine coast.

Simultaneously, German knights extended their domains across the Elbe and then, in the thirteenth century, having been checked in their eastward expansion by a consolidated Polish state, leapfrogged to Prussia and thence along the Baltic coast as far as the Gulf of Finland. The second phase of this expansion was carried through by the Teutonic Order, a crusading society of knights specially organized for the purpose. German settlers occupied Prussia; elsewhere the knights subjected local peoples — Lithuanians, Latvians, Estonians — but populated the towns for the most part with German immigrants. In fact, German and German-ized (often Jewish) townsmen outstripped German rural settlement everywhere along this eastward frontier, penetrating Poland, Bohemia, and Hungary where Slavic and Magyar peasants worked the fields.

This enormous economic and military success provided a basis for an equally remarkable elaboration of high culture. Romanesque gave way to Gothic art with an energy and driving self-confidence that is reminiscent of the pride and skill with which classical Greek art burst forth to cele-brate the perfection of the polis. But it was Latin Christian civilization, embodied in a series of great cathedrals, that demanded celebration in the thirteenth century; and townsmen's pride, reinforced by the piety of poor peasants and of lordly rent-receivers of high and low degree, found full-throated expression in lofty naves and the tracery of Gothic windows and spires. The power and exuberance of Gothic art paralleled the development of rational theology at the University of Paris, itself a new institution devoted as much to the definition and discovery of truth as to its propagation.

The buoyancy and sublime self-confidence that characterized the cul-ture of northwestern Europe in the thirteenth century was sustained by the massive economic and military successes which continued to reward Frankish efforts to cope with nature and with men of alien culture. In such circumstances Latin Christians could afford to be curious and were wil-ling and ready to interrogate ancients and moderns who had anything interesting to say. The reception of Aristotelian philosophy and of Greek science in Paris in the thirteenth century is the great example of this openness to novelty and of faith in human reason as a guide to nature and the universe. The reception of Roman law in Bologna and at other centers (mainly in Italy) was a second and equally pregnant demonstration of faith in reason as a guide to ordering society. In addition, Arabic poetry, Celtic myths, pagan antiquity, whether Roman or German — all pro-vided stimuli for the flowering of European literatures.

Institutional inventiveness was no less striking. Guilds, parliaments, and innumerable other corporations for the conduct of economic, religious, and political affairs proliferated freely. These corporations allowed individuals to cooperate effectively across time and space and the aptitude Latin Christians exhibited for this form of endeavor magnified their power and multiplied efficiency as compared to anything attainable in communities where men were less able or willing to trust one another. The all-but-universal training peasants had in cooperation through joint tillage of open fields probably underlay and reinforced such aptitudes; at any rate the dense multiplication of cooperative associations capable of ordering and compartmentalizing human activity seems clearly to coincide with the distribution of moldboard tillage in Europe. Beyond those limits, distrust of persons beyond the circle of blood relationship tended to interfere with the smooth functioning of such corporations, and an excessive and masculine valuation of personal self-assertion often proved incompatible with voluntary acceptance of subordinate roles in corporate undertakings.

Consolidation of comparatively large kingdoms in both France and England was another illustration of the vigor of institutional inventiveness that characterized the heartlands of this northwestern style of civilization. But territorial sovereignties, however delineated on the ground, never achieved the unambiguous primacy among human associations that they had been accorded among the ancient Greeks. Overlapping jurisdictions were the rule. In particular, the claims of the Church to universal sway — if not over bodies, at least over souls — tempered and often conflicted with secular rulers' power. Local and customary ties between knight and peasant, landlord and tenants, also countervailed centralizing, bureaucratic tendencies; and in the Germanies and part of Italy, the overarching claims of an emperor met effective opposition from lesser territorial princes on the one hand, and from rival claims to universal authority issuing from the popes in Rome on the other.

Assuredly, the brilliant achievements of Latin Christendom in the tenth to the thirteenth centuries deserve the attention historians have lavished upon this age. Modern Western civilization, which bestrode the entire world like a colossus in the eighteenth and nineteenth centuries, grew from these roots. The medieval history of the Seine, Rhine, and Thames basins have therefore a peculiar importance for those who hope to understand our own times. Nor is modern reverence for the achievements of the thirteenth century in northwestern Europe simply a matter of retrospection. Men in the age itself and in the century that followed recognized the attractiveness of what had been so triumphantly generated in the soil of northern France. The reception of Gothic art and of Parisian scholasticism in Italy itself, not to mention the diffusion of these styles of art and of thought throughout central and eastern Europe as far as the limits of moldboard cultivation, proves it. The *reconquista* of Spain by knights armed and trained *à la Franca*, and the subjugation of the

Celtic fringes of the British Isles by Norman conquerors and churchmen between the twelfth and fourteenth centuries also attested the enduring power of the Frankish style of life. The capture of Constantinople in 1204 by knights of the Fourth Crusade, and the establishment of a number of Frankish principalities in the Levant thereafter, was yet another demonstration of the power Europe's Far West had achieved. Frankish styles of warfare and courtly culture even made modest inroads among the Greeks and other Balkan Christians in the thirteenth and fourteenth centuries. Russia itself turned back the knightly assault only by accepting Mongol rule.

Yet it is a defect of perspective to treat this brilliant Frankish civilization as the only important cultural model in medieval Europe. At the beginning of the period with which we are dealing, cultural primacy clearly belonged to Byzantium; by 1300, primacy was about to focus on central and northern Italy, where a galaxy of city-states and the restored papacy (after 1378) soon outstripped trans-Alpine Europe as a seat of successful cultural innovation. Even in military matters, the supremacy of knightly tactics, the special badge of Frankish prowess in the battlefield, was nearing an end by the close of the thirteenth century, when the great frontier boom in the Seine, Rhine, and Thames valleys came finally to a halt.

Before considering this second phase of Europe's medieval development (1300–1500), something should be said of the ebb and flow and interactions of Spanish Islam, Byzantine Christendom, and the steppe cultures of eastern Europe. Spanish Moslem culture and the Islamic steppe culture are often regarded as non-European, despite the undeniable fact that they existed for many centuries on soil that is conventionally defined as part of Europe. This exclusion reflects religious prejudice of very long standing which identified everything admirable with Christianity and abhorred Islam as infidelity. The further fact that Russian and Spanish national sentiment matured in opposition to the Moslem presence on soil that eventually fell to these two outposts and guardians of Christian truth, east and west, also colors historical scholarship with often unconsciously preserved, but pervasive, denigration of Islam. When one becomes aware of such bias it is hard not to overreact. My remarks with respect to both Moslem cultures should therefore be understood as extremely tentative.

First, Spain: Moslem Spain achieved a high level of prosperity and civilization in the tenth century. Moslem law dictated full toleration for Christians and Jews, both of which communities played an active part, along with Arabs and Berbers, in the development of literature and learning. Cordoba, the capital, rivaled Constantinople in size and magnificence; the Umayyad court consciously and on the whole successfully set out to rival the Abassids of Baghdad as patrons of art and learning.

Conquest by fanatical North African sectarians — Almoravids after 1056, Almohades after 1145 — did not entirely eclipse Spain's intellectual culture, as the life dates and successful public career of Averroes (ca. 1126–1198) in Cordoba attest. Yet the fanaticism of the Almoravids forced the family of another distinguished Spaniard, the Jew Maimonides (1135–1204), to take refuge in Cairo; and after 1212, when a Christian coalition defeated the Almohade forces in a decisive battle (Las Navas de Tolosa), the great days of Spanish Moslem civilization were over. Yet Christian fanaticism, like the Islamic fanaticism of the Berbers which had preceded it, did not prevent the three great faiths — Christian, Moslem, and Jewish — which had coexisted so successfully under the Umayyad caliphs in the tenth century, from continuing to survive side by side peacefully enough until the fifteenth century.

I can only guess as to why the Spanish bridgehead of Moslem culture never took deep root in central and northern Spain, and collapsed as completely as it did after 1212. Perhaps the high development of Moslem civilization was so tied in with irrigation agriculture as to inhibit transition to rain-watered lands. Irrigation was certainly important around Cordoba. Yet the heavy capital outlay required for building canals and their laborious maintenance after they had been constructed had little appeal in lands adequately watered by rain. Hence in regions northward from the valley of the Guadalquivir, where more rain fell, there was less incentive to build up a canal system like that which sustained the dense settlements around Cordoba. Moreover, such an irrigation system was doubly vulnerable. In time — sometimes centuries, sometimes much less, depending on how rapidly salt was left behind by the evaporating water — fields began to lose fertility, poisoned by accumulating salt. In addition, marauders can cut canals quite easily, condemning wide regions to sterility unless the system can be repaired within a few weeks. Any general breakdown of public order in the Guadalquivir Valley was therefore likely to be fatal to the dense populations that had sustained Spanish Islam at its peak. Perhaps this is in fact what happened. At any rate, what remained after 1212 was a struggling remnant even though the patient labor of Moorish peasants made the sun-drenched, water-shy region around Granada, where Islamic princes ruled until 1492, bloom like a garden, even without the waters of the Guadalquivir to feed large-scale irrigation works of the sort that had been possible before.

An important change in maritime affairs in the Mediterranean also affected the Moslems of Spain adversely. Italian shipping successfully challenged Moslem seafarers in the central Mediterranean soon after 1000. By the end of the century, the Norman conquest of Sicily (completed 1091) made it difficult for Moslem ships to traverse the entire length of the inland sea safely. This tended to cut Spain and the rest of the Maghreb off from the main centers of Islamic culture. The surviving

Moslem principalities of the Islamic Far West were thus condemned to a more remote and provincial existence than had been the case when Moslem shipping moved freely from one end of the Mediterranean to the other. Caravans, of course, remained but the sea had, for the most part, become Christian, to Italy's great advantage and Spain's loss.[5]

The decay of Spain as an active center of Islamic civilization after 1212 was in some measure compensated for by developments in North Africa, where such notable figures as the geographer and traveler, Ibn Battuta (1304–1377) and the great historian, Ibn Khaldun (1332–1406) were born and educated. But Spanish Islam also had a powerful afterglow in Christian Europe. The doctors of Paris, for example, who were discovering Aristotle, for the most part through translations made in Spain from Arabic versions of his writings, also accorded respectful attention to the works of Averroes, the Commentator. In Spain itself, despite Christian prejudices against Moslems, a few rulers, chief among them Alfonso X, the Wise (reigned 1252–1284),King of Castile, did something to carry on the tradition of royal patronage of learning. In the field of *belles lettres*, Arabic verse forms and music stimulated the troubadours of Catalonia and southern France to develop a more polished, genteel, and sensual poesy than had been known before in Latin Christendom. Styles of Christian piety and mysticism in Spain also took something from Moslem Sufi traditions, as is particularly evident in the writings of Raymond Lull. Indeed, it is worth wondering whether the distinctive and persistent traits that distinguish Spanish Catholicism from that of other parts of Latin Christendom do not owe a good deal to borrowing from, as well as rivalry with, the faith and fanaticism of Islam.

Yet the Christians of the Latin west took only bits and pieces from the Moslem treasury in Spain; the real heir of Spanish Islam was Africa. Indeed, Moslem high cultures in North and West Africa bore much the same relation to Spain as Russian culture bore to Byzantium. There are other interesting parallels between Cordoba and Byzantium. The downward curve of Byzantine fortunes and cultural influence that set in toward the close of the eleventh century paralleled chronologically the disasters that descended on Moslem Spain. It is also noteworthy that Cordoba and Byzantium succumbed to the same executioners. For just as crusading

---

[5] Shortage of suitable ships' timbers within Moslem territory was a major reason for their loss of command of the sea. This, in turn, was a result of the failure of Islamic civilization to establish itself securely on well-watered soil. Moslem affinity, so evident in Spain, to intensive irrigation-oasis techniques of agriculture condemned Islam to having to import timber from better-watered regions. This put Moslem seafarers at a crippling disadvantage as compared to dwellers on the northern side of the Mediterranean as soon as essential skills of navigation and ship construction established themselves among the Christians of those coasts. Hence the two main technological weaknesses of Spanish Islam can be traced back to the fineness of the adjustment Spanish Moslems made to a semidesert environment. Irrigation agriculture was so productive that it made transference to other landscapes unattractive and, for a long time, entirely unnecessary.

Christian knights, many of them recent arrivals in Spain from beyond the Pyrenees, destroyed the prosperity of Cordoba after 1212, so also crusaders from France and Flanders captured and sacked Constantinople in 1204, administering a blow to the economy and society of Byzantium from which the empire never recovered.

Though Latin Christian crusaders therefore had the dubious honor of administering the *coup de grâce* to the high civilizations that had hitherto flourished at either end of the Mediterranean, they were not solely responsible. In Spain, for instance, the Almoravid and Almohade conquerors had injected a barbarous Moslem fanaticism into Spanish life that had disruptive consequences long before an approximately equally barbarous Christian fanaticism finished the job. Byzantium, too, faced Turkish nomad attackers pressing forward from the east who were almost as dangerous as the rude Frankish knights and sailors coming from the west.

There was another interesting parallel between what happened in Spain and what happened in Byzantine territory. For just as the Franks appear to have disrupted a delicate irrigation system in southern Spain and thus made Moslem recovery impossible, so also the advancing Turkish nomads rolled back the frontier of agricultural settlement in Asia Minor and the Ukraine, thereby depriving Byzantine authorities of essential resources which in earlier centuries had permitted the embattled masters of Constantinople to survive as a great and civilized power. North of the Black Sea, an influx of Turkish tribesmen in the mid-eleventh century damaged whatever agriculture had previously existed on the Ukrainian grasslands and river bottoms. More important, the tribesmen seized command of the strategic areas along the river banks where falls and rapids made it necessary for boatmen to come ashore and use ropes to haul their vessels past the danger. By intercepting and plundering river flotillas at these vulnerable points, the Turkish nomads soon made communication between Byzantine and Russian lands in the north as precarious as sea communication between Moslem Spain and the eastern Mediterranean was becoming at precisely the same time. Russia, like the Moslem Far West, became remote, half cut off from the invigorating force of Byzantine culture which had initially nourished the beginnings of civilization in the northern forests.

This Turkish advance across the Ukrainian steppes constituted a severe blow to Byzantine prosperity and security, cutting down the economic as well as the cultural hinterland available to nourish the capital in the Bosporus. Far more damaging, however, was Byzantium's loss of the interior of Asia Minor to other Turkish bands. This took place in the decades before and after the Battle of Manzikert (1071). As the Turks advanced, agriculture retreated from the broad valleys and upland plateaus of the peninsula. Most of the interior of Asia Minor became a grassland similar to the Ukrainian steppe itself, while the Christian peasantry, which time and again had served as a valuable reservoir of fighting manpower for Byzantium, disappeared. Tax income diminished *pari passu*, of course; so did supplies of various raw materials that had traditionally filtered down from the interior to the coastal ports. Without these resources, Byzantium limped on one leg, so to speak, and could no longer, as had often happened before, call upon the resources of Asia Minor to repel attack in the Balkans, and vice versa. Since the same foe could not attack both the Balkans and Asia Minor simultaneously, crises on the one front seldom coincided with crises on the other. This had been the great secret of Byzantium's survival; but after about 1100 that possibility had permanently disappeared.

No one knows why the nomads were able to displace peasant cultivators on such a scale. Numbers may have had something to do with the case, if it is true that the size of migrating Turkmen hordes that arrived in Asia Minor in the eleventh century were greater than in earlier times. On the other hand it is possible that the agriculture and town life of the interior regions of Asia Minor were suffering from a creeping crisis, owing to exhaustion of wood supplies. Without a supply of wood for fuel, construction, tool-making, etc., agriculture and city life were literally impossible; nomads had from time immemorial adjusted their habits to an almost total absence of wood supplies. The climate of the interior regions of Asia Minor made forest growth precarious, and increasingly destructive peasant efforts to find enough wood to keep going in traditional lines may have quite literally prepared the way for nomad occupancy by destroying the last remnants of tree growth in one region after another.

Whatever the truth may be about what took place in Asia Minor to undermine Greek Christendom in that region so profoundly, another important change, this one in the regime of the seas, acted against Byzantine interests as powerfully as it did against those of Spanish Islam. The rise of Italian shipping to dominion over the central Mediterranean meant that the profits of trade gravitated away from Byzantine toward Italian ports. More than that, from 1081, when the Byzantine emperor accorded the Venetians special exemption from the ordinary excise taxes collected in Byzantine ports, the Greek government lost an important source of revenue and gave the Italians (for other cities soon extorted similar rights from the Byzantines) a crushing trade advantage over their own subjects.

To be sure, Emperor Alexis I Comnenus (reigned 1081–1118) adroitly exploited the prowess of the Franks who responded to the papal summons for a crusade in 1097–1099 to regain lost provinces in Asia Minor. Some of his heirs worked hard to restore Byzantine defenses, imitating Frankish knighthood and hiring knights from the Latin west in some number. But insufficient cash income restricted what the emperor could do along these lines, and the alternative of infeudation risked fatal insubordination. There was no escape from this dilemma as long as Turkish nomads continued to eat away the Christian peasantry of Asia Minor, and Italian merchants continued to dominate Byzantine sea trade, while enjoying exemption from excise taxes. Hence it was a hollow shell that fell in 1204 before the combined forces of Venice and the Frankish knights who had joined the Fourth Crusade.

Yet the economic and political disruption of Byzantium did not lead to cultural decay. First in exile from their capital at Nicaea, and then after 1261 at Constantinople itself, Greek rulers styling themselves emperors of Rome maintained a brilliant court culture, more self-consciously Greek and more keenly aware of their pagan ancestors than had been the case in earlier ages. Some interesting convergences occurred between the tastes and interests of Byzantine courtiers and those of their humanist contemporaries in Italy. But creeping secularism and acute concern for elegance of language and of manners generated a volcanic opposition among the lower classes of Orthodox Christendom. In the fourteenth century impassioned monks, who saw God in their mystic visions, won control of the Greek Orthodox Church. The result was to widen and deepen all that separated Orthodox Christianity from Latin Christianity. Moreover, in asserting their doctrinal and ecclesiastical independence, the monks rejuvenated Orthodoxy and gave that faith a new and power-ful missionary impulse. New styles of art and new styles of piety went hand in hand, spreading out from Mount Athos where monkish mysticism had its headquarters. The movement penetrated Bulgaria, where pious and learned men devised a standardized Slavonic literary language to propagate their faith. Thence it penetrated westward into Serbia and northward to Russia. In both these lands, new monastic establishments became extremely influential centers from which important aspects of late Byzantine civilization radiated. As in the case of Moslem Spain, therefore, the decay of material power and wealth did not bring an end to cultural influence. On the contrary, it was in the declining days of economic weakness and political upheaval that both Byzantine and Span-ish Moslem culture achieved their maximal geographic dispersion.

The penetration of a monastic version of Byzantine civilization into Russia and the Balkan interior was facilitated by a notable commercial development that took place in all the lands draining into the Black Sea during the thirteenth and fourteenth centuries. Soon after the victory of 1204, most of the Frankish knights went home, carrying bits of plunder with them. The Venetians, however, remained, and set out to exploit the commercial possibilities opened by their new position. Before 1204, Byzantine policy had always kept the Black Sea closed to Italian ships. After 1204, for the first time the same vessels that sailed the central Mediterranean and Aegean could move also into the Black Sea, penetrating as far as the mouth of the Don at the head of the Sea of Azov. This meant a vast expansion of the commercial hinterland available to Venice. For a while disturbed political conditions in the Black Sea region hindered the development of trade; and in 1261 the Venetians lost control of Constantinople, when a *coup de main* engineered partly by Genoese, restored a Greek emperor to the Byzantine throne. But Genoese took over where the Venetians had left off, and for the next century these two cities struggled for control of the Black Sea trade. Sometimes they fought all-out wars; more often they resorted to force only on a limited scale or in special circumstances.

What made the Black Sea trade so valuable was this: in the generation after the Italians first broke through into the Black Sea, Mongol conquerors unified and pacified the Russian lands and most of Asia. The Mongol conquest of Russia and the Ukrainian steppes (1237–1240) brought a highly efficient administration to that part of the world. The new rulers were quite aware of the advantages flourishing trade could bring to their courts and armies. In particular, the tribute system they imposed upon the subject Russian principalities invited the development of relatively massive export of northern products — e.g. furs and wax — in exchange for items that could not be supplied by their unskilled subjects. The Volga served as the natural conduit for the concentration of the Russian tribute. The Mongol conquerors therefore located their headquarters along the lower reaches of that stream. From this center, the rulers of the Golden Horde, as the westernmost branch of the Mongol empire is commonly called, maintained systematic communications with China to the east, Iran to the south, and the valleys of the Don and Dnieper to the west. Military and political considerations required a highly organized postal system capable of carrying urgent messages at a gallop across the whole of Asia. Lengthy packtrains, toiling more slowly across the same vast distances, followed naturally enough in the wake of the Mongol pacification.

Hence, for about a century, roughly between 1250 and 1350, the Italian vessels arriving in the Crimea and at other points along the north and east coasts of the Black Sea were able to enter into commercial relations with a vast hinterland extending eastward all the way to China as well as northward to the upwaters of the Dnieper, Don, and Volga. Genoa was more successful in this trade than Venice, though it was a Venetian, the famous Marco Polo (1254–1324), who left the most vivid and persuasive account of how a bold and resolute man might make his fortune and see the world in the process by venturing along the Mongol trade routes.

After some hesitation, the khans of the Golden Horde officially (and rather tepidly) espoused Islam. With Islam came some of the trappings of Moslem civilization. But nomadic habits and ideals died hard: for a long time the khans shifted their headquarters, summer and winter, migrating up and down the banks of the Volga according to the season. Arts and crafts compatible with the life of mounted warriors certainly flourished among the Mongols; but the accoutrements of civilized urban society could have only slender development among a people and at a court that clung tenaciously to migratory patterns of life.

Yet this much is clear: the charms of settled civilization were insufficient to wean the Mongols from their own unique style of modified nomadry. Pride in their extraordinary military accomplishment re-inforced this conservatism. But the fact was that before they appeared in Europe at all, the Mongols had borrowed a good deal from civilized neighbors, Chinese as well as Moslem. They should not therefore be dismissed as crude barbarians. Thus, for example, Mongol administrative, tax, and military systems reflected Genghis Khan's familiarity with Chinese bureaucratic practice. The Mongols' inclination to reinsure against divine displeasure by adherence to a plurality of forms of worship tantalized Christian missionaries who visited the Great Khan's court in the thirteenth century; but what scandalized and puzzled Christians of the past does not seem irrational or particularly barbarous in an age when we are able, like the Mongols of old, to appreciate some of the charms and reflect upon the rival claims to theological truths advanced by the different civilizations of Eurasia in the thirteenth and subsequent centuries. About art and literature it is difficult to speak: too much has been lost to allow a summary evaluation, though a few surviving scraps show that, at least by the fifteenth century, a thoroughly professional style of painting flourished at Mongol courts on the lower Volga and in central Asia. Like Mongol administration, this art showed strong affinities with China. Even though Mongol high culture was always narrowly restricted, affecting only the court and the yurts of a few notables, Mongols and Italians found it easy to do business with each other. For a century or so, as long as the political unity of the steppe empire held, Italian merchants were able to tap the riches of the whole of Asia through Black Sea ports and reestablished a southward flow of forest products, grain, fish, and slaves from the Ukrainian and Russian hinterlands of the kind that the Byzantines had monopolized in earlier centuries.

This greatly expanded field of trade was an important stimulant to Italy's prosperity. Capital accumulated very fast: larger and larger operations became possible. As a result, not long after 1300, nearly all Europe (and some of Asia as well) came to be tied into a far denser commercial net than ever before. Italian merchants, bankers, and ships, collaborating with the Mongol trade and tribute system, acted as the organizing element in the whole complex. The main sufferers were Orthodox Christians, condemned to pay tribute to the Mongols in the north, and condemned in the south to see the profits of trade and imperial power pass from their grasp and lodge instead in the hands of Venetian, Genoese, and Pisan interlopers.

In the fourteenth century, northwestern Europe was incorporated into the busy Italians' web as well. English sheep farms, Spanish herdsmen, Flemish spinners and weavers all became suppliers of raw material for Italian manufacturers. Sharp-eyed financiers and entrepreneurs from Italy organized or reorganized salt mines in Poland, tin mines in Cornwall, and alum mines in Anatolia, and linked them all into the new, widened trade network from which they profited greatly.

The key breakthrough date that permitted merging the trade and finance of the Mediterranean–Black Sea regions with that of northwestern Europe was 1290. In that year a Genoese sea captain attacked and defeated a Moroccan naval force that had until then closed the Straits of Gibraltar to Christian ships. In the following decades, first Genoese and then Venetian vessels began to ply the Atlantic waters regularly. With the establishment of a dependable maritime connection between Europe's northern seas and the Mediterranean, the superior skill, capital resources, and organization of the Italian merchant communities soon gave them dominant positions in northwest Europe's big business. As a result of Italian enterprise, therefore, in the first half of the fourteenth century, the economies of Spain, England, France, and the Low Countries became a subordinate though important part of a truly pan-European market.

Interregional specialization allowed massive import of commodities in short supply locally. In principle, this permitted northwestern Europe to overcome the impasse created by the approaching exhaustion of virgin forest land. But it took a while for the necessary adjustments to work themselves out. Men had to move into new occupations and find ways to pay for massive deliveries of coarse goods like grain and timber from distant parts. Marketing and production of these and other commodities had to be increased to meet the demand. The Black Death, 1347–1351, may have slowed these adjustments. It certainly killed off a very substantial proportion of the inhabitants of northwestern Europe. Population in some localities did not regain pre-1346 densities until the sixteenth century. Hence it was only after 1500 that northwestern Europe began fully to react to the potentialities interregional trade offered for supplementing its local resources not merely with Italian luxuries, but with articles of mass consumption. Before that time management of European interregional exchanges remained mainly in Italian hands.

At first glance, the strict discipline of Mongol encampments and the noisy confusion of the city-states of northern Italy seem to have nothing in common. Yet both were able, in very different ways, to mobilize human and material resources for consciously defined goals more efficiently and on a larger scale than had been done before.

The Mongol army and administration was bureaucratic through and through. Men were appointed and promoted to office on the basis of performance, and the test of frequent battle provided a relatively straightforward basis for recognition of merit. Strangers and conquered peoples were fed into the Mongol command system — witness the career of Marco Polo in China — wherever their skills or experience seemed useful. Genghis Khan and his heirs also appreciated technological improvements, as is shown by their ready resort to gunpowder and other siege weapons borrowed from China.

But generally speaking, the tactics and equipment of horse archers had been perfected long before the thirteenth century. Technological changes were therefore marginal. The great novelty sustaining Mongol power lay in the realm of bureaucratic command and organizational structures. In 1241, when the Mongol army headed westward, columns advanced on either side of the Carpathians, yet the two maintained regular contact by couriers, so that a single commander could (and did) direct the movements of both forces. Until World War I, no other European commander was able to control such far-flung forces or coordinate movements across such difficult terrain. This capacity to communicate, and through communication to command and coordinate masses of men at a distance, explained both Mongol victories in the field and the cohesion, however precarious, of the vast empire their victories won.

The upthrust of the Italian city-states — chiefly Venice, Genoa, Milan, and Florence — also rested on superior means of coordinating human activity at a distance across time and space. But instead of a military command system run on bureaucratic principles, the Italians relied upon an elaborate network of contractual and corporate relationships, which allowed a gifted and lucky individual to make a fortune very quickly and measured efficiency not by success in battle but by capital accumulation. And like the Mongols, the Italian business community developed a keen eye for useful technological improvements, i.e. for anything that promised to increase profits or reduce costs. Indeed, without a far-reaching technical advance in matters nautical, the extraordinary expansion of Italian business from the thirteenth to the fifteenth century could not have occurred. Larger ships, steered by sternpost rudders, equipped with multiple sails and masts, and decked over against bad weather, made it safe to sail the seas at any time of year. Instead of beaching ships in the fall and launching them again in spring, as had been customary before the thirteenth century, Italian (and other European shipmasters) now kept their vessels at sea all year round, with only such stopovers in port as were necessary to take on and unload cargo or to wait for a favoring wind, or for pirates to go away.

Simultaneously, use of larger containers — e.g. barrels instead of amphorae for carrying wine — cheapened the transport of commodities.

Handling tuns of wine, like the handling of a heavy rudder or raising a mainsail, depended on mechanical advantage secured through use of block and tackle. The magnification of human muscles by this simple but important device probably lay at the heart of the entire nautical revolution of the thirteenth century.

The new ships also needed protection and found it through the development of crossbows. These weapons also magnified human muscle power by using mechanical advantage to bend bows too heavy for straight pull. A well-aimed bolt from such a weapon penetrated armor easily; and when this fact became apparent, the supremacy of the knight in battle ended abruptly wherever a corps of crossbowmen and the artisan skills needed to produce these weapons in sufficient numbers existed. This happened in 1282 in the Mediterranean (the Sicilian Vespers). In the more backward lands of northern Europe, the overthrow of knighthood as the decisive element in battle came almost two centuries later at the Battle of Nancy, 1477, when Swiss infantry spitted the charging chivalry of Burgundy on a serried array of long-hafted pikes. By bracing the butts of their pikes against the ground the Swiss discovered a simple and effective way to convert the momentum of a charging knight from a supreme asset into a suicidal liability. Thereby they ended the supremacy of heavy cavalry in northwestern Europe just as it had earlier been ended in Mediterranean lands by the more sophisticated technology of the crossbow.

Between 1280 and 1330, larger and more seaworthy vessels, protected by efficient missile weapons, spread rapidly through all the European seas. Italians pioneered most, though not all, of the improvements and took the lead in exploiting the new commercial possibilities such ships opened. The critical change was that long-distance carriage of coarser, cheaper goods became economic. Bulk commodities such as raw wool, salt, grain, timber, alum, and iron became worth transporting from one end of Europe to the other, given existing price differentials; and Italian (mainly Genoese and Florentine) businessmen eagerly organized the financial marketing and transport facilities needed to make such long hauls pay off. Older exchange patterns involving long-distance transport of relatively expensive goods — spices, cloth, luxury manufacture, etc. — also increased in volume; but the real novelty of the economic pattern woven through all the waterways of Europe by Italian seamen and merchants in the fourteenth and fifteenth centuries was the increased importance of cheap bulk commodities.

Under such a regime industrial specialization and interregional economic integration opened up all the advantages Adam Smith was later to analyze so persuasively, and did so for a larger number of Europeans than had been conceivable before. The marvelous development of northwestern Europe between the tenth and thirteenth centuries had been a frontier phenomenon, based on multiplication of locally almost self-sufficient units in what started as waste forest lands. Towns, with a few square miles of surrounding countryside, were the important units in economic matters; local feudal officers and knights in residence in innumerable villages were the politically important units. But with the arrival of cheaper shipping and of Italian entrepreneurial expertise, economic integration on a far larger scale began to thrive. Correspondingly, larger political units — whether national monarchies, as in France and England, or the papal monarchy in all Latin Christendom — solidified and extended their control in ways that affected the daily lives of far more human beings than had been possible in earlier times.

The connection between the expanded interregional economic specialization and political consolidation was very close. Indeed, the Italians were able to penetrate northwestern Europe economically, owing in large part to the protection they had from local rulers, for whom they performed various services in return. Not only could Italians supply luxuries and administrative *savoir-faire*, they also had money to lend. Edward III of England (reigned 1327–1377), for example, found it far easier to borrow from Lombard moneylenders than it was to get his own subjects to pay the costs of his court and of the armies he sent to France to fight what came to be called the Hundred Years War (1337–1453). So much did he borrow from "Lombards" that when he repudiated his debts the news precipitated a serious financial crisis in Florence and other Italian money markets. Financial relations between the papacy and Italian banking firms were even closer; and agents dispatched from Rome to administer papal revenues in the far corners of Latin Christendom, carried with them much of the business acumen that stood the Italians in such good stead wherever they encountered less commercially sophisticated populations.

At home in Italy, too, the relationship between public authority and capitalist entrepreneur was vital to the economic success that came to the Italians. Cities like Venice and Genoa were governed by men who shared the commercial spirit to the full. Confiscatory taxation was not in question: indeed, from many points of view city government was itself managed like a business enterprise. State policy and commercial policy were scarcely distinguishable. Private capital was tapped for public purposes in time of emergency through loans. Interest payments on the Venetian public debt were so reliable that subscription to it became a favored form of investment for anyone, citizen or stranger, who sought a secure income on his capital. As for Genoa, when the commune fell on evil days financially, most of the powers of government were transferred to what had begun as a private company, the famous Bank of San Giorgio.

Self-governing commercial and industrial cities existed also in Germany, and in the fifteenth and sixteenth centuries some of them became seats of capitalist enterprise on an important scale. In particular, German businessmen based in Augsburg and other south German towns opened up a series of mining enterprises in central Europe, working eastward from the Harz Mountains of Saxony to the mountains of Bohemia and Transylvania. Silver and iron were the most important metals put into circulation through these efforts. Mining techniques improved rapidly; deeper and deeper mines were opened, and the Germans became the most accomplished miners in Europe — and, for that matter, in the world. A more copious supply of metals and at cheaper cost became thenceforward one of Europe's most important advantages over the other civilizations of the earth.

Farther north, other German businessmen based in Lübeck and adjacent towns took the lead in exploiting the possibilities of a new pattern of Baltic trade. As happened earlier in northwestern Europe, the development of the southern and eastern coasts of the Baltic from the fourteenth to the sixteenth century depended on the stabilization of a new technological and ecological pattern in what had formerly been a thinly inhabited frontier region. The critical factor was an ample supply of cheap salt, as a result of its discovery and exploitation in Poland and elsewhere. With enough cheap salt, herring and cabbage could be preserved indefinitely in brine, and a relatively cheap and nutritious diet — rye bread, cabbage, and an occasional herring on feast days — became available to the population all year round.[6] Salt, of course, had to be paid for. This was managed by developing an export trade in grain and timber — precisely the commodities needed in the older, densely populated lands of northwestern Europe.

Unlike the patterns of life of the tenth to the thirteenth century, this new Baltic and east European economy required relatively long-distance movement of coarse commodities. Salt, grain, and timber, the key items, all had to travel far to market. Away from the coast itself, where German merchants took charge, organization of these exchanges fell mainly into the hands of large estate owners or their agents (often Jews). The entire region draining into the Baltic from the Gulf of Finland to the base of the Danish peninsula thus acquired a distinctive social structure in which the landed aristocracy played a far more important managerial role than was true elsewhere in Europe.

The Baltic region in turn linked up with the Russian river system through Novgorod. As Mongol power weakened, owing largely to the

---

[6] Rye bread alone lacked sufficient protein and vitamins and could not sustain a healthy population through the relatively long winters of the Baltic regions without supplement. In early times, hunting provided such a supplement, but this required a very thin population. The virtue of cabbage and herring was that relatively dense populations could find suitable nourishment from these sources. Incidentally, in western Europe protein-rich beans and peas played a similar role in supplementing the cereal diet available to the common people. These legumes, however, did not flourish in the poorer soils and shorter growing seasons of the Baltic coastlands.

decay of the bureaucratic rationality that had characterized the Mongol state in its prime, Russian commodities began to flow westward to the Baltic as well as southward toward the Caspian and Black seas. Less was siphoned off by the Mongol overlords, and more remained to be exchanged for iron and other commodities available through the Baltic trade net.

The upshot of these and other less spectacular developments was to integrate the everyday activity of a very substantial proportion of the entire population of all Europe into a single whole, regulated by market relations that focused in a few dozen cities, chief among them those of northern Italy. Strangers living hundreds or even thousands of miles apart combined to produce a result that some businessman, living perchance in still a third locality, planned and intended, though the participants in the process (including the business entrepreneurs) were not necessarily aware of how all the distant and necessary connections were in fact established and maintained.

Until after 1500, Italians remained the chief managers of Europe's interregional integration. They were masters of business organization. Partnerships and family-scale enterprises were supplemented by state undertakings and by joint stock companies. Some companies even became territorial rulers (and plantation managers) in island colonies of the eastern Mediterranean. Indeed, almost all the organizational devices later employed by Dutch and English entrepreneurs to develop trade and industry on a transoceanic scale after 1500 were developed first by Italian businessmen who had an empire to exploit within the Mediterranean from the time of the First Crusade until the Turks in the east and the Spaniards in the west squeezed the Italians out of most of their managerial roles at either end of the inland sea by 1500.

Assuredly, between 1300 and 1500, the capitalist spirit — whether manifested in plantation slavery, accounting techniques, bank credit and cycles of boom and bust, impersonal manipulative use of other human beings, or restless experiment with new techniques, materials, and products — had ample expression in the great Italian cities of Tuscany and of the Po Valley.

Italy's primacy was never secure, to be sure. Throughout trans-Alpine Europe local sentiment nearly always disliked the slippery skills Italian entrepreneurs applied so successfully. Whenever local rulers could secure equivalent services from their own subjects, the Italians lost their principal protectors and could expect to be squeezed out. This, in effect, was what happened among the Turks, who found a suitable supply of Greek, Armenian, Jewish, and Moslem businessmen among the populations of the Levant who were capable of performing all the commercial functions Italians had almost monopolized along the eastern Mediterranean coasts since 1204 or earlier.

The resulting setback to Italian prosperity was serious. Like the Byzantine Empire after it lost control of the interior of Asia Minor, the Italian cities lost the eastern half of their hinterland as the Turks advanced; and after 1453, having seized Constantinople and extinguished the last shadow of the Roman Empire in the east, the sultan closed the Black Sea to Italian ships. Constantinople, in short, resumed its former role as imperial mistress and monopolistic market for all the products of the Black Sea coastlands. Elsewhere, in the Aegean and (after 1520) in Syria and Egypt, Ottoman commercial policy also restricted Italian economic activities very sharply.

Simultaneously, Spain, England, France, and Germany were also pushing back Italian economic influence upon their respective lands, partly by state action, partly through the development of local competition. Yet as the scope of Italian economic management decreased, Italian leadership in Europe shifted on to a different plane. Reception of what we know as Italian Renaissance culture in trans-Alpine Europe became a really live possibility precisely in proportion as local economic life began to achieve an Italian level of complexity and sophistication. Hence, for a century or more after Italian cities ceased to exercise economic primacy in Europe (roughly after 1500), Italian cultural influence upon the trans-Alpine hinterland of Europe continued and, indeed, increased in importance.

This sort of "ecological" succession may be taken as normal. The spread of classical Greek culture throughout the Mediterranean came after the economic power of Athens and the olive and wine-exporting region around the Aegean had broken down. Latin thought and letters penetrated the western provinces of the Roman Empire when Italy's economy was already in trouble, thanks to the spread of wine and oil production in Spain and Gaul. We have just seen how the culture of Moslem Spain and Byzantium began to attract distant peoples more strongly after military and economic disaster had struck the heartlands of both those civilizations. Similarly, the diffusion of Gothic art and scholastic philosophy beyond the boundaries of northwestern Europe occurred after the overthrow of the knight's supremacy in the Mediterranean and at a time when the economic transformation of the northwestern forest lands into fields was beginning to press against its natural limits, thanks to the exhaustion of fresh forests.

There is little I need say here about the peculiar qualities of the civilization of the Italian Renaissance. Italian writers of the fourteenth century developed an intense admiration for Roman antiquity and a corresponding disdain for both Byzantine and "Gothic" styles of civilization. Such value judgments supported the notion of rebirth that remains implicit in our historical terminology. The politics of northern Italy between 1300 and 1500 did in fact somewhat resemble the struggles among the city-states of ancient Greece, and the development toward monarchical rule (everywhere but at Venice) seemed to recapitulate the political experience of classical antiquity. This was why the study of ancient authors had such importance for Machiavelli and others. But in most respects the resemblances between antiquity and the experience of the Italian city-states were superficial, and the differences profound. The relationship is well reflected in art. Take sculpture, for example, where the influence of ancient models was strongest because numerous antique statues, more or less intact, survived to be studied and admired. Yet any of Michelangelo's works, his "David", for instance, though it may share such an obvious external as nudity with the art of ancient Rome, nevertheless differs profoundly in spirit or meaning.

If one tries to express the difference between the art of Michelangelo and that of ancient Greece and Rome, it seems fair to suggest that the heart of the matter lies in a kind of self-consciousness that informed the Renaissance artist's work. Michelangelo chose a style deliberately; the ancient sculptors knew only one tradition of art and remained captive within it, not by choice but from ignorance.

This, indeed, seems to me an example of the most important, central, and underlying difference between classical antiquity and the civilization of the Italian Renaissance. The Italian world was pluralistic in a far more pervasive fashion than had been true in antiquity. Pagan Rome, so praised by Italian humanists, knew only one model of high culture — that of Greece; and only a small class of rich and powerful men were in a position to share in that culture actively. By the fourteenth and fifteenth centuries, educated men of Europe were at least dimly aware of multiple civilizations, knowing something of India and China as well as of Islam and of pagan antiquity.

More than this, within Europe itself a far greater internal variety and complexity existed. The polarization between a handful of rich — mainly passive receivers of rents and tax income — and the poverty-stricken multitudes, which had prevailed through most of antiquity, created a far simpler, more brittle social structure than that which prevailed in medieval Europe. There corporate organizations proliferated endlessly, all the way from the work group that accompanied each plow team into the fields to the vast corporation of the Latin Church itself. Villages and towns, business enterprises, guilds, military companies, religious orders, territorial governments, estates of the realm, incipient nations, and still other forms of corporate groupings fell in between the professedly universal Church and the humble plow team. Amid such pluralism, overlapping membership was the rule rather than the exception. Conflict and internal friction were the result of indefinite multiplication of corporate entities, as the interests of one group seldom coincided exactly with those of others, and corporate organization gave increased weight to the will of even the poorer and weaker classes.

Intellectual pluralism was sustained by the corporate complexity of society. Think, for instance, of the rivalry between Dominicans and Franciscans as a factor in diversifying the tenets of scholastic philosophy, or reflect on how Machiavelli and Savonarola coexisted in the same city of Florence, each sustained by a milieu in which his ideas found an appropriate, encouraging resonance. In a society in which variety had been institutionalized as extensively as took place in the major centers of Renaissance culture, most men had to make far more, and more important, deliberate choices as to what to believe, how to act, what to do, than commonly occurred in simpler, less pluralistic settings. The self-consciousness we read into the stone figures coming from Michelangelo's chisel says as much to anyone with eyes attuned to the difference between his art and that of the Roman sculptors he studied — and transcended.

To sum up: by 1500 Europe was well on its way to modernity, if we take the distinctive hallmark of modernity to be pervasive pluralism of society and culture. Centers of economic and cultural dominance within Europe had oscillated sharply since 900, with the rise of northwestern Europe and of Russia, the sudden irruption of a Mongol power into eastern Europe, the decay of Moslem Spain and of Byzantium, and the concentration of wealth, power, and creativity in Italy. Yet by the end of the period, weaknesses in Italy's position in Europe as a whole had become evident, with the consolidation of Ottoman, Spanish, and other comparatively vast territorial states. Italian power continued to manifest itself for a century and more; but after 1500 new patterns became important enough to justify taking that date as a major watershed between what are traditionally and appropriately called medieval and more modern times.

EUROPE SINCE 1500

By 1500 the city-states of northern Italy were already recoiling before the land power and enhanced administrative efficiency of the Ottoman Empire to the east and of the Spanish Empire to the west. At the very beginning of the sixteenth century, this shift of power entered a critical phase, when both Turkey and Spain built formidable navies, on a scale that far outstripped the material resources available to Venice or any other Italian city. The war between Venice and the Turks, 1499–1503, marked the turning point, for it was then that the maritime skill of the Venetians for the first time failed to make up for inferior numbers. Thereafter within the Mediterranean only the Spaniards were in a position to oppose the Ottomans on anything approaching even terms. The result was a series of naval campaigns, lasting from 1516, when Constantinople first extended its naval power to the western Mediterranean with the capture of Algiers, until 1581, when the protagonists made what turned out to be a lasting truce with each other in order to turn attention to more critical frontiers.

In spite of sporadic efforts to substitute quality for quantity by pioneering improvements in naval design (e.g. the Venetian invention of heavy-gunned galleasses that did so well at Lepanto in 1571), the Italian navies were reduced to auxiliary roles in the sixteenth-century contest between Spain and Turkey for command of the Mediterranean. Moreover, the decay of Italian naval power undermined the mercantile basis of Italian prosperity. The economic hinterlands of Venice, Milan, Florence, and Genoa tended to shrink back toward their respective territorial possessions in northern Italy. Only remnants of the interregional economic dominion of the fourteenth and fifteenth centuries survived — traffic across the Alps in luxury goods, and a limited export of specialized skills and services to all of Europe by, for example, bankers, music masters, engineers, architects, and acrobats.

Thus geopolitical roles within the Mediterranean were once more reversed. Spain and Constantinople, whose decay as centers of civilization had permitted the rise of Italy in the eleventh century, became again seats of powerful states and high cultures that were able to pinch out the city-states of Italy by mobilizing far superior resources from vastly larger territories — territories which had, until the administrative consolidation of Spain and of the Ottoman Empire, acted as important economic hinterlands for the Italians. As a result, after about 1500, the Italian cities had increasingly to get along on local resources and ceased to exert dominating influence in anything but the definition of good taste in art, music, manners, and, for much of Europe, religion.

This fundamental setback to Italian prosperity was magnified by armed invasion. First the French (1494) and then the Spanish (1502) intruded upon the fair land of Italy and, having quarreled, precipitated prolonged and bitter warfare. Fighting ended in 1559, when the French recognized Spanish preponderance in the whole of Italy by the Treaty of Cateau-Cambresis. For two full generations the Italian states, which had been fully sovereign and accustomed to lead the whole of Europe, suffered repeatedly from pillage and the humiliation of helplessness in the face of superior foreign military force. By 1559 those which were not outright provinces of the Spanish Empire, like Naples and Milan, retained precarious independence more on sufferance of the potent foreigners than by virtue of their own strength.

The Renaissance spirit that had flourished so strongly in Italy suffered fatal erosion as one after another of the great centers of art and luxury fell prey to plundering soldiers from beyond the Alps. The sack of Rome in 1527 by the army of Charles V pretty well snuffed out the circle of patrons and performers who had made the papal court the major center of Renaissance thought and art in the first decades of the sixteenth century. Thereafter Venice alone remained hospitable to Renaissance attitudes and values, while the rest of Italy (as well as many Venetians) fell in with the Catholic effort to define and then enforce authoritative religious truth.

The vision of a saving truth, to be served by all right-thinking men with all the force of their being, was in its way just as compelling as the multifaceted vision of human potentiality that had glittered in Italian courts and countinghouses at the height of the Renaissance. It was in part a natural, necessary, and logical reaction against the inadequacy of the Renaissance vision of mankind as maker of his own fate and fortune. For in an age when disaster after disaster descended upon Italy, it was all too obvious that men, whether as individuals or gathered together in cities, did not control their own fate and were in fact playthings of forces utterly beyond their control.

But circumstances pushing Italians and the other peoples of Europe to abandon the individualistic, assertive ideals of Renaissance culture and seek instead some authoritative formulation of faith and a reliable routine of piety were far broader than anything happening in Italy alone. In the decades on either side of 1500, a series of sharp and sudden disjunctions with earlier patterns of experience struck at Europeans everywhere and in all walks of life. This, indeed, is what justifies making a new era of European history begin at that time.

First and foremost among these disruptive novelties was the political upheaval that accompanied the spread of the cannon and the other gunpowder weapons. Indeed the rise of the Ottoman state in the eastern Mediterranean and the rapid magnification of Spanish power in its western reaches were related to the gunpowder revolution in armaments. For a ruler who controlled a well-stocked artillery park could make his will prevail across comparatively enormous distances as soon as cannon became capable of knocking breaches in even the best fortified castles or city walls within a few hours of their emplacement. This meant that local defenses became vulnerable as never before to whoever commanded a few big guns and had the means to carry them to the scene of action (or cast them on the spot, as the Turks did at the siege of Constantinople in 1453).

Aside from strengthening the Ottoman and Spanish empires, the most conspicuous consequence of the gunpowder revolution on European soil was the consolidation of Muscovy in the northeast. The ingathering of the Russian lands by Ivan III, Grand Duke of Moscow (ruled 1462–1505), and his successor Basil III (ruled 1505–1533) created a vast empire, which grew to extraordinary proportions because cannon, easily transported by river, gave the Muscovite ruler the means to batter down local defenses of such ancient rivals as Novgorod, Tver, and Pskov with (at least comparative) ease. Having asserted dominion over all the Russian lands, the Muscovite power next turned its weapons against the remnant of the Mongol Empire on the Volga, with the result that by 1557, Ivan IV, the Terrible (reigned 1533–1584), extended his reach all the way to the Caspian. Thereafter, Siberia presented no insuperable obstacle. Portaging from one river system to the next, Cossack fur traders and explorers equipped with no more than a few handguns and their native hardihood, carried Russian sovereignty all the way to the Pacific by 1637. Only the Mongol Empire which had preceded it in more southerly parts of Asia, and the contemporary Spanish Empire of the New World, have ever compared in territorial extent to the Russian Empire that thus sprang into being.

In western Europe, however, the weapons revolution of early modern times misfired. The Hapsburg Empire of Charles V (ruled 1519–1558) looked for a while as though it might provide the kernel around which a state territorially comparable to that of Muscovy or Turkey[7] might crystallize. In this part of the world mining and metallurgy had developed more fully than anywhere else. As a result, it was not possible to monopolize access to the new master weapons of the age. Gunmetal and skilled gunfounders were in sufficient supply so that Charles V could never prevent his rivals from equipping their armies about as well as he could equip his own. Then, about the middle of the sixteenth century, revetted fortifications effectively proof against cannon fire were developed (mainly in Italy). With this, the balance of forces shifted sharply in favor of more local sovereigns, who could rely on modest garrisons stationed in barrier fortresses to defend them effectively against any and every force that could be brought against them. Nevertheless to survive under these conditions, European rulers had to devote enormous effort to fortifications, and to equipping and reequipping their armies with cannon and other expensive armaments. Such devices, unused, were liable to rust: hence European rulers were often tempted to engage in the "sport of kings" by provoking war. The upshot was an extremely volatile situation in which Europe's rulers, through their jockeying for wealth, power, and glory, kept society in turmoil. Elsewhere in the civilized world far vaster states maintained an effective monopoly of heavy weapons in a single hand, and did not need to devote nearly so much attention to armament and competitive mobilization of resources for war.

Consolidation of these rival states maintained an unstable and variegated pattern in northwestern Europe. Political divisions tended to reinforce cultural divergences. In particular, instead of continuing to rely on Latin as the common language for learning and administration, as had

---

[7]   Not to mention Manchu China, Tokugawa Japan, and Mughal India, all of which consolidated hitherto unequaled territorial dominions by use of cannon.

generally been the case in the Middle Ages, about a dozen different tongues achieved the dignity of serving as literary and administrative media. Multiplication of these mutually incomprehensible literary languages created, or at least encouraged, cultural and intellectual divergences among national groups. On the other hand, within the boundaries of a single state, local differences tended to diminish, though common sovereignty did not always lead to decay of regional peculiarities, as the history of Wales and Ireland, after centuries of English rule, attests.

The political pluralism of early modern Europe was, I think, fundamental and distinctive. When all the rest of the civilized world reacted to the enhanced power cannon gave to a central authority by consolidating vast, imperial states, western and central Europe instead reinforced dozens of local sovereignties, each consciously competing with its neighbors both in peace and, most especially, in war. Such a political structure acted like a forced draft in a forge, fanning the flames of rival ideologies, and nurturing any spark of technical innovation that promised some advantage in the competition among states.

There was also a most important maritime aspect to the gunpowder revolution. Ships equipped with heavy guns could defend themselves at a distance quite effectively. As a result, when European sailors learned just before 1500 to navigate across oceanic distances, their ships proved far more formidable in naval battle than any others afloat. Hence the intruders, even though few in number and far from home, found it easy enough to come and go at will, using force or threat of force as a principal stock in trade in dealings with both Asian and Amerindian populations. How effective European naval gunnery could be was demonstrated in 1509 at the Battle of Diu (off the west coast of India) where a few Portuguese ships destroyed a far larger fleet without ever allowing their Moslem enemies to bring their numerical superiority to bear by closing and boarding, as traditional tactics in both the Mediterranean and Indian oceans required.[8]

Easy dominion of the high seas, in turn, lured Europeans, especially those living on or near the Atlantic coasts, to transoceanic adventure. A swarm of explorers, missionaries, and merchants therefore continuously brought new things to the attention of their stay-at-home contemporaries throughout the sixteenth and seventeenth centuries. By about 1550, colonial and trans-Atlantic commercial enterprises began to assume real

[8] To survive along the stormy shoreline of the North Atlantic, ships had to be built strongly to withstand the shock of wind and wave. It proved easy for such vessels to take the recoil of cannon with no damage. But vessels designed for less stormy seas shook apart after a few shots had been fired. Hence, to match European cannonade at sea a whole new art of shipbuilding had to be acquired: and this no Asian people — not even the Japanese — undertook. Europe's supremacy at sea 1500–1900, is comparable to the supremacy of knights in land battle, 900–1300, and lasted just about as long.

importance, and the scale of European activities — both warlike and peaceful — in the Atlantic, Indian, and Pacific oceans continued to grow thereafter at a rapid rate.

New wealth, information, techniques, and ideas flooded into Europe as a result, and it became increasingly difficult to believe (though most men did until the mid-seventeenth century) that all important truth had been discovered by or revealed long ago to a small segment of mankind. On the other hand, to cut loose from the secular learning of the classics and from the sacred truths of Christianity or Islam was more than Europeans could easily bear. Somewhere, somehow, truth and certainty had to be found — or so almost everyone agreed.

On top of everything else, the Spaniards upset the price system of Europe when they opened up extremely productive silver mines in Mexico and Peru. As the supply of silver increased, prices surged upward, because goods did not multiply in proportion to the increase of coin. No one understood what was happening; and everyone was convinced, as prices rose and traditional economic relationships of all kinds came under harsh new stresses, that the cause of it all had to be evil, greedy men who somewhere, somehow, were unjustly taking more than was rightfully theirs. Real hardships, inflicted up and down the social scale by laggard readjustments of wage, rent, and tax rates, were thus compounded by a pervasive sense of grievance, though no agreement could be reached on exactly who was to blame.

Political, economic, and intellectual volatility, one piled on top of the other, set the stage for the desperate, revolutionary thrust after saving truth which characterized the sixteenth and early seventeenth centuries more than most ages of European history. The force and scale of such movements was in turn magnified by the invention of printing (1450's) which made communication of abstract ideas and technical information much easier than before and democratized, if not learning, at least ideology. Luther's reformation of the Christian church is the archetypal example of this response to the distressing conditions of the age, but there were other comparable movements in every part of Europe. Those that mattered — including Lutheranism — prospered in alliance with political authorities. Indeed, the major states of Europe each became firmly identified with a reformed, purified version of religious truth. Political loyalty and religious conformity tended therefore to be identified with each other because a subject who adhered to a foreign faith was likely also to prefer obedience to a foreign ruler who had taken that form of faith under his protection.

In eastern and southern Europe, rulers and religious leaders were more nearly successful than in the northwest. In Spain, for example, the identification between emotionally intense Catholicism and the imperial power of Spanish kings led to systematic expulsion of Moslems and Jews from the peninsula. Even converts fell under suspicion, and many of them also fled, fearing the Spanish Inquisition. Muscovy too rooted out heresy with fire and sword; in fact, the Grand Duke Basil III (ruled 1505–1533) deliberately borrowed Spanish methods of dealing with heretics as reported to him by a Hapsburg ambassador.

The Ottoman empire was different, inasmuch as the sacred law of Islam expressly commanded toleration for Jews and Christians who agreed to pay a head tax as a sign of their subjection. After 1499, however, when an incandescent sectarian challenge to the legitimacy of Ottoman rule flared into sudden prominence in Azerbaijan and adjacent regions, the Ottoman government set out to reinforce Sunni orthodoxy among their Moslem subjects. Overt adherence to rival forms of the faith provoked bloody repression in the first decades of the sixteenth century, but after 1520, when Suleiman the Lawgiver came to the throne (ruled 1520–1566), violent persecution gave way to administrative containment and constraint of heterodoxy. Such relaxation was possible because Suleiman's successful resumption of victorious war against Christendom effectively confirmed the sultan's claim to legitimacy in the eyes of pious Moslems everywhere. Yet the sectarian challenge refused to die away. Instead, the Ottoman sultans had to confront a religious rival on their eastern flank in the form of the Safavid state. The Safavids claimed to be the legitimate successors to the Prophet, and as such the sole rightful leaders of Islam. Such a neighbor was more troublesome to the sultans than their Christian enemies to the west, because war between fellow Moslems, though far from new, still ran profoundly counter to what pious adherents of Islam believed to be right. The posture of the Ottoman state thus remained ambiguous. As champion of Islam *vis-à-vis* Christian Europe, the sultans filled a thoroughly congenial and traditionally honorable role. But as champions of Sunni orthodoxy, the same sultans found themselves quarreling with fellow Moslems with a venom the pious everywhere deplored.

In northwestern and central Europe, efforts of religious reformers and political rulers aimed at the sort of religious uniformity that was in fact attained in Spain and Muscovy. But the patchwork pattern of political sovereignty that existed in the Germanies meant that religious uniformity could not prevail. Rival rulers, espousing rival versions of the true faith, fought one another to a standstill. Hence, although religious uniformity was imposed within each jurisdiction as a matter of course, in central Europe as a whole, a variegated Lutheran, Calvinist, and Catholic patchwork emerged by 1648, when the sputtering hope of imposing a single truth on all Germans faded away in frustration.

As for France and England, the two largest states of western Europe, both allowed considerable religious dissent, more by accident than by design. By the time Louis XIV of France got around to revoking the Edict of Nantes (1685), whereby his grandfather had guaranteed French

Calvinists religious and political privileges, the fierce anxieties that had fired religious controversy in the sixteenth century had begun to dissipate, so that French officialdom stopped short of Spanish and Muscovite rigor in hunting down and punishing the dissenting remnant within France. The English government adopted an even more lenient policy after 1688, partly at least in imitation of Dutch practice. In the sixteenth century, the absence of an effective central government among the embattled provinces of the northern Netherlands resulted in a policy of religious toleration. This, in turn, attracted persecuted minorities from most of Europe, many of whom contributed to the surprising surge of commercial prosperity that raised Holland and its associated provinces to the status of a great power in the seventeenth century.

If we try to survey the ebb and flow of events in Europe as a whole between 1500 and 1650 or thereabouts, it is possible to view the various and discrepant efforts men made to find and enforce a single saving truth as so many forms of reaction against professionalization and pluralism (especially as manifested in religious indifference if not outright skepticism) that had come to prominence in Italy during the high Renaissance. In Turkey and Muscovy, religious reaction started explicitly from rejection of Italian cultural influence in high places. Sultan Mehmed the Conqueror (ruled 1452–1480) presided over a religiously tolerant court at which Italian experts offered their services in many different capacities. Reaction set in after his death, and was then magnified enormously by the Safavid sectarian challenge. As a result, later sultans ceased to employ Italians and relied exclusively on skills and ideas available among their own subjects.[9]

In Muscovy, similarly, Ivan III (ruled 1462–1505) opened his court to Italian influence through his marriage to Sophia Paleologos, who, though descended from the last Byzantine emperors, was entirely Italian in her education and culture. He imported Italian artillerists and other experts, and toward the end of his life was suspected of tolerating a court clique of "Judaizers," whose ideas were perhaps also inspired from abroad. Reaction set in even before Ivan's death, when his heir, Basil III, set himself up as protector of Orthodoxy in every jot and tittle. Moreover, the Orthodoxy he so jealously guarded had already survived an earlier insidious assault from Italy. For at the Council of Florence (1439), prelates of the Russian church had agreed to union with the pope, only to be repudiated on their return to Moscow. Thereafter, Russian Orthodoxy came to be identified with a punctilious preservation of existing ritual and

[9]   The displacement of Italian experts from the sultan's court was facilitated by the influx of Jews fleeing Spain after 1492. Some Spanish Jews had full education in the arts and skills of Christian Europe and were willing, indeed eager, to put their knowledge at the sultan's disposal, particularly after their enemy, the government of Spain, became also the enemy of the sultan. Jews acted as experts in residence for all matters pertaining to Christian Europe until Greeks displaced them in the mid-seventeenth century.

a deep-seated suspicion of everything alien. It was to this obscurantist tradition that Basil III returned at the beginning of the sixteenth century.

Even in western Europe, the element of reaction against Italian influence was not lacking. Luther's youthful encounter with what he felt to be scandalous laxity at the papal court is well known. Moreover, the later appeal of Lutheranism among his fellow Germans rested in part on widespread popular revulsion against the way clever and unscrupulous Italians exploited German simplicity and piety for their own advantage. In Spain, too, the strenuous Catholic reform carried through by Cardinal Ximenes (1437–1517) fed upon xenophobia provoked by Italian as well as by Jewish and Moslem activity (especially economic activity) in Spain.

Yet even those who rejected aspects of Italian Renaissance culture accepted other sides thereof. Basil III did not throw out the fortification experts his father had imported from Italy but used their skills to make the Moscow Kremlin one of the most impregnable (as well as one of the most beautiful) strongholds of Europe. Similarly, Cardinal Ximenes patronized the preparation and publication of a famous polyglot Bible, that drew upon techniques of philological scholarship perfected by the humanists of Italy. And German Protestantism too, in the person of Philip Melanchthon and others, incorporated much of the fruit of humanistic learning into the tradition of the Lutheran church, just as Calvin later did for the more rigorously reformed churches of Europe.

As in many cultural encounters, to reject Italian influence successfully it was frequently necessary to resort to the Biblical tactic of "spoiling the Egyptians," that is, to borrow enough from the foreigners to be able to argue back effectively, whether with words and texts, or with the harsher music of big guns. Different parts of Europe arrived at different compromises between the impulse to throw off corrupting foreign influences and the recognized need to borrow in order to catch up and overtake the standard set by Italian achievements.

Generally speaking, the reception of Italian taste and learning in France, Spain, and England was relatively broad, presumably because there were substantial groups in the population of those lands who were ready to respond to the attractiveness of Italian models, yet were saved from excessive defensiveness by their sense of belonging to a great and powerful state and nation that had nothing to fear any more from Italians. Shakespeare's free and easy use of Italian plots and settings for many of his plays illustrates well the fruitful relationships such attitudes permitted.

In eastern Europe, groups ready and able to profit from Italian skills were few and weak. As a result, within the pale of Latin Christendom, the eastward reception of Italian Renaissance culture was more the work of missionaries based in Rome than of local elites. The missionary drive got into high gear throughout the Hapsburg and Polish lands in the 1570's

Success was dramatic, so that by the 1640's a "baroque" form of Catholicism had established its sway over all but a stubborn Calvinist remnant among the Magyar gentry. This great missionary effort brought to Austria, Hungary, and Poland a dogmatically structured version of Italian Renaissance culture, as modified by Catholic reaction to the doctrinal challenges of Protestantism. The intellectual and artistic power of this culture was very great. Impressive learning, combining medieval scholasticism with humanistic philology, was marshaled to defend papal definitions of dogma and ritual practice, and the intense conviction with which Catholic (especially Jesuit) missionaries adhered to their faith persuaded many waverers. In addition, the establishment of schools in which secular as well as sacred instruction was intellectually more rigorous and up to date than anything previously offered to lay students became an important part of the Jesuit recipe for winning Protestants and other schismatics back to the Catholic faith. Finally, the emotional timbre and artistic expression of this culture were also powerful. Even sin had its place. The ideal of rigorous sexual repression found its complement in the license of carnival, and the confessional offered a ready remedy for practically any personal shortcoming.

So powerful, in fact, was the appeal of the reformed Catholic culture that Orthodox Christians in the Balkans and in Russia could not escape its attraction. Early in the seventeenth century, Greek prelates in Constantinople and other centers launched their own campaign to "spoil the Egyptians" by importing into the Greek world a version of Italian higher education. Preserved and elaborated within the Venetian dominions, this learning had the double virtue in Greek eyes of being Aristotelian (and therefore in a sense their own, merely reappropriated after a lapse of centuries) and anti-papal (for the Jesuits had been unable to capture or modulate the scientific naturalism that dominated the University of Padua in the sixteenth and early seventeenth centuries). The result was that during the ensuing century a few strategically placed Greeks received a rigorous scientific education and found themselves in a position to act as intermediaries between the Turks (who had ceased to pay attention to new winds of doctrine or even to new technologies originating in Christian Europe) and their increasingly formidable enemies in the west.

Muscovite reaction to the challenge of papal Catholicism was more stormy. Educational upgrading at Kiev and elsewhere made it all too clear that Russian Orthodoxy was not everywhere the same. Minor variations in ritual had somehow crept in, but local practices had warm support from pious and dedicated men, who saw in any change, even the most trifling, an evidence of the abandonment of Orthodoxy. In such a situation the only logical way to decide what was truly Orthodox was to consult Greek texts of the fathers and decrees of early councils. But this, it soon became clear, meant some changes in Russian practices; and many

Russians, the so-called "Old Believers", refused to accept the logic that compelled others to undertake official reform and standardization of ritual. The result was a profound schism in the Russian church. By forcing all those most attached to unchanging Orthodoxy into the ranks of the Old Believers, the schism in effect paralyzed resistance to a further wave of technical modernization launched by Peter the Great at the end of the seventeenth century. Tsar Peter could afford complete disregard for the sensibilities of Orthodox believers because the logic of the pious position required them to await the Second Coming of Christ to set things right in a world where the approaching apocalypse was clearly indicated by the apostasy of the very men — tsar and patriarch — whom God had appointed to protect the one, true Orthodox Christian faith.

By the time Peter the Great (reigned 1689–1725) came to the throne of Russia, however, Italy had ceased to be the main center of European cultural creativity. Both Renaissance and Catholic reform had spent their force, being incorporated into the cultural inheritance of trans-Alpine Europe in greater or less measure. Instead, a new center had defined itself in northwestern Europe, occupying almost exactly the same territorial heartland as had provided the basis for the "Gothic" civilization of the tenth to the thirteenth century. The change that had come to the cultural landscape of Europe was symbolized by the fact that when Peter decided to visit the west he headed for Holland, not for northern Italy as a man on a similar mission would certainly have done two hundred or even one hundred years before.

What happened to bring this fundamental shift about? First, and most obviously, Italy and all other Mediterranean lands were faced by a crippling economic crisis at the beginning of the seventeenth century. Population growth outran food supplies, and the problem was compounded by widespread destruction of woodlands. Plague and other forms of disease, of course, brought population quickly into line with available food supplies; only in exceptional circumstances were Mediterranean cities able to pay for grain imported from the Baltic, as happened briefly but dramatically in the 1590's. However, restoration of a precarious food–population balance did nothing to bring back an adequate wood supply. Fuel, therefore, became scarce and expensive, handicapping industry of almost every kind. The Mediterranean lands have yet to recover from this setback. Early in the seventeenth century, both large-scale commerce and large-scale industry deserted the crowded shores of Europe's southern seas. Only the development of continent-wide electrical power grids in the second half of the twentieth century promises to redress the fuel shortage handicap under which Mediterranean Europe has had to labor ever since the later sixteenth century.

To be sure, neither Spain to the west nor Ottoman lands to the east were as densely populated as Italy, and some obvious possibilities — irrigation agriculture, for example — could have raised the food-producing capacity of Spain and European Turkey enormously. But social conditions did not reward peasant industriousness sufficiently to make attractive the heavy investment such cultivation requires, and neither government officials nor private landlords had the technical knowledge and entrepreneurial imagination to marshal the requisite peasant labor by force. Instead, barren hillsides and treeless plains attested ecological disaster, brought on and perpetuated by political conditions and public attitudes toward work and property as well as by brute pressure of population — human, sheep, and (not least) goat.

The social effect of the Mediterranean food and fuel crisis was to check the growth of cities and keep a pool of underemployed masses of people in the countryside. There, at least, hungry mouths were close to whatever food there was. Poverty, ignorance, and idleness multiplied under such a regime. Undernourished, unskilled peasants dominated the landscape by sheer weight of numbers. Under such conditions, everything that had made Italy and the Mediterranean the center of European civilization weakened and faded away, not least intellectual and artistic creativity.

Pervasive poverty certainly hurt Italian, Spanish, and Ottoman high culture from the seventeenth century onward. Diminishing means restricted opportunities of all kinds. Yet poverty by itself does not seem an adequate explanation for the suddenness of Italy's intellectual collapse. In 1609–1610, when Galileo turned his new invention, the telescope, to the skies and announced startling new astronomical discoveries week after week to all the world, the University of Padua, where he was then professor, was also the leading center of medical study in Europe. Twenty-five years later, Galileo was under house arrest for failure to heed an earlier ecclesiastical warning against the heretical notion that the earth revolved around the sun, and the great days of Paduan science were gone forever, as new centers rose north of the Alps to attract students and teachers of the caliber that had once made Padua famous.

What happened was this: the very success with which Roman Catholics of the sixteenth century carried through their effort to chart the entire universe and define man's place in it created an authoritative doctrine which collided unyieldingly with new data and new ideas at the beginning of the seventeenth century. The completeness of the moral-intellectual systems of truth, generated both by baroque Catholicism and by official Ottoman Islam had paradoxical results. Authoritative and relatively unambiguous answers to all important questions were what men wanted and what these systems provided so convincingly. Herein lay their strength, an essential aspect of their appeal to troubled minds. But on the principle that a chain of reasoning, like a chain of iron, is no stronger than its weakest link, completeness also created radical weakness. Dissent on any point automatically called the authority of the entire belief system into question. After all, the same authorities and the same procedures for determining truth guaranteed each and every doctrine and prescribed behavior. Hence when theological experts declared that the sun went round the earth, evidence and arguments to the contrary, no matter how persuasive, had to be denied, as Galileo discovered to his distress in 1616 and again in 1632.

Under such circumstances, a wise and prudent man refrained from expressing doubts, even to himself, and instead sought out a niche, readily found within the established system of belief and conduct, where he could be reasonably comfortable. Sin, even the sin of self-will and intellectual pride, had its appropriate remedy already provided for. Thus heirs of such rich and coherent intellectual traditions, whether Moslem or Christian, usually persuaded themselves that intellectual conformity and reverent respect for established truths were morally right and necessary. The most intelligent and sensitive individuals, who under other circumstances might have taken the lead in developing new ideas, were exactly those who comprehended best the delicate interdependence of the entire belief structure, and who were therefore most eager to defend it against clumsy, irreverent specialists, like Galileo, who cared far too much for their own opinions. Moreover, his and other similarly novel and heretical views were intrinsically liable to error, being based on faulty and imperfect sensory observation rather than on logical reasoning from self-evident first principles.

No doubt economic and intellectual conditions of Mediterranean lands in the early seventeenth century acted subtly one upon another. Had economic circumstances not been so constricted, perhaps conformity to dogmatic authority in matters intellectual would not have been so pervasive; conversely, if pious explanations and religious remedy for economic hardship had not been so impressively at hand, men might have searched harder for economic and political alternatives. But as things were, economic setback and the hardening of dogmatic definitions of permissible belief advanced simultaneously in Spain, Italy, and Ottoman lands. Creativity in art lasted longer, particularly in music (Turkish as well as Italian), which, being innocent of doctrinal content, escaped even the most officious efforts at thought control.

The impasse confronting Mediterranean Europe in the seventeenth century was all the more conspicuous because at about the same time two other regions of Europe were beginning to enjoy the advantages of a rapidly expanding economy. In the northwest, Holland, England, and France embarked on successful trans-Atlantic colonization soon after the turn of the century, and all three nations also made substantial gains in the Indian Ocean as well. With the decay of Spanish and Portuguese energies and power, these northerners moved in and started to take a far more aggressive part in settling North America, exploiting India and the Spice

Islands (Moluccas), developing sugar plantations in the Caribbean, and in other ways pursuing and expanding economic empire overseas. It seems fair to say that techniques for organizing overseas enterprises which in the fourteenth century had been part of the Italians' secret — stock companies, plantation management, financial accountancy, etc. — had become fully domesticated in the north by 1600 and were put to work by Dutch and English businessmen with the same brilliant success that had earlier come to businessmen of Genoa and Florence.

Two important technical developments underpinned the seventeenth century upsurge of northern wealth. One was agricultural: Dutch and English farmers of the seventeenth century, by systematic experiment and a good deal of trial and error, discovered how to get along without fallowing one third or more of the arable land each year. Fallowing had been fundamental to traditional moldboard cultivation. It kept the plow busy in early summer when the grain was ripening; more than that, plowing the fields destroyed weeds, which would otherwise have accumulated in the soil so thickly as to crowd out the grain. The same result, it was discovered, could be achieved by repeated tillage between rows of turnips. Turnips could then be fed to stock in the wintertime, allowing the farmer to support more and stronger animals than the traditional method had permitted. An alternative was to plant alfalfa or some other leguminous crop; it, too, provided fine winter fodder, kept back weeds by its early, vigorous growth, and simultaneously deposited nitrogen in the soil, thus enhancing fertility for the next year or two. These and related improvements, e.g. in plow design, mechanical seeders, harrows, and the like, allowed the production of more food per acre and per agricultural laborer than had been possible before. A corollary was that a larger percentage of total population became available for tasks unrelated to food production.

Fuel shortage of the sort which hit the Mediterranean so hard (and which may have been partly or even largely responsible for the setback to northwest European prosperity in the fourteenth century) was solved even more decisively by the growing exploitation of coal. England had particular advantages here because coalfields existed immediately adjacent to navigable water at places like Newcastle, conveniently located with respect to London and other North Sea ports. Timber, especially oak suitable for shipbuilding, remained in critically short supply and had to be jealously guarded. Moreover, until the eighteenth century, coal could not be used to smelt iron because sulphur and other chemicals from the coal entered the iron and made it uselessly brittle. For that reason Sweden and distant Russia became major iron producers because their forests provided an ample supply of charcoal at a time when western Europe had depleted its forest resources to a point that made smelting difficult. Coal was therefore not a perfect substitute for wood. Nevertheless it relieved most of the problems which crippled industry in the Mediterranean, and allowed the coal-rich north to use the labor released from the task of raising food for a wide variety of new industrial (and commercial) activities.

With food and fuel supplies thus more or less satisfactorily assured, northwestern Europe was in a position to take over the dominating economic role northern Italy had formerly played *vis-à-vis* the rest of the continent. Raw materials in scant supply at the center could be imported: grain, timber, and iron from the Baltic, or from North American colonies were matched by new or newly important commodities such as sugar from the Caribbean, tobacco from Virginia, cotton from India, tea from China. Naval supremacy, resting first with the Dutch, and after 1688 with the English, backed up commercial domination of oceanic routes as well as of Europe's coastal waters, including the Mediterranean.

England's insularity was particularly advantageous, for control of the narrow seas along the English coasts made elaborate military investments unnecessary. Accordingly, wealth actually increased more rapidly than taxes, benefiting private enterprises and persons, and encouraging accumulation of capital in the hands of men of quite modest circumstance through the exercise of the far-famed "Puritan ethic". At the top of the social scale, the rich, too, got richer, sometimes spectacularly so by profiting from increments of land value or by speculating in large-scale ventures far afield. A wealthy aristocracy and business oligarchy together with a relatively numerous collocation of gentry, farmers, shopkeepers, and professional men thus took shape in England, giving the social hierarchy a distinctive, middle-class bulge which has lasted into the twentieth century.

These solid successes in the northwest were matched by a large-scale frontier boom in the east. Until the seventeenth century, the steppes of the Ukraine, Rumania, and Hungary mostly remained open grasslands occupied by grazing herds with a few men tending them. Cultivators had been unable to survive, even in the most promising soils, because of slave and booty raids launched at frequent intervals by Tartar horsemen. The Tartars were remnants and heirs of the once formidable Mongol Empire, based, after 1577, only in the Crimea and subordinate, in a vague way, to the Ottoman sultan.

Tartar predation depended on finding the frontiers of agricultural settlement poorly defended. As handguns became available in greater numbers, and as a better organized military establishment took form in Austria on the one flank and in Muscovy on the other (Polish armies, while sometimes formidable, were never well organized), the balance slowly but surely tipped against the Tartars. Settlers advanced, by trickles at first, later in a flood. After 1667, when Russia annexed most of the Ukraine, and 1699, when the Hapsburgs asserted control over most of

Hungary, the eastward movement came firmly and finally under the direction of official bureaucracies of the major east European states. Even the Turks, though driven from Hungary and the Ukraine, were nonetheless able to open the Rumanian grasslands to cultivation on a wholesale scale. Resulting surpluses nourished either the sultan's capital on the Bosporus or the sultan's armies, wherever they might be engaged in war. City and camp alike paid for Rumanian grain with monies collected as tax and tribute from the Christian (after 1711, Greek) rulers whom the Turks appointed to govern the provinces. The food problem that had troubled Constaninople, like all the other big cities of the Mediterranean at the beginning of the seventeenth century, was thus triumphantly solved in the latter part of the same century. Ottoman armies, likewise, achieved a new lease on life thanks to the availability of a much enlarged food supply. The so-called Kiuprili revival of offensive war against Crete, Russia, and Austria, climaxing in the second unsuccessful Ottoman siege of Vienna in 1683, would not have been possible without the massive development of Rumanian agricultural resources.

Generally speaking, the pioneers who broke the sod in southeast Europe were poorly equipped and careless husbandmen. But the black soil of the west Eurasian steppe is among the world's best, especially for wheat. Hence even technically sloppy cultivation often produced fine harvests. After 1774, when Russian ships gained the right to travel freely through the Turkish straits and enter the Mediterranean, massive wheat exports from Odessa and other Black Sea ports became available to relieve the chronic Mediterranean food shortage insofar as Mediterranean peoples had means to buy. Previously, the growing amount of grain produced along Russia's southern frontier supplied the north, and in particular fed Russian soldiers and state officials, not to mention iron workers in the Urals and other less important industrial work forces elsewhere. The Russian river network made delivery of grain across long distances a practicable proposition. Boats in summer and sleighs in winter could carry relatively large loads quite cheaply. Austrian development of Hungary was less etatist and less effective; indeed the problem of marketing Hungarian grain was not solved effectively until the nineteenth century.

Obviously the spectacular frontier development of Russia and the no less spectacular industrial-commercial development of northwestern Europe put the intermediary regions of the continent under special pressure. Poles and Swedes, though they participated in the early stages of the frontier development in the east, (Poland, agriculturally, in the Ukraine; Sweden, in timber and iron) failed to organize state power strong enough to cope with the Muscovite autocracy. In the eighteenth century both these states therefore became little more than Russian puppets. Many German states descended to the same status *vis-à-vis*

Germany's western neighbor, France. But Prussia and, to a lesser extent, Austria managed to mobilize sufficient resources from local populations to sustain an army and supply system that made those states rank as great powers by the middle of the eighteenth century. Prussia's secret was superior administration and a distinctive Spartan ruthlessness in subordinating private and corporate interests to the overriding needs of the state. The harsh memory left by the Thirty Years' War, when Prussian land had been plundered for years on end by occupying foreign troops, provided the initial stimulus to the development of the Prussian militarized administration. Austria benefited similarly from its role as principal guardian of Christian Europe against the Turks, for corporate and private resistance to paying taxes or rendering services in war against the infidel was noticeably less than when the emperor sought means with which to fight fellow Christians.

Generally speaking, the increase in the Russian state's resources through frontier development, and the increase of Austrian and Prussian state power through superior administrative manipulation more or less kept pace during the seventeenth and eighteenth centuries. Expressed differently, deficiencies of Russia's administrative articulation and defects of Russian technical skills approximately were compensated for by the superior geographic and demographic base upon which Russian state power rested. But during the reign of Catherine II, the Great (1762–1796), Russia began to catch up with her western neighbors in technical and administrative matters and definitively outstripped the Turks.

The upthrust of Russian power and civilization threatened toward the close of the eighteenth century to upset the existing fivefold great power structure of interstate relations. In the preceding century the consolidation of the French monarchy after a generation of religious and civil wars, 1562–1598, had threatened to do the same. But French power was eventually contained by a Dutch-English-Austrian alliance, though not until long drawn-out struggles against the French had strained Dutch resources to the limit and undermined the commercial dominance Amsterdam had enjoyed at the beginning of the seventeenth century.

The repeated adjustments of the international balance of power in the seventeenth and eighteenth centuries through war and diplomacy were indeed a minor triumph for rationality and calculation in human affairs. Far more important for European civilization as a whole was the way rulers and administrators rationalized the application of violence by bureaucratizing armies. The principles were age-old: in the seventh century B.C., ancient Assyrian kings set up regular career promotion patterns for their army officers and paid them enough, in booty and otherwise, to make the careers attractive. The Roman and Byzantine imperial administrators had likewise been familiar with the concept of a standing army, commanded by officers who were appointed, paid, and promoted by the emperor or his delegated agent. The Italian cities in the late fifteenth and sixteenth centuries also supported professional military establishments, but few city administrations, except the Venetian, had enough cash and enough continuity of purpose and policy to create a permanent professional force of trained men, available winter and summer, in peace as well as in war.

Military professionalism instead took a mainly private form. From the time of the Hundred Years' War (1337–1453) self-appointed individual captains set out to raise a troop or company and offered their services to whoever had means to pay. As long as Europe's rulers could not afford to support large military establishments on a permanent basis, this arrangement continued to prevail, for it offered the possibility of putting large and well-trained forces in the field at short notice. On the other hand, a successful captain was likely to be tempted to seize power for himself, as the careers of many Italian condottieri of the fourteenth and fifteenth centuries demonstrated. Short of this, discharged soldiers, even if dismissed with all arrears of pay settled were liable to plunder their former employers' subjects, especially if the onset of peace threatened future employment. Calling upon mercenaries could therefore become far more costly than anything provided for in the initial contract.

This fact burned itself into the minds of Europe's rulers in the course of the Thirty Years' War, which devastated much of Germany (1618–1648). In the early stages of that struggle, private military enterprises enjoyed unparalleled opportunities, and the scale of their armies exceeded anything known before. But by 1634, Emperor Ferdinand II felt his power threatened by Albrecht von Wallenstein, the most successful military leader in his service. The emperor first succeeded in dismissing and then concurred in the assassination of his overmighty servant; thereafter all Europe's major rulers bent systematic efforts to assure loyalty and obedience, reducing military entrepreneurial commands to the relatively small scale of a single regiment, and endeavoring to surround the contract for military service with a semisacred aura by assimilating it to the ancient feudal oath of homage and fealty which knights had once offered to their liege lords.

When the war ended, France, Austria, and other major European states all maintained a few regiments on a standby basis, as much to overawe potential rebelliousness at home as to guard against foreign threats. Little by little, promotion, pay, and other perquisites of the officer class came to depend less on the colonel of the regiment and more on the decisions of some clerk in the central offices of government. Simultaneously, systematic efforts were made to ritualize and reinforce the personal link between monarchs and the officers of the army. Kings began to wear military uniforms on all sorts of public occasions; royal parades and reviews multiplied; young officers were assigned decorative and ritual functions at court; royal princes were often raised as cadets, and so forth. The result was extremely successful. Unruly aristocrats of past ages enrolled their sons in the royal armies gladly enough; the possibility of private war and local rebellion, which had remained an ever present reality of European politics through the sixteenth and early seventeenth centuries, ceased to be an important consideration, save in remote fringe regions like the Scottish Highlands (risings, 1715, 1745), eastern Hungary (risings, 1703–1711), or the Don-Volga frontier (rising, 1773–1775).

The French army quickly became the most powerful and best administered of Europe. Ministers who spent their lives nursing the royal income to make it capable of sustaining the cost of court and army quickly came to the conclusion that a plundering army was too expensive to be endured. Plundering took men away from the field of battle and weakened discipline. More important, it reduced for years afterward the tax value of the land through which the army passed and made annexations of devastated territory scarcely worthwhile from a fiscal point of view, at least until after years of peace had allowed gradual recovery. Hence it became royal policy to supply the French armies with food and other necessities from magazines located along the route of march. This limited mobility, but on the other hand it made war worthwhile, at least as long as the French faced weaker forces in the field, as was true, generally speaking, until 1689. By then the French policy and the reasons for it had become general — in principle if not always in practice — among Europe's Christian princes. Only the Turks adhered to an older custom of allowing irregular troops to plunder almost indiscriminately, within as well as beyond the Ottoman frontier.

From the point of view of the ordinary subject, however burdensome taxes required for the support of a regular standing army might be, they were nonetheless preferable to risking ruin at the hands of marauding soldiery. Overall, the result was a significant reduction of the incidence of violence in most Europeans' lives. At the same time the controlled, deliberate application of force on the field of battle increased in scale and effectiveness as trained men, using carefully thought-out tactics and equipped with weapons designed and redesigned in the light of battle experience, confronted one another at frequent intervals, at the will of their kings and commanders.

Nor were the triumphs of early modern military administration merely rational. Close order drill, like the drill of the ancient Greek phalanx or the training necessary to allow Swiss pikemen to keep their place in maneuvers, had powerful psychological effects upon soldiers subjected to endless repetition of prescribed movements, performed in unison. Such movements had a rational purpose, of course. Properly done, they assured that soldiers kept formation in march and deployed to maximize fire-front without delay on the field of battle. Even more important, with sufficient training the complicated movements required to load, aim, and fire a musket could be performed reliably and in minimal time by every soldier, despite the confusion and excitement of battle. Endless practice kept idle hands busy, even in wintertime. But more than this, such rhythmic muscular movements created a visceral feeling of solidarity among those participating in the drill that far transcended any rational response. This was what sustained military discipline and allowed the cultivation of a profound and (at least at first glance) surprising *esprit de corps*. Such acts probably stir echoes of men's earliest sociality. Close order drill, in fact, probably summoned back to life the shades of ancient hunting bands, whose members danced around the campfire before and after every hunt, moving their muscles in unison, building up a spirit of camaraderie and creating courage in the face of anticipated danger by collective incantation, expressed through both voice and gesture. Countless European drill sergeants achieved comparable results, despite the fact that they usually started with extremely unpromising human material. Caging violence by such sleight of hand surely deserves to rank among the more remarkable achievements of Europe's Old Regime.

Proof of the power accruing to European armies through such training and administrative practices was their success in wars with other peoples. As mentioned already, the Ottoman Turks and the nomads of the steppes were both clearly outclassed by the end of the seventeenth century. India, too, was unable to resist European military forces by the eighteenth century, but in the Far East the military establishments of imperial China and imperial Japan were still capable of holding Europeans at arm's length. Nowhere else in the entire world was there a force to rival armies that European states maintained as a matter of course.

In matters of art and intellect, the autonomy of professionalized specialists which had attained such substantial development among the Italian cities of the high Renaissance never disappeared, even when the drive to cage all truth in a single authoritative formula was at its apex. It was, not unnaturally, in the parts of Europe where the governmental authorities met with least success in establishing and enforcing a pattern of total truth that professional autonomy best survived and began to flourish and proliferate soonest. Holland had begun to be hospitable to the professional pluralism characteristic of the Renaissance before that spirit faded from its last place of refuge in Italy (Venice), about 1630. Descartes, for example, prudently took up residence in Amsterdam and cautiously waited to see just what might happen to Galileo before venturing in 1637 to publish the first fruits of his own scientific and philosophical researches, whose compatibility with Catholic doctrine he carefully affirmed but did not care to test by living in an officially Catholic country such as his native France.

In 1660 the restoration of Charles II to the English throne precipitated a powerful revulsion in England against Puritan efforts to constrain human life to an authoritative interpretation of God's will. The result was to uncork professionalized license — whether on the stage, in personal conduct, or in investigation of how to improve tillage, measure gas pressure, or unravel the mystery of the universe with the help of ecstatic visions. New communication networks sprang up to connect kindred spirits. These ranged all the way from George Fox's Society of Friends (formally organized 1669) to the Royal Society of London, founded in 1660, whose published *Transactions* quickly became a means of conveying new data, stimulating new researches, and exciting new thoughts in all who read them. Similar societies took form in other European countries, though Catholic governments did not usually permit religious fellowships such as the Quakers to flourish freely. Counterparts of the Royal Society of London, however, became fashionable throughout Europe, many of them endowed or founded by kings and princes who were eager to win fame as patrons of learning. Such societies exchanged publications with the Royal Society and with each other; in addition, a vigorous private network of correspondence allowed Europe's leading scientists, mathematicians and philosophers to exchange news and views of professional interest wherever they might happen to be living at the time.

Under these circumstances natural science flourished as never before. A community of inquirers and experimenters spread across Europe as far east as Saint Petersburg and across the oceans to distant Philadelphia and Lima. The major centers of scientific research remained, however, in England, France, and Holland, where social structures, educational establishments, and increasing wealth all helped to sustain such activities.

The great monument of the age was Isaac Newton's radically simple mathematical analysis of the behavior of moving bodies, whether celestial like earth, sun, and moon, or terrestrial like cannonballs and falling apples. By bringing all such cases under the same simple formulae, Newton broke through, once and for all, the separation traditional European physics had made between things celestial and things of this earth. The blow to older, theologically certified views was correspondingly severe; and yet the demonstrated accuracy of Newton's formulae, tested over and over again both by astronomical observations and by ballistic research, could not be easily dismissed by anyone who understood the argument. Newtonianism therefore spread, and as it did so, radical adjustments in religion had to follow. Characteristically, a religion of the heart, eschewing dogmatic and doctrinal definition and seeking holiness through private devotions, could accommodate Newtonian science easily enough, by simply sloughing off all the unimportant astronomical and other beliefs Christians of earlier times had accepted but now found to be erroneous. In parts of Europe where such pietistic traditions were already strong, the "Enlightenment" arrived in the eighteenth century without interfering too much with religious faith and practice. This was the case in Protestant Germany and also in England. Where such movements had been officially suppressed, as in most of Catholic and Orthodox Europe, however, the Enlightenment collided head-on with a stout carapace of ecclesiastically certified doctrine. In time it was the ecclesiastical carapace that cracked, giving way, usually, to some form of radical unbelief, whether deism or atheism.

Political and economic theory, history, drama, and belles lettres all flourished. The most influential writers clustered mainly in England and France, with Dutch and Germans sometimes important. The same was true of painting, though Italy's fame as a center of the visual arts was not entirely eclipsed by the rise of Dutch and French schools. Music was different, for in that domain Italian creativity lasted into the eighteenth century; and when musical primacy shifted north of the Alps it was Germany, particularly Catholic Germany, that took the lead in creating what the nineteenth century already called "classical" music.

The custom whereby the music of the eighteenth century is called classical is suggestive, for there is a sense, surely, in which the entire social and cultural universe developed in Europe by the early decades of the eighteenth century was potentially "classical." That is to say, the balances of the early eighteenth century within society and between states, together with rules agreed upon by all important artists and thinkers for applying rational and conventional checks to raw human impulse might have been accepted as normative for all true civilization by subsequent generations. Something like this is what had happened in imperial Rome of the first Christian centuries, when classical culture par excellence spread so widely and sterilely throughout the Mediterranean lands. But, in fact, modern Europe soon became the scene of further revolutionary upheavals, for the collapse of the Old Regime in France in 1789 signaled the collapse of the eighteenth-century pattern of European society and civilization as a whole, and launched the continent on yet another chapter of its stormy history.

The revolution in France had such importance partly because the aspirations summed up in the slogan "Liberty, Equality, Fraternity" were widely shared in Europe of the day, and beyond Europe's confines in the Americas, too. Indeed, the American Revolution preceded and helped to precipitate the great revolution in France; similarly, there were important and energetic groups among the Belgian, German, and Italian populations — not to mention the Poles — who received the French as liberators, even when they came with arms in hand and began to requisition supplies left and right from liberated or conquered neighboring peoples. The force of such responses to revolutionary ideas and practices meant that most of the changes the revolution brought were irreversible, even when men deeply opposed to revolutionary ideals came to power after 1815.

Ideology and its appeal was not the only reason for the revolutionary success. By sweeping away innumerable corporate privileges and local monopolies on positions of power and pecuniary reward, the revolutionaries opened a career to talent that allowed men of unusual capacity to come from "nowhere" and make their fortunes — whether in civil life, or, most flamboyantly, in the ranks of the army. This meant, of course, that all who rose rapidly in social status became defenders of the revolution. Organized and conscious of their individual and collective interest in preventing restoration of old privileges and monopolies, the newcomers easily outweighed those who had profited from the arrangements of the Old Regime, even when restoration became the slogan of the day.

Finally, the reorganization of society and public administration that the revolutionaries carried through increased the capacity of European governments to mobilize men and resources to accomplish agreed-upon purposes. This increment of power, as compared to anything rulers of the Old Regime had been able to command, provided the ultimate argument that made the revolutionary changes irreversible, and, indeed, forced even Napoleon's most inveterate enemies to imitate at least some of the innovations the revolution had brought.

Speaking generally, what the French revolutionaries did was to sweep away obstacles to manipulation of men and resources by a single national command center. Peculiar local practices and immunities were systematically suppressed. Administrative uniformity brought equal taxation in all parts of the country; this meant a vast increment of disposable income at the center. After revolutionary legislation had been codified and applied throughout France, individual citizens confronted the august embodiment of the nation, as it were, face to face, without the protecting integument of corporate identities and roles which had all (except the Church) been swept away as part of the abominable aristocratic privilege that had hamstrung French government for so long. In actual fact, what a citizen confronted was an agent of the central government — representative on mission, prefect, tax collector, recruiting sergeant, or someone else — who in the name of the people demanded goods and services on a far more massive scale than royal agents had ever tried to do. But as citizens and part of the sovereign people from whom all authority descended, loyal Frenchmen had no logical recourse, and most did as they were told willingly enough.

The enhanced power such a regime could attain was most clearly apparent in military matters. The right to command the services of all adult males as soldiers was taken for granted by the National Convention of 1793, when it decreed the famous *Levée en masse*. Other societies had acted on the same assumption in the past — the Roman republic not least, which in fact offered the revolutionaries their favorite historical model. But the art of war as developed in Europe between 1650 and 1789 had made universal conscription inconceivable. Under the Old Regime a few had specialized as soldiers; most paid taxes to support them. The innovation of the revolutionary era was to make something close to universal military service for men of active years possible by expanding production of military supplies at home on the one hand, and by relying on captured material and the conscripted manufacturing resources of most of Europe on the other to supply the swollen French forces. Where before the division of labor between soldier and civilian had been organized within national and state boundaries, under Napoleon the tendency was for French soldiers (and soldiers in French service from other nations) to rely on the rest of continental Europe for their support.

An enormous increase in the size of armies was one result. Short, decisive campaigns were another, for such enormous armies could not long remain in the field, being too large to depend upon supplies brought up regularly from the rear. Nevertheless, a series of swift, sudden victories, followed by replenishment of supplies at the expense of the conquered army and population, allowed swollen French forces to remain in existence for something like twenty years, until Napoleon found himself lured onto ground where local resources were inadequate for the support of really large armies — Spain to the south and Russia to the east.

Among Napoleon's enemies, too, an international division of labor asserted itself strongly. Austria, Prussia, and Russia, sporadic allies of Great Britain against Napoleon, maintained larger armies than their own resources would have permitted, thanks to British subsidies, which in turn permitted the respective continental governments and peoples to buy British-made goods, many of which assisted, directly or indirectly, in prosecuting the war.

Thus the two leading nations of western Europe took opposite roles between 1792 and 1815. The French specialized as soldiers and administrators and drew support from a broad band of adjacent German and Italian territory, while the British specialized as manufacturers for (among other customers) the rulers and soldiers of central and eastern Europe.

Of the two, the British role proved the more durable. French domination, however disguised by revolutionary phrases, inevitably galled the pride of those they lorded it over. Moreover, revolutionary principles were double-edged: if fraternity made Frenchmen so powerful, perhaps a touch of the same elixir would produce similar results for Spaniards or even for the much put-upon, constantly-fought-over, Germans. Powerful German national sentiment actually was stirred up against the French in 1813–1814. It was not the least of the ways in which royalty learned from revolutionaries how to mobilize popular support more effectively than before. The British, on the other hand, expanded their industrial capacity very rapidly throughout the wars, and when peace came were in a position to supply more and cheaper goods than anyone else — an advantage which not all governments and states were prepared to pass up, though some did set up tariffs and quotas aimed at shutting out British manufactures. Despite such reactions to their dominating economic position, the British emerged as the "workshop of the world," whereas after 1815, France was no longer the ruler of Europe — merely a threat to its political stability, against which the monarchs and peoples of the rest of Europe stood keenly on guard.

Yet on a longer time scale, the innovations in political ideals and practice associated with the French Revolution and the innovations in economic organization and practice associated with the English Industrial Revolution were alike inasmuch as both proved exportable; and once well rooted beyond their original territory, their spread diluted the primacy they had conferred on France and Britain at the beginning of the nineteenth century.

There was another parallel between the French Revolution and the Industrial Revolution. For just as the ultimate success of revolutionary principles had been validated by the superior power they allowed French rulers to exert, so, too, the industrial changes that took place in England from about 1750 also multiplied European power enormously. This was most clearly evident in contacts with peoples of other cultures; but the rapid advances of industrialization also profoundly altered domestic and international relations within Europe.

Indeed, industrialization and the adjustment it provoked in human societies interacted throughout the nineteenth century with the ideological and political inheritances from the French Revolution to create a tumultuously changeable age. The leading fact of that age was simple: Europe achieved dominance over all the other peoples of the earth to a degree unexampled in earlier world history. From about the middle of the century that relatively small promontory of Asia we call Europe began to act as pacesetter and metropolitan center for the entire globe. All the other major civilizations of mankind (with the possible exception of Japan) suffered irremediable moral and practical collapse. This transformation of world cultural relations set the stage for our own age, when global cosmopolitanism seems to prick the great powers of the earth along remarkably parallel paths of development.

The exact circumstances whereby the accumulation of capital and openness to technological innovation reached critical concentration in parts of England about 1750 deserve all the minute analysis recent scholarship has directed to the matter. Here I wish merely to emphasize three basic parameters: population, food, and fuel. All three increased dramatically. Factors affecting population were extremely complex and remain debatable. One matter deserves particular attention: the changing incidence of disease arising not only from changing conditions of life but also from altered patterns of human contacts and hence of paths of infection.

The increases in supplies of food and fuel can be understood more easily. Innumerable small improvements cumulatively added greatly to the productivity of Europe's fields between 1750 and, say, 1850. By far the most significant single change was the spread of potato cultivation which became important in continental Europe for the first time during the Seven Years' War and spread to important new territories during the long disturbances of the Napoleonic period. In cooler regions and on sandy soils where cereal crops did not yield well, the potato multiplied caloric yield per acre as much as four times. Without such an expansion of food supply Europe's early industrialization could not have occurred as it did.

Equally indispensable was a vast increase in fuel. Discovery and exploitation of coal measures, first in Great Britain and then on the continent, met this need. Moreover, the gradual development of reliable and effective methods for coking coal between 1709 and the 1820's provided an abundant substitute for charcoal in smelting iron, thus making possible Europe's age of coal and iron.

Another important dimension of the Industrial Revolution was the way in which war and mobilization for war encouraged departures from familiar manufacturing routines and expanded the scale of production. In the second half of the eighteenth century, military demands acted like a vast bellows speeding up reactions of every kind in the industrial sector of the British economy. The Seven Years' War was a landmark: it required a more strenuous mobilization of home resources than Britain had ever before undertaken; and the pattern of subsidy to the Prussians, allowing Frederick the Great to maintain a larger army than he could otherwise have done, set a precedent for the longer and more important subsidies of the Napoleonic period.

Cutbacks and sudden discontinuance of government orders were almost as important as sudden increases in demand from the same source. Such cutbacks tended to weed out the inefficient firms and rewarded the technologically progressive and well managed by allowing them to survive until a new round of government orders restored sudden prosperity. Private enterprise and private marketing, of course, mattered; indeed, in some lines, like cotton manufacture, which was one of the most dramatic and is one of the best studied aspects of the British Industrial Revolution, the private dimension predominated. Only by giving due weight to other manufactures, some of which increased in scale without altering technology very notably, does the role of government orders and military consumption become apparent. Moreover, subsidy payments to foreign governments opened markets in Europe for Manchester cotton cloth, as well as for other commodities which were not purchased directly by military or official agents but circulated instead through normal civil channels of trade.

The worldwide as well as pan-European importance of the Industrial Revolution scarcely needs to be emphasized. Generally speaking, before about 1750, the margin of superiority that Europeans had over other civilized peoples of the world was primarily naval and military. When it came to trade, the artisan products of Moslem, Indian, and Chinese workshops commanded a larger market in Europe than European manufactures could command in Asia. Woolen cloth (in cooler regions) plus raw metals (of which Europeans had a superior supply, thanks to their expertness as miners) were about all that civilized foreigners found worth buying from the West. As a result, force and threat of force constituted an important element in European overseas trade throughout the Old Regime. In particular, compulsory labor played a very conspicuous part in European overseas economic activity both in the form of the slave plantations of the New World and in the form of semifree artisan and agricultural production in India and Indonesia.

After about 1750, however, and definitively by 1800, European (i.e. British) workshops were in a position to offer cheaper and better goods than local artisans could produce, even in such civilized regions as India and the Middle East. By about 1850 or so, the same was true of China. This allowed European penetration of the Asian and African continents to proceed more rapidly and in a different fashion than before. Cheap European goods upset social structures wherever artisan populations had been important. Distressed artisans who could not compete in price or quality with imported European goods provoked acute internal conflicts; such disorders facilitated and sometimes invited European political-military intervention.

Within Europe, the political and legal upheavals connected with the French Revolution and the economic upheavals connected with the Industrial Revolution tended to reinforce each other between 1815 and 1870. Individuals and groups actively promoting one sort of change often supported the other, too; opponents, similarly, tended to resist both movements. Yet there was no necessary connection between liberal democratic forms of government and industrialism. As both innovations spread eastward through Europe in the course of the nineteenth century, gaps began to show clearly. In the Balkans and in Russia, for instance, industrialism implanted by government fiat and financed by foreign capital outran liberal patterns of government; simultaneously, liberal political ideals and practice outdistanced industrialism in Italy and, uncertainly, also in Spain.

Yet in the nineteenth century itself, manifestations of the fragility of the connection between political liberalism and industrialism seemed unimportant and atypical, and could be attributed to transitory deficiencies in local skills and traditions. Most western Europeans agreed, after the convulsion of the Napoleonic period had subsided, that even if constitutions and political command structures were manmade and thus subject to human will, there still remained a "natural" economic order which functioned best when human nature and calculated individual self-interest directed behavior. According to this vision of the human condition, governments ought to leave economic processes alone insofar as possible; private persons, pursuing what they saw to be their own best interest, could be trusted to manage the economy better than it could be managed by any government official.

Complete laissez-faire never existed, even in Great Britain where the doctrine was strongest and where traditions of administrative control of behavior were weaker than anywhere else in Europe. Moreover, as more and more people began to live in towns and work in industry or related service occupations, a host of new corporate bodies began to grow, within which individuals eagerly found refuge from the uncertainties and hardships of industrial urbanization. Larger and larger business enterprises, legally incorporated so as to assume many of the legal rights of a person, were only one of the new forms of corporate life — though a very important one. There was, in addition, a veritable forest of benevolent and self-help societies, municipal government agencies, labor unions, social gatherings like the chapels and pubs of Great Britain, together with socialist and other political parties (especially on the continent) that grew up within the context of new industrial cities and towns. These and other corporate groupings cushioned the confrontation between sovereign people and private citizen which had been so pronounced during the first stages of the French Revolution. In time, these new privileged corporations and vested interests grew to be quite as formidable as those of the Old Regime. They often had the effect of slowing down the pace of industrial change — or at least of reducing the personal strain and the occasional disasters that industrialism, especially in its early phases, often provoked.

After about 1870, a slowdown of British economic development set in, at least by comparison with what happened in the newly arisen industrial centers of Germany and the United States. The Americans recapitulated the British model of industrialization and improved upon it mainly by enlarging the scale of operation. Larger markets, larger machinery, larger business organizations, greater raw material resources, a more elastic labor force, thanks to mass immigration from Europe — in these and similar respects the United States far outstripped the British between 1870 and 1914.

Quantitavely, the Germans also surpassed Britain in many lines of production by 1914. More important for the future, though, was the fact that the Germans departed from British patterns of industrialization in some important ways. First of all, the role of government officials and of a handful of great banks that worked hand in hand with government was far greater in Germany than had been the case in Great Britain. The role of officialdom and of a managerial elite in close contact with officialdom was even greater in Russia, when that country began to industrialize on a significant scale after 1890; the same was true of Japan. Indeed, in the twentieth century it became clear that the German pattern of active manipulation of economic policy by an educated elite of government officials was a far more viable export model for industrialism than the original British pattern, which left so much to private pecuniary initiative of a sort that in most societies was either entirely lacking or else confined to penalized religious minorities — Jews, Armenians, Parsis, and the like.

A second way in which German industrial patterns differed from the British was the greater importance Germans accorded to advanced academic training in science and technology. Chemists, trained in university laboratories, began by inventing new coal tar dyes for each season's high fashion, so that a lady could appear annually in clothes of a hue literally never seen before. Before long, chemists discovered and learned how to mass produce other new substances as diverse and important as nitrogenous fertilizers, dynamite, celluloid, and aspirin. Thanks largely to their superior educational system, Germans soon took and held the lead in such innovations. For the same reason, by 1914, the German electrical industry led the world, and German artillery was bigger and better than anyone else's.

Yet even in Germany before World War I the linkage between academic science and research on the one hand and industrial practice on the other was relatively weak. Prejudices on both sides prevented more than sporadic interaction between academic theory and the grime and sweat of industrial processing. Many inventions resulted from the tinkering of some ingenious mechanic working by himself with meager capital and only an elementary education. Yet toward the very end of the nineteenth century, a few big businesses began to set up laboratories where highly trained men were employed to improve existing techniques by testing alternatives systematically, seeking, along the way, for promising applications of physical and chemical theory to manufacturing processes.

Britain's loss, around 1870, of industrial primacy to Germany and the United States was matched by a similar eclipse of France and of the political ideals associated with the French revolutionary and republican tradition. Defeat in the Franco-Prussian War (1870–1871) led to the unification of Germany, not by the people under liberal leaders, but by Bismarck and the Prussian army, acting in defiance of the expressed will of the elected representatives of the people. Simultaneously, in France, the revolutionary rising of the people in Paris led to a violent parting of the ways between bourgeois republicans and socialist revolutionaries. Most of the rest of Europe soon followed suit. Thus the liberal, revolutionary, and republican ideals that had been handed down from 1793 split into jarring fragments, exactly at the time when an unrepentant reactionary, Chancellor Bismarck, showed how it was possible to manipulate public opinion so as to strengthen the power of kings and emperors and other remainders from Europe's Old Regime.

Internationally, the polarity between eastern reaction and western reform, which had defined Europe's diplomatic structure between the 1820's and the 1860's, was swept away, so that by 1907, a common fear of Germany persuaded autocratic Russia to ally itself with republican France and liberal Britain, despite innumerable points of friction along their respective imperial frontiers and spheres of influence overseas. Domestically the practical compromise between managed politics and "natural" economics which had emerged after the Napoleonic wars in western European lands also blurred and nearly broke down. Economics was politicized in the name of social reform. Questions of economic policy tended to supplant constitutional quarrels as the most acrimonious foci of political debate.

The further east in Europe, the more active state officials remained or became in all aspects of economic management. Russian industrialization and railroad building, for example, were at least semisocialist from the start. Revolutionary socialism and revolutionary nationalism also tended to become more persuasive as one went from west to east, at least partly because the managerial elites of eastern Europe were more authoritarian and systematically excluded certain national groups. By the end of the nineteenth century, Russia therefore presented the spectacle of two rival elites competing — often violently by bomb and hangman's noose — for command of the country's political and economic management. Ironically, the more successful the existing government was in advancing industrialization and modernization, the larger became the volatile urban population to whom the socialist elite was able to appeal. In Ottoman and Hapsburg lands, on the other hand, revolutionary rhetoric found nationalist slogans more congenial, though the resultant political mobilization of lower against upper classes within existing social hierarchies was very similar to that which socialists so vigorously undertook in Germany and Russia.

Nevertheless it took the unexpected strain and human catastrophe of

World War I to erase the boundary between politics and economics in all of Europe (except, perhaps, Switzerland) and to push the polarities of eastern Europe over the edge of revolution. By the end of the war, the United States had become the patron of nationalist revolution in southeast Europe, dragging reluctant British and French authorities along, whereas Russia had become the patron of class war, reproaching the desperately embarrassed socialist parties of western and central Europe for failure to join wholeheartedly in the revolutionary cause their spokesmen had so loudly and proudly proclaimed before the war.

It is rash and perhaps unnecessary to say anything here about the intellectual and cultural flowering of Europe in the nineteenth century. Institutional structures within which innovative thoughts were encouraged and facilitated by such master instruments as libraries and laboratories multiplied enormously, and the outpouring of new ideas and projects was correspondingly vast. Professionalization ran rampant; experts in one profession lost touch with those of others save in rare instances. Pullulating confusion rather than any visible overarching intellectual structure resulted, although just as there was a "European" art style until the first decade of the twentieth century that bound all the painters of Europe together in a loose but real way, so, too, there may have been a "European" intellectual style of which we are still too much the heirs to be able to recognize it clearly. The art style, inherited from the Renaissance of Italy, was discarded by avant-garde painters in the decade before World War I who rejected the master device of perspective and abandoned the ideal of making a painting resemble optical experience closely. In similar fashion it is conceivable that future ages will recognize an abandonment of a long-established "European" intellectual style at about the same time. Certainly the discovery of unconscious levels of psychic activity and the limitations this discovery imposes on rational management of human as well as of nonhuman affairs marks a notable change in outlook. Yet reason has its way of outwitting unreason: the discovery of irrational levels of psychic life was itself a triumph of reasoning; and effective manipulation of such impulses to achieve consciously established goals is perhaps a reasonable dream, though the moral and practical dilemmas that actual achievement of such skills would create among men boggles the imagination. Who would manipulate whom? And for what purposes?

However future ages may assess the intellectual and artistic achievements of nineteenth-century Europe, it seems certain that the massive variety of what was achieved will remain impressive. It was perhaps a golden age when Europe dominated the entire world, as no one center had ever done before, not merely politically and militarily, but far more significantly in scientific, technological, and intellectual matters. France and England remained extremely active; Germany rivaled and in some fields overtook the two older centers of high culture; and the adjacent regions of Europe all participated (along with European emigrants established overseas) in marginal but often significant ways.

The difficulty of passing anything like a firm and confident judgment upon nineteenth-century European high culture is compounded as one approaches closer to our own time. Political and social as well as intellectual and artistic events of the past half century are still too recent to allow any sort of confident analysis on a scale appropriate to a hasty overview of the whole of Europe's past such as this. Yet an attempt seems needed for completeness, even though the reader should understand how tentative any statements must be because the course of future events remains unknowable.

As of 1979, at least, it looks as though Europe's political history since 1917 were dominated by two conflicting yet complementary processes. One was the growth of American and Russian wealth, power, and influence. This tended to supplant the dominance northwestern Europe had exercised over all neighboring lands since about 1850. On the other hand, the consolidation of western Europe, first into national and more recently into transnational political-economic units, tended to redress the balance in favor of the older metropolitan center. It is still too soon to know which way Europe's future will lastingly incline.

The United States and Russia began to catch up with western Europe industrially and in other respects even before 1914. This reenacted a familiar frontier phenomenon. Peoples near the margins of a civilization have often been able to take advantage of access to larger blocs of territory. Applying techniques of manpower and resource management as worked out at the metropolitan center to new ground and on a larger scale has repeatedly allowed such frontier polities to eclipse the power and wealth attainable by any one political unit at the center itself.

The twentieth-century variation upon this well-worn theme of world history was remarkable mainly because of the way Russia seemed to be reenacting earlier efforts to catch up with western European nations, only to fall behind again. As remarked above, toward the end of the eighteenth century Russia was clearly overtaking the organizational and technical levels of central and western Europe's Old Regime, only to be left behind by the new energies and resources so successfully tapped by the French Revolution on the one hand and by the Industrial Revolution on the other. In 1917, Russia had her own revolution, analogous to the French in the sense that the revolutionary regime soon proved able to mobilize far greater resources from the Russian population than the Tsars ever did. Moreover, the Communists have been eager to advance the industrial development of Russia, both for dogmatic reasons and because industrial skills enormously enhance military and other forms of governmental power. They have been marvelously successful, yet it is not clear that existing Russian command patterns will be able to bear the strain of conscripting human and material resources for state purposes indefinitely. Indeed it is hard to see how the Communist Party can expect to pass on to future generations the ideals and aspirations that made the sacrifices of the revolutionary generation bearable, any more than the officials and landowners of Catherine II's time were able to pass on to their sons the attitudes that inspired the builders of Russia in the century after Peter the Great's revolutionary assault upon tradition.

Western Europe's twentieth-century political development seems at least as remarkable as the rise of Russian and American power centers, east and west. World War I quickly overturned the nineteenth-century patterns of socioeconomic management. Military conscription soon led the principal belligerent nations to planned allocations of civilian manpower too. Supply shortages at the front led to planned armaments production, raw material controls, fuel allocations, and so on. A command economy, in short, supplanted free market economic relations and achieved otherwise impossible results. In principle, though reality, of course, always fell short, it was as though an entire nation coalesced into a single vast business enterprise, managed in such a way as to maximize output of war goods and services.

The brutal result, involving the squalid death of millions in the trenches of the western front, led French and British governments between the wars to reject the new managerial roles they had explored reluctantly enough from 1914 to 1918. In Russia, however, from the time the first Five Year Plan was instituted (1928), the Communist regime made the type of economic command planning that had been used in western nations during World War I a normal peacetime condition. Soon thereafter, German Nazi and American New Deal responses to the Depression of the 1930's introduced somewhat less drastic but nonetheless real variations upon the wartime model.

World War II (1939–1945) widened the range of mobilization and improved upon World War I methods in two main respects. First of all, transnational coordination became normal. The British and Americans managed a common war effort particularly well between 1941 and 1945, and by 1944, the Russians too, owed a great deal to supplies from the United States. What Britain had done so successfully from behind the island's then impenetrable water barrier in the Napoleonic period, the United States did again from behind the Atlantic from 1941 to 1945: subsidizing the Russians so that they could maintain a far larger force in the field than would have been possible on the strength of Russian resources alone. Yet the two parties never achieved agreement on war aims, and after the common enemy had been overthrown the alliance quickly split apart.

Nazi racial and nationalist doctrines notwithstanding, the European continent also witnessed a remarkable transnational economic and administrative integration during the latter phases of World War II. Having conquered most of Europe by 1942, the Nazis began to draw upon the manpower and material resources of the entire area under their command to supply German armies. Their position resembled that of the French during the Napoleonic wars, with the difference that Hitler's professed political principles were repulsive to all who could not qualify as members of the master race, so that the appeal that French revolutionary principles had exerted upon fraternal (if subject) peoples was almost totally lacking.

Yet memories of Europe's wartime economic pattern could not be wiped away, and when economic boom conditions returned to western Europe after 1948, men who had worked as slave laborers in German factories during the war were ready enough to return to Germany again as factory workers and led thousands of others after them. In fact, the postwar success of the Common Market clearly built upon recollections of the massive transnational migrations that had taken place under Hitler, when prisoners of war as well as civilian slave laborers had crisscrossed Europe by the hundreds of thousands. The breakdown of national barriers, raised so high during the nineteenth and early twentieth centuries, thus appears as the ironic and altogether unexpected but probably the most lasting monument to Hitler's maniacal career.

The second way in which World War II mobilization improved upon earlier patterns was the greater scope planners gave to systematic, organized invention. To be sure, there were beginnings from 1916 to 1918, when rapid evolution of airplane design and the creation of such a radically new weapon as the tank took place. But deliberate invention remained marginal in World War I. In World War II, on the contrary, all major belligerents invested much effort in planning new weapons and achieved some startling results. The most dramatic and important was the controlled release of nuclear energy (1942), achieved through collaboration between a vast American corporation and a company of physicists gathered from European as well as American universities and research institutes. Other major inventions — rockets, jet airplanes, radar, and the like — came into being under similar circumstances, as a result of systematic collaboration between academic theorists and the best engineers and technologists that could be assembled and set to work on the task.

The effect of such organized invention was to reverse older relationships between the inventor and the marketing of his invention. Under the pressure of war needs, men first decided what was needed to accomplish some purpose, then assigned experts to solve the technical problems inherent in producing a suitable device that would have the desired performance characteristics. The ultimate consumers waited impatiently until the tangible product of such inventive collaboration finally became available. Instead of making an invention first and then having to overcome systematic resistance to the proposed change, now change was taken for granted, actively desired by the managerial elite, and facilitated by everything administrative action could achieve.

Planned economies and planned invention proved relatively easy to achieve in war, since the goal of victory and the steps likely to contribute to it were relatively clear to all concerned, as well as being acceptable to almost everyone — on both sides. In peace, agreement was harder to achieve. Hence, after World War II, governmental mobilization of manpower and resources according to plan remained sporadic in western Europe, being mainly confined to the design and redesign of weapons systems. But business corporations, military planners, and social reformers all recognize what can be done by large-scale concentrations of effort and intelligence for devising new ways of doing things. The malleability of society and the economy seemed about as great as the malleability of government itself. This made choices difficult, while depriving custom of any claim to more than tentative legitimacy.

Despite all such uncertainties, since 1948, the heartland of western European civilization as it defined itself between 1600 and 1900 has prospered greatly, and in intellectual and technical matters is not noticeably laggard in comparison with anywhere else, with the possible exception of Japan. The loss of political control over colonies of Africa and Asia did not noticeably diminish European standing in the world. On the contrary, the colonies achieved independence, thanks partly to anticolonial currents of thought within the leading nations of Europe, and thanks partly to the clamor raised by local leaders who had mastered elements of European thought and culture and demanded for their own people a chance to join the community of nations as juridical equals.

In eastern Europe, to be sure, a kind of semicolonial regime was set up immediately after the war by Russian armies and political agents, and Russian influence over the satellite governments of eastern Europe remains strong a full generation later. American activity in western European lands was somewhat less heavy-handed but no less dominating, at least to begin with. Yet it is not clear that Europeans, both those located in the Russian sphere of influence and those living in the American ambit, will not again assert their effective independence. It looks as though the nationalism of eastern European peoples were inhibiting effective transnational economic integration among the Communist states — despite Marxist internationalist principles; whereas the growing solidity of transnational structures in western Europe — if the process of consolidation continues for another generation or longer — may create a power center comprising French, British, German, and Italian nations, together with a fringe of others, whose strength would compare favorably with that of any other in the world.

It will require a century or so to achieve the necessary perspective to sustain a firm judgment on Europe's twentieth-century pattern of development. Evaluation of comtemporary thought, letters, and art as created in Europe will take even longer. The story is unfinished. As for all living things, the future is uncertain. In our ignorance of what is yet to come, what has just happened remains profoundly enigmatic, pregnant with seeds of all the future.

APPENDIX 1: PROFESSOR McNEILL'S REPLY TO VERBAL CRITICISM OF HIS PAPER[10]

The author has tried to give a historical overview of the evolution of European societies. He believes that there exists at any given point a relationship between the development of a civilization, the geographical distribution of resources, and transport capabilities. The accumulation of wealth favors the development of culture. This concentration of wealth and political, military, and economic power entails the flourishing of culture, which imposes itself upon other, less evolved, neighboring civilizations. Italy and the Mediterranean region have been underestimated in regard to their influence on European civilization. Looking at it from the anthropological point of view, Professor McNeill puts the problem in a synoptic presentation of the facts and the possible connections between anthropology and history. In point of fact, since the only existing records have been composed by men of letters, it is important to have recourse to complementary works, based upon nonwritten, archaeological, archives, in order better to know about the life of former peoples. The writer was unaware only that maritime power and the beginnings of industrialization in Tuscany were related to wind energy and underlines the necessity for further work on this question.

Professor Bromley has examined the report from the historian's point of view and regrets the lack of historicism that is shown among Western anthropologists and ethnologists, and in particular the author's lack of comprehension of the path followed by European politics. McNeill begins by apologizing for calling the U.S.S.R. "Russia"; in spite of the fact that the Great Russians were in a dominant position before and after 1917, the term is incorrect. The author agreed that he understated class feuding in the Middle Ages and in previous times, this being omitted although perfectly well known. The conflicting interests of the social classes have manifested themselves in feuding and violence in European and world history. He acknowledged equally his having passed silently over ethnogenesis, feeling unable to treat the structural relations which unify all aspects of European prehistory.

The Europeanist conception of history extolled by Professor Vulcanesco is of great interest: national ethnocentrism will perhaps weaken in favor of a pan-Europeanist conscience, but this remains more or less in the realm of prediction.

[10]   This text is a résumé, made from tapes and from simultaneous translations, of the Congress discussion. The statements are however not exactly transcribed from their original formulations, nor are they in full. We have strived to retain the substance, abridged and simplified by the editor, who of course takes full responsibility for doing this.

In reply to the thoughts of J. Halpern, Professor McNeill thought that only an American, from the fact of distance, would be able to see the history of Europe as a single whole. With regard to the nomads, we possess too few archaeological traces. In addition he was obliged because of the time to schematize and took no account of demographic studies. Perhaps one day he will write a history of Europe in which he will make good the gaps which have been pointed out to him.

Finally, in response to the last interventions, Professor McNeill pointed out that in the course of the last generation the archives of Italian cities have been used to the full. Spanish records, very difficult to obtain, could very probably furnish similar material. Also, the Ottoman Empire possesses an extraordinary stock of as yet untouched archives. Perhaps one day it will be possible to establish the social and economic history of the Ottoman Empire, but the task is enormous. Some social anthropologists have been working in Europe on the fringes of history; the future will without doubt bring some discoveries in the field of institutional history.

APPENDIX 2: PROFESSOR McNEILL'S REPLY TO WRITTEN CRITICISM OF HIS PAPER

In response to all objections, Professor McNeill emphasizes that he has placed the accent upon the ecological and technological aspects of European history, a viewpoint rarely adopted by historians. To Franck Bourdier, who regrets the lack of a place given to prehistory, the author blames his lack of knowledge of the subject, nevertheless expressing surprise at the affirmation of the preeminence of European prehistoric man as catalytic of the evolution of all humanity. Taking into account the interest shown by W. A. Douglass in the relationships between colonial empires and national consolidation in Europe, he intends to get to the core of the issue in underlining the important role played by ethnic minorities in the foundation of these empires, in contention with the accusation made against him of falling into the liberal tradition of historical interpretation.

In accordance with J. Friedl's objection, he admits that his work could not be considered as an implement for anthropology, being beyond the bounds of the subject — the science of everyday man. Likewise he acknowledged, along with M. Gavazzi, the small place given to Slavic history as well as to the history of the moldboard plow.

In agreement with W. P. Lehmann regarding the probable role of social organization and individuals of the elite classes throughout history, he replies to T. F. Nemee that Nemee underrates what has been said about the neolithic revolution, acculturation, etc. Regretting, as does J. Nemeskéri, the absence of solid demographic foundations, he cannot help but think that the philosophy of history and culture developed by A. Nesheim is more optimistic than his own.

Having left himself open to criticism from P. J. Pelto, who reproaches him for explaining historical events from the technological study of an isolated fact, Professor McNeill points out that in fact the various consequences of a technical achievement produced by a vanished society are past recall, a fact which renders it impossible for a perfect appreciation of the changes exhibited through this achievement. To conclude, as a specialist in this problem, he stands categorically against the use of statistics relating to the potato.

Regarding the subjective theories of D. Rodnick, A. Steensberg is in opposition to such theories of evolution of the plow and of its fundamental role in the development of northwestern Europe.

Lack of space was the cause of his silence regarding the role of the Etruscans, the Scythians, the Celts and the Slavs — an omission pointed out by J. Kandert. One single formula is not valid for all cultures and would be a distortion of reality. Concerning the Fall of Rome, internal factors were certainly of importance, but the author tried his best to put the emphasis upon elements normally neglected by historians. He insists upon this in his response to S. Khera, at the same time doubting her statement, according to which there would have been in the past many an affluent society with a leisure class constituting a potential audience.

To conclude, in reply to P. Leser's question concerning the plow, he agrees that his account has accorded too little attention to the role of this instrument, and that as far as other details are concerned it would be necessary to refer to the text of his conference discussion.

REFERENCE

SLICHER VAN BATH, B. H.
1963   *Yield ratios, 810–1820*. School of Agrarian History Publication 10. Wageningen, Netherlands: State Agricultural University.

Ethnological Cartography and Atlases

BRANIMIR BRATANIĆ

*To the memory of António Jorge Dias
(1907–1973), distinguished scholar, dependable collaborator in common research work,
good man, and friend.*

RÉSUMÉ: LA CARTOGRAPHIE ET LES ATLAS ETHNO-LOGIQUES

A l'occasion de la publication de l'*Atlas ethnologique de l'Europe et des pays voisins*, Bratanić tente de formuler plus explicitement les principes généraux en vue de la préparation scientifique et technique des cartes générales, principes tels qu'on pouvait les déduire des travaux des pionniers dans ce domaine.
    1. Chaque science doit élaborer sa méthode propre, libre d'influences extérieures, même lorsque, à un degré supérieur, la synthèse de plusieurs sciences ainsi que la confrontation de diverses théories sont nécessaires.
    2. La présence d'un corpus organisé de connaissances est la précondition de toute science en évolution. Ce corpus ne s'obtient pas seulement par l'observation et l'enregistrement de phénomènes, mais aussi par leur ordonnancement et leur classification, tout en ne se préoccupant pas trop, à ce stade, de l'interprétation.
    3. L'ethnologie, science empirique, phénoménologique, historique, compara-tive et humaniste ne peut mériter ces adjectifs que grâce à la méthode d'une technique heuristique indirecte, c'est-à-dire, la méthode rétrogressive qui, graduellement et intuitivement, remonte du présent au passé.
    4. La cartographie ethnologique est l'un des outils de la recherche heuristique, et elle ne fournit pas seulement de simples illustrations ou résumés des travaux précédents. Il n'est pas possible non plus de représenter une culture vivante par quelques cartes. Ce n'est qu'en réunissant, classant, comparant de grandes quan-tités de matériaux systématiquement établis que la cartographie ethnologique doit parvenir à une interprétation et acquérir une haute valeur en tant que méthode. Si ingrate qu'elle paraisse, cette tâche est indispensable pour donner

I am grateful to professor Paul Leser for pointing out to me some passages, by Sir William Jones and Charles Darwin, of which I have made use in this paper.

une vue rapide et simple des cultures traditionnelles des peuples et de leurs relations effectives.

5. Leur typologie, aussi claires et détaillées que doivent être les cartes, n'est qu'heuristique et non génétique interprétative. C'est pourquoi une bonne carte de recherches doit présenter sa matière de façon telle qu'il soit possible de tirer des conclusions des *diverses et caractéristiques distributions de phénomènes de culture dans l'espace*.

6. Il y a de telles différences entre les méthodes d'investigation pour les régions de petit étendue et pour celles de surface plus importante, qu'on distingue entre la "microcartographie" et la "macrocartographie" ethnologiques. Il est de plus nécessaire d'établir la typologie qui convient afin que la comparabilité des phénomènes de culture soit assurée et de vérifier que ces phénomènes ethnologiques soient aptes au traitement de la cartographie.

7. Enfin, le problème le plus épineux est de clarifier celui du "présent ethnologique," c'est-à-dire de définir le "moment" de l'histoire culturelle que la carte doit représenter, étant entendu que la culture préindustrielle doit constituer la matière d'une carte ethnologique, culture qui disparait, plus ou moins vite selon les pays, dans la civilisation urbaine. Est-il alors possible de comparer des faits que séparent des dizaines, voire parfois des centaines d'années? L'idée d'"intégration descriptive" (ou intégration conceptuelle) de Kroeber peut constituer le dénominateur commun: c'est-à-dire que ". . . l'histoire n'est pas seulement une séquence chronologique d'évènements. Mais aussi tout ce qui est arrivé, créé et qui demeure, en tant que résultat ou produit du processus historique et qui continue à vivre, à changer, à bouger, à son rythme propre, en tant qu'exemple concret de vie culturelle."

Ainsi sera-t-il possible d'utiliser les données réunies par deux ou trois générations d'informateurs, toutes les précautions critiques étant assurées par un témoignage ethnologique, de même que d'obtenir une meilleure interprétation.

En résumé, c'est en étendant les frontières temporelles du présent ethnologique, afin de délimiter un modèle défini de phénomène culturel, que sera acquise la possibilité de tirer des conclusions plus significatives et de meilleures interprétations qu'il ne l'aurait été à l'intérieur de strictes limites chronologiques.

8. En tant que science, la cartographie tend à apporter une connaissance nouvelle et à en découvrir les moyens, à travers un long et difficile travail d'interprétation. De fermes principes de méthode sont la base indispensable de tout travail préparatoire: sélection des thèmes, réunion des matériaux, élaboration des cartes. En un mot, il s'agit d'une sorte d'hypothèse à vérifier continuellement par des travaux postérieurs, sans surtout négliger d'anciennes méthodes qui ont fait leurs preuves, comme l'ethnologie historique.

Un important appareil de notes et une bibliographie assez détaillée complètent cet article.

There has been rapid progress in ethnological cartography in the last eight or nine years.[1] Eleven ethnological atlases have published their

[1]   About older endeavors and results, encompassing also the linguistic-ethnographic atlases in Switzerland and in Latin countries see Weiss (1950), Erixon (1955), Bratanić (1959a, 1965, 1970), Zender (1959), and Barabás (1963). For our purpose the most important is Barabás' book, which reviews "the spatial way of viewing" in ethnology, from the first theoretical thinkers (Adolf Bastian, Lewis Henry Morgan, Edward Burnett Tylor, Friedrich Ratzel, Leo Frobenius, Fritz Graebner, Wilhelm Schmidt, Kazimierz Moszyński) to the beginning of modern atlases. The state of cartographic work until 1960 is critically analyzed. Unfortunately the book is entirely in Hungarian, not in one of the great world languages, and the German summary does not give sufficient help.

maps until now[2] and thirteen further ones are in various phases of preparation.[3] Moreover, the common *Ethnological atlas of Europe and its bordering countries* (i.p.)[4] is being intensively prepared, and its first trial maps are to be published soon. Thirty-two countries, until now, have collaborated in this common international undertaking.[5] Much energy, time, professional skill, and also financial means have been spent on these efforts. The mentioned instances of concrete work in so many countries, notwithstanding their different social, economic, and political structure, and on such a broad international basis, give sufficient evidence to prove that the purpose must be a worthy and an attainable one.

By practice and theoretical reasoning, general principles for scientific and technical preparation ethnological maps and atlases have been laid down, and these can be regarded as common experience. It is remarkable how the most important of these principles have been, at various times and in various circumstances, independently expressed in the writings of experienced specialists conducting concrete work on comprehensive atlases (Gajek 1947, 1958, 1971; Weiss 1950; Zender 1959; Bratanić 1959a, 1970;[6] Barabás 1963). The common work on the atlas has both

[2] Those (chronologically) of Germany (Harmjanz and Röhr 1937–1940; Zender 1958), Switzerland (Geiger et al. 1950), Sweden (Erixon 1957; Campbell and Nyman, i.p.), Poland (*Polski atlas etnograficzny* 1953–1971), Netherlands and Flemish Belgium (Meertens et al. 1959), Austria (Burgstaller et al. 1959), Yugoslavia (*Etnološki atlas Jugoslavije* 1960), Russia (Tolstov 1967), Hungary (*Magyar néprajzi atlasz* 1967), Portugal (Dias and Galhano 1968), and Greece (*Atlas tēs Hellēnikēs laografias* 1970).

[3] Those of Finland, since 1962 (*Suomen kansankulttuurin kartasto*, i.p.); Rumania, since 1965 (*Atlasul etnografic al României*, i.p.); Slovakia, since 1966 (*Etnografický atlas Slovenska*, i.p.); Luxembourg, since 1968 (*Atlas der Luxemburger Volkskunde*, i.p.); Czechoslovakia, since 1965, where the systematic work has been temporarily suspended; Denmark; Scotland (*Scottish ethnological atlas*, i.p.); Ireland, for both the Republic of Ireland and Northern Ireland (*Irish ethnological atlas*, i.p.); Egypt; and four atlases in the U.S.S.R. (Ukraine, Byelorussia, and Moldavia; central Asia and Kazakhstan; the Baltic states; and Caucasia).

[4] Besides Europe, the atlas encompasses North Africa and southwestern Asia, from Morocco to Iran.

[5] They are Albania, Austria, Belgium, Bulgaria, Cyprus, Czechoslovakia, Denmark, Egypt, England, Finland, France, Federal Republic of Germany, German Democratic Republic, Greece, Hungary, the Republic of Ireland, Iceland, Italy, Luxembourg, Netherlands, Northern Ireland, Norway, Poland, Portugal, Rumania, Scotland, Spain, Sweden, Switzerland, Turkey, U.S.S.R., and Yugoslavia. Experts from these countries cooperate by providing materials, drafts for maps, and by attending regular working meetings of the organizing commission of the atlas. Four such meetings have taken place until the time of writing (at Zagreb in 1966, Bonn in 1968, Helsinki in 1970, and Stockholm in 1972), and for the first three of them published reports exist (*Arbeitskonferenz* 1968, 1970, 1972). The whole undertaking has been from 1966 conducted by the Permanent International Atlas Committee (with two coordination centers, Bonn and Zagreb) which has done all coordinating and preparatory work since 1953 (Bratanić 1965). A turning point in these endeavors was a two-day symposium at the VIIth ICAES in Moscow in 1964, which was to initiate the regular international working conferences.

[6] This last paper is, really, only the introduction (about a fifth part) to a comprehensive survey of methodological, organizational, and technical principles of cartographic work in ethnology, read at the congress, partly in its eighteenth section ("Géographie ethnique"), and partly in the special symposium "Méthodes de rédaction des atlas ethnographiques."

provided the possibility and more strongly stressed the necessity to for-
mulate these principles more explicitly and more definitely. They have
also been fixed officially by resolutions of the regular meetings of the atlas
(*Arbeitskonferenz* 1968, 1970, 1972). On the other hand, they are not
new at all, and can be found in works of the pioneers — Bastian, Morgan,
Tylor, Graebner, Schmidt, A. L. Kroeber, as well as with other eminent
scholars such as Moszyński and S. A. Tokarev, to name only a few. What
is new, is that they are being *applied*, at last, in a planned, systematic,
concrete, and coordinated work on a grand scale. This implies not only a
firm scientific method, with clear aims and with consciousness of its
theoretical suppositions, but also considerable organizational effort and,
as a consequence, such human qualities of collaborators which, in addition to those required of every scientist, will make possible a long-
lasting and trustworthy[7] common work. It also means that there is a wish
and ability to continue, to build upon what has been achieved hitherto, to
try to come to an end, not to begin from scratch every time when a new
idea arises.

GENERAL PRINCIPLES

1.   Every science which deserves the name must make its contribution to
the increase of our knowledge *independently* (Weiss 1950:5; Bratanić
1960:226–227) — that is it must furnish something not known before,
new facts and new conclusions. It is a methodological necessity that such
results be elaborated in every science by a method of its own, free from
any other influence, bias or persuasion, even in those cases when, on a
higher level, for the ultimate solution of a problem a confrontation and
coordination of the contributions of several sciences, a common synthesis, is needed (Weiss 1950:5; Bratanić 1960:227). The respective arguments, as well as those for choosing a scientific aim and an appropriate
method in general, must be weighed according to their validity, cogency,
and importance for research, not counted by the number of their temporary supporters. There can be no voting in science (Bratanić, in
Arbeitskonferenz 1972:45).

2.   "Possession of an *organized corpus of knowledge* of phenomena is
precondition of any soundly growing science" (Kroeber 1963:150;
emphasis added). This holds also for a historical approach, and "without
such a series of corpuses, and a willingness to examine and organize each

---

Unfortunately, the other four fifths of that paper, which was in German have not been
published, except for a brief summary of it in Russian (Bruk 1970:519–520).
[7]   As Kroeber said of biologists, "trusting each other — by having common methods, a
common front of attack" (1963:164).

one comparatively, there can be no historic interpretation of nature on any of its levels; there can be only pseudohistoric guess" (Kroeber 1963:171).[8] Such a corpus is obtained not only by observing and recording phenomena, but also by ordering and classifying them (Kroeber 1953:362). Although one, in this humble task of patiently ordering "large masses of observations" (Kroeber 1963:158), at "an earlier stage" of research (Kroeber 1953:363), does not need to "worry too much about interpretation" (Kroeber 1963:150), it is the indispensable basis for all following interpretation in every empirical science. For "the distinction is false, both in natural science and in humanistics, between a higher theoretical understanding and a lower order of merely informational knowledge" (Kroeber 1963:150).

3. Ethnology, being an empirical, phenomenological, historical, comparative, and humanistic science of the *cultural aspect* within what has been called the "sociocultural range," that is of culture and of its bearers, has also its own ways to gain knowledge. Today there is no need to demonstrate or to prove the scientific character of such an ethnology any more.[9] Like linguistics, it has its descriptive, comparative, and historical part (Gleason 1955:11). And to arrive at historical results,[10] ethnology must make use, in concrete research, of an *indirect heuristic method and technique*.[11] This is the well-known retrogressive method which, in reconstructing the history of traditional nonliterate cultures, proceeds gradually and systematically from the present to the past, from the known to the unknown, and by which historical ethnology becomes an inductive and empirical science in the proper sense of the word, while its results attain something of that sureness which is in natural sciences obtained by

---

[8]   For the necessity of "an adequately large and growing body of compared knowledge" (Kroeber 1963:171) in ethnological cartography, compare also Bratanić (1959a:11, 13) and Bratanić in Bruk (1970:519, 531), where the dangers of skipping some important information, in case of scarce data, are especially emphasized (Bruk 1970:531).
[9]   Tylor took early pains to found his "science of culture." And for a humanistic discipline *par excellence*, the "human history, in the ordinary sense of the word," Kroeber in our times has shown it brilliantly: "It is recorded and sifted knowledge, always organized with reference to time and space, usually organized also with regard to significance, and as far as possible concerned with cause and effect" (1963:181). And he includes it even "within the confines of natural science," because it is "dealing with what is customary, predictable within its limits, and therefore regular" (1963:184). The same holds, of course, also for ethnology — compare too, what Tylor said of "ethnography" (1929 [1871]:12). And modern general dictionaries define "science" in such a way that it can encompass also the humanistic disciplines (see, for example, *Webster's new international dictionary*, third edition, s.v. "science," meanings 2 and 3).
[10] "The time, place and circumstances of the origin and further development of any institution, invention, or cultural form must be considered a legitimate and potentially soluble problem of inquiry through analytic comparison" (Kroeber 1963:164).
[11] "Es ist nicht bestimmt, daß die direkte Methode immer auch die erfolgreichste ist. In diesem Fall bedeutet es, daß die Klärung vielleicht unbedeutender Themen zur Lösung der grundlegenden Probleme führen kann" (Barabás 1970:507).

experiment (Bratanić 1959a:12, 18). The factual state of things gained in this way is still open to an explicative interpretation.

4. A special heuristic research tool of ethnology is *ethnological cartography*.[12] As an instrument of research it is no independent method, but a technique in the frame of the cultural-historical method in ethnology already mentioned. All experts agree today that the purpose of ethnological maps is not to provide mere illustrations,[13] "summaries of investigations done already elsewhere" or "illustrations of the points of view or ways of thinking preconceived in the text" (Bratanić 1959b:44). It would be also quite mistaken of us, and impossible for us to try to present the living culture of a people in its whole by a number of maps. These are the *"Plakatkarten"*: "research maps, no mere illustrative expedients which can be read, like posters, at the first glance" (Weiss 1950:xiv, 93). They give us a kind of an ordered corpus of knowledge, but not only this, solely by ordering, classification, and typological treatment of a large quantity of systematically collected material,[14] mapping tech-

[12]   The term "ethnological cartography," which is today in general use among specialists and experts, denotes simply the making of maps with an ethnological aim and point of view. The formerly often used term "ethnogeography," sometimes also "ethnic geography" (analogous to "Sprachgeographie," "géographie linguistique," or "geolinguistics" — Weiss 1950:2; Weijnen 1972:3, 9), is not adequate, since ethnological cartography has nothing to do with the science of geography as such. Likewise, there is no "geographical method" in ethnology. The point in question is merely the *spatial* distribution of ethnological phenomena. This has already been stated clearly by Weiss: "Die 'geographische Methode' in der Volkskunde bedeutet . . . kartographische Darstellungstechnik und *räumliche Betrachtungsweise* im Rahmen der volkskundlichen Methode . . ." (1950:2; emphasis added). Still better, with respect to the order of ideas, this is expressed in the title of his first chapter: "Räumliche Betrachtungsweise und kartographische Darstellung in der Volkskunde." For the importance of distinguishing between this "spatial way of viewing" and a "geographical method" Weiss cites the view of geographers themselves, according to which one should not talk of a "geographic method in ethnology," nor of a "language geography," because the "räumliche Betrachtung und die kartographische Darstellung von geisteswissenschaftlichen Forschungsgegenständen im Rahmen der betreffenden geisteswissenschaftlichen Disziplin noch keine 'Geographie' und noch keine 'geographische Methode' sei, und weil *das Verbreitungsproblem überhaupt nicht als Kriterium geographischer Forschung gelten könne"* (1950:2; original emphasis). Thus, ethnological cartography is a special, independent research procedure in ethnology. If it is viewed as a special subdivision or subdiscipline of historical ethnology, it could be rather designated (which is not really necessary) as "ethnological chorology" — analogous to "chorology" in biology; or, which is not so good, as "ethnological topology" — analogous to "topolinguistics" — "Topolinguistik (Weijnen 1972:9, 11); or to the distinction between the "topological" and "geographical" positions in archaeology (Kroeber 1963:135). It is also necessary to distinguish between this *thematic* ethnological cartography and the *ethnic* mapping (mapping of peoples) which are different things (Barabás in Bruk 1970:520).
[13]   A beautifully executed map is, of course always a welcome means for better illustration of a fact pointed at, or of a point raised in a discussion; but there is a danger that we might act like that medieval bishop who turned the pages of a beautifully illuminated codex in admiration without reading or understanding its contents.
[14]   In a sense, the treatment of such a mass of data has something in common with statistical procedures, and can, up to a limit and for gaining a general orientation, in fact be given a statistical treatment. But it must be stressed that in ethnology, because of its historical

nique in ethnology must lead, without special endeavor, to some interpretation, and attains thereby a high methodical value (Bratanić 1959a:12, 18; 1970:394). Thus, certain selected and scientifically productive themes are being investigated all at once, comparatively and systematically, *in a large area* (*Flächenforschung*), as opposed to *Punktforschung*, the intensive study of a complex whole of cultural phenomena in one place (Bratanić 1959a:11, 17). It is natural that this type of research must put emphasis on "a census of items of culture content," on formal properties of cultural phenomena, and not on "persons and their relations" (Kroeber 1954:290).[15] Although ethnological cartography represents only one of the possible ways of gaining knowledge in ethnological research, although it cannot give us all what we can expect from modern ethnology, it is methodically and practically for some of its ultimate scientific aims, especially for ethnological reconstruction of cultural history, simply indispensable (Weiss 1950:3; Bratanić 1959a:11, 17; 1961:70; 1970:394; Barabás 1963:177).

The task is to some minds thankless; to others it is fascinating; but if anthropology refuses to accept it, no one will have illumination on a large [perhaps the largest] part of the total story of mankind. . . . This is a laborious method, is beset by several pitfalls, and is easily abused . . . But it is a method of indirect and circumstantial evidence, such as the rest of science uses; and at least there are no witnesses to lie or distort testimony — any distortion is by the investigator (Kroeber 1948:538–542).

For other goals in ethnology, maps are, as a rule, not necessary tools of research, although even in such cases they can serve as illustrations of some theses obtained by other means. In any case, ethnological cartography is the quickest, simplest, and clearest way to get an objective idea of the traditional cultures of peoples, and of their actual connections and relations (Bratanić 1959a:18; 1967:1). Thus, the results of ethnological cartography might also, by the way, help to clear away injurious ethnocentrism in practical life.

5.   An ethnological map and an ethnological atlas are *instruments of research*, as has been said before (see, for example, Weiss 1950:93; Bratanić 1959a:12, 18; 1970:394; and the resolution in *Arbeitskonferenz* 1968:26, 28). But they are also a sort of scientific "half-product" (Bratanić 1959a:12, 18; 1970:395). They offer a clear survey of ordered facts and their sources. Therefore they have also a considerable

---

character and therefore of the inevitable incompleteness of its data, statistics can never have such importance and exactness as it has in natural sciences.
[15]   This practical and methodical point of view does not preclude the possibility of other aims in anthropology or ethnology, and it is independent of any extremistic theory of the (ontological) nature of culture.

documentary value.[16] They also set up problems. But they represent no summaries of final conclusions or solutions of problems[17] (Bratanić 1959a:12, 18; also Weiss 1950:93). Their typology must be clear and detailed as much as possible (Bratanić in *Arbeitskonferenz* 1970:98), but it is a *heuristic typology*, not an interpretative genetic one (Bratanić in Bruk 1970:520; and Bruk 1973:3).[18] A genuine, correctly designed research map ought to present its material in such a way that it will be possible to draw corresponding conclusions from various and characteristic *distributions of culture phenomena in space*. This is the most important, pivotal property of ethnological cartography,[19] and it was, in principle, known and stated long ago. Tylor very early thought that "the ethnographer's business is to classify . . . details with a view to making out their distribution in geography and history, and the relations which exist among them" (1929 [1871]:8).[20] "This placing of phenomena in space is an indispensable need in all the historical sciences," says Kroeber (1948:541), and he also quotes R. H. Lowie: "When we do not know the distribution of a phenomenon, we know nothing that is theoretically significant (1948:542). And Kroeber has a whole chapter showing clearly that the distributions are the starting point for historical interpretation (1948:538–571; especially the summary on pp. 568–571). In another passage speaking about archaeology, Kroeber formulates it as "the *conversion of space relations into time relations* of relative sequence" (1963:135; emphasis added). This principle is based on the supposition that the picture of forms and their distribution on a map reflect very complicated historical events (Bratanić 1970:395).[21]

[16]   This documentary value has been stressed especially by Weiss (1950:93); Bratanić (1959a:11, 17; 1970:394); Bratanić in Bruk (1970:519); and Barabás (1963:179). The possibility of thus controlling the evidence and later conclusions was emphasized by Bratanić (1959a:11, 17; 1959b:44). And this moment has an important role also in the technical execution of ethnological maps of the "first order" (analytical maps).
[17]   As it has been sometimes affirmed, e.g. by Bruk and M. G. Rabinovič in Bruk (1970:511).
[18]   On genetic and heuristic typologies see Bratanić (1963:512–514, especially p. 514) and also Kroeber (1948:542).
[19]   Barabás calls it "the core, the most important special research method of ethnological and ethnographical investigations with historical aims" (1970:504).
[20]   Geography in the first place, then comes "history." We would say today "in space" and "in time."
[21]   Other experts in ethnological cartography share, of course, this view, especially Barabás (1963:177; 1970:504), Gajek (1958:19), Zender (1959:4, 5), Bruk and Rabinovič (Bruk 1970:511) and others. Linguists, too, have taken the same point of view, sometimes referring to ethnologists (Weijnen 1972:14; Bruk 1973:17). And even in natural sciences and in philosophy of science this way of thinking is legitimate. Reichenbach, mentioning that "Darwin made the inference that the *systematic order* of coexisting species represents the *historical order* of their genesis," says: "The inference is good inductive logic" (1951:197). And he further concludes: "So we shall always depend on an inference from systematic order to historical order, a cross-inference from the order of the simultaneous to the order of succession" (1951:198). And especially in geology: "It appears legitimate to identify the spatial order of the strata with the time order of their deposition" (1951:198).

6.   There is a methodical difference between the cartographical investigation of very small areas and that of larger ones. We can even speak of an ethnological *"microcartography"* and of such a *"macrocartography,"* which is largely analogous to Kroeber's distinguishing between "microscope" and "telescope" (or "macroscopic") approaches to historical problems in ethnology (Kroeber 1963:133, 134; and also 1952:108). The first approach deals with culture traits characteristic of a small area, compares them with, and tries to explain them by, the known facts of geographical (climatological, pedological, and so on), economic, sociological, historical, and psychological nature, and the like. There is, however, always great danger of the so-called "local interpretation" in such endeavors to explain facts of culture. This local interpretation often becomes, analogous to "folk etymology" in linguistics, a "folk interpretation" in the science of history and in ethnology, which, not so rarely, means that it is demonstrably false. "Narrowly restricted local interpretation (since Malinowski and his followers having become fatally general in ethnology) is mostly just as risky as the folk etymology" (Paul Leser in *Arbeitskonferenz* 1970:19). For ethnological comparison, on the other hand, only the second kind, macrocartography — especially a macrocartography of "microthemes" — has any real value (Bratanić in Bruk 1970:520). It is only such a "macrocartographical" distribution map "that qualifies us for a methodically admissible interpretation" (Leser in *Arbeitskonferenz* 1970:20). In any case, there must be also some prerequisites fulfilled. First, the *comparability* of the phenomena of the culture mapped must be secured. This means that in selecting the material for mapping — if possible, even in collecting it — the qualities of form of phenomena (in which sense also certain functional properties may be used), as well as the lexical and semantic characteristics of their names, must be well defined.[22] In other words, the *proper typology* must be made. The mere existence, or nonexistence, of formal qualities which do not depend on circumstances necessarily demanding just such a form (the purpose or function of the phenomenon, available or necessary material in things, and the like) poses sufficient ethnological and historical problems, and therefore this kind of question is in the foreground (Weiss 1950:55). The identity, or strong similarity, of form established in this way, whenever or wherever, is most important. These formal, sometimes quite accidental, nonfunctional details (microtopics) can be as important for the reconstruction of the history of peoples and their cultures, as the now rare relics from former times.[23] This has been expressed many times by various authors, among them eminent scholars and philosophers of

---

[22]   Linguists also agree that the "vocabulaire dialectal" is "une source importante pour la recherche culturelle et historique" (Weijnen 1972:14), and therefore they also begin with lexicology (1972:16).

[23]   This is no romanticism, as some would maintain, but simple methodological necessity.

science.[24] Secondly, *suitability for cartographical treatment* is not the same for all ethnological phenomena, for especially those with their distribution confined to one limited area do not belong on an ethnological research map (Bratanić 1959a:13; Bratanić in Bruk 1970:520). On the contrary, those phenomena "which appear as an essential part of the culture of most groups of men" are most apt for cartographical treatment (Bratanić in *Arbeitskonferenz* 1972:46).[25] And above all, the widely distributed phenomena of culture must be, in our times, led back to a sort of *common denominator* which only will allow a meaningful comparison and interpretation of their various forms (Bratanić in Bruk 1970:519). For successful comparing of the historically originated cultural properties of different peoples, especially for research in the scope of the *Ethnological atlas of Europe*, the *traditional preindustrial culture*, in its various forms of appearance, proved the only possibility of such a common denominator.[26] Without such measures we would always risk the danger of involving ourselves in quite another problem, namely in the advance of urban civilization — a qualitatively and historically entirely different thing — and in the receding of traditional folk cultures, at various times and in various places, which is for ethnology of peripheral interest only, and does not require to be investigated cartographically at all.[27] For a consideration in terms of large areas and for the investigation of far-reaching connections, only old, preindustrial folk culture comes into question if meaningful results are to be expected.

7.   The thorniest problem of ethnological cartography, that of the "*ethnological present*," must be specifically clarified. It is easy to understand

[24]   In 1786 Sir William Jones had already envisaged "some common source" for six of the main Indo-European languages on the grounds of a detailed "stronger affinity . . . than could possibly have been produced by accident" (Waterman 1963:15, 16). Darwin even spoke about "a multitude of points" many of which were "of so unimportant or of so singular a nature, that it is extremely improbable that they should have been independently acquired (1878:178, 179). Compare also Kroeber's "minutiae": "this is inherent in the method . . . from sharply definable minimal units: to let patterns emerge from broad collocation of exact items" (1952:265). Bratanić adds that "we can hardly know in advance which phenomenon and which place have a scientific significance" (1959a:13, 18). Barabás mentions the importance of "insignificant themes" and of "smaller part questions" which "can express more clearly the former relations" (1970:507), while Weiss (1950:58) speaks about "historically interesting relics." Ethnological importance, then, and cartographical productivity "cannot be always properly predicted" (Weiss 1950:33).
[25]   The same, says Weijnen, is true of linguistics: "ce qu'on est à peu près assuré de trouver dans toutes les régions" (1972:17).
[26]   This standpoint was expressed officially in the first resolution of 1966 (*Arbeitskonferenz* 1968:26, 28), as well as before and after by individual experts — by Zender (1959:5; and in *Arbeitskonferenz* 1970:96; and 1972:16) and by Bratanić (in Bruk 1970:519). Similarly, linguists do not include in the basic map of their planned European atlas "des langues de culture" (Weijnen 1972:23). It is to be added, briefly at this point, that by "preindustrial culture" only a culture *form* is meant, not a definitive chronological period which might be expressed in years.
[27]   The so-called "maps of regression" are primarily illustrative maps.

that an ethnological map represents a profile, a cross section in time, a "moment"[28] in what is happening in cultural history. But the question instantly arises: which "moment" an ethnological map should present. If we have agreed, and few will have not, that the old traditional folk culture is the proper object of historical investigations in ethnology, we can understand that traditional preindustrial culture ought to make the contents of an ethnological map. But this preindustrial culture has been continually retreating before the urban civilization, in one country earlier and faster, in another later and slower. That which in one people is alive today, disappeared from actual use in another a hundred or more years ago, perhaps. How can we compare two such cultures? Which chronological "moment" should we select for comparison (if this is possible at all)? The questions are wrongly posed. They rest upon two basic and fatal misunderstandings: first, there is the tenacious residue of that apparently ineradicable notion that a map must be an illustration of something (here, say, of a condition of culture in a definite cross section of time); second, that history is merely a sequence of chronologically connected events. We know already that ethnological maps are instruments of research and not illustrations; and this may suffice to clear away the first misunderstanding. But can we really compare things many decades or even centuries apart? We can, if we have an idea of history which allows that; and we must, if there is to be an indispensable common denominator with respect to time, like that which has already been fixed with respect to contents — the traditional preindustrial culture. Fortunately, these two common denominators largely coincide if we apply Kroeber's idea of *"descriptive integration"*[29] (or "conceptual integra-

---

[28]   Meaning "a definite period or point in a course of events" not an "instant" or "a comparatively brief period of time" (*Webster's new international dictionary*, third edition, s.v. "moment"). And in any case, even language borders, at any given time, are very indeterminate and uncertain (Weijnen 1972:3, 24; Leser in *Arbeitskonferenz* 1970: 18).
[29]   As expressed by Kroeber many times and in various places since 1935 (e.g. 1953:151). "The establishment of time sequences is a normal, but not fundamental, feature of the historic approach" (Kroeber 1952:71). Described by it is a historical time span (Kroeber's example is the Middle Ages), regardless of its beginning or end expressed in years, but forming a definite and meaningful unit with regard to its contents (Bratanić in *Arbeitskonferenz* 1972:27). "The essence is the characteristic delineation of groups of phenomena in context, into which both time and space factors enter," but "either of these two considerations can be temporarily suppressed by being held constant by the historian, if circumstances *or his objective* warrant" (Kroeber 1952:102; emphasis added). The phenomena can be thus "placed in time . . . but not diachronic internally" (Kroeber: 1963:4). The idea was for most people difficult to understand (even Kroeber's teacher Franz Boas did not understand it) and unacceptable. Kroeber himself says in this connection: "When I expressed myself on this point I have used the term 'historical.' However the idea of sequence of time as the essential factor in history is so deeply implanted that, no matter how often you affirm that the historical approach is not necessarily chronological, the impression remains. The term 'descriptive integration' is much more effective . . ." (1953:151). But progress of clarification is slow, and "it will be no doubt better speeded by cooperative attempts than by wrangling" (Kroeber 1952:102).

tion")[30] as a valid historical concept. To put it very briefly, and as the present writer has understood it, the core of this notion is not only that history is a chronological sequence of events, a process (what it surely is), but also that what has happened, originated and remained as a result or product of the historical process, and continues to live, to change, to "move" at its own pace as a concrete pattern of cultural life, this pattern being the most important thing. In this way we are able not only to use the recollections of two or three generations of informants (Zender in *Arbeitskonferenz* 1972:30; cf. Bratanić on p. 36), a legitimate means, provided that there is also critical caution, of procuring ethnological evidence, but also to gain a better possibility of proper interpretation of this evidence. Also all disturbing questions of synchronic and diachronic treatment,[31] of dynamics[32] and statics in ethnological cartography thereby lose their meaning. The correct interpretation of a spatial-temporal picture of ethnological facts on a map can show, behind an apparently static structure, peculiar latent historical dynamics. The properly construed ethnological map gives us always, in a sense a "kinemato-gram,"[33] the dynamics of which are revealed only by sensible interpreta-tion. Historical occurrences come about and leave their effects in long spans of time. It could be said that the history of culture is being played in "long waves," but one must have an ear for this kind of historical music. The shorter time intervals are, usually, not sufficient to create more significant culture conditions. Therefore, taken ethnologically, it would not make much sense to repeat cartographical investigations — as it is not so rarely deemed necessary — in smaller time spans, nothing to say how much waste of time, energy, and money this would cause. The carto-graphical picture shows us, it is true, a "moment" in the course of cultural development, but such a "virtual" moment can last for a hundred or two hundred years (Kroeber 1963:181–184) and still more, but this is, to be sure, of very little importance for cultural history. The "ethnological pre-sent" is just somewhat different from the present of a man's life. And, on the other hand, we should not use the terms "dynamics" and "statics" as

[30]   Kroeber (1952:70), meaning a "conceptually reconstructive or integrative process."
[31]   Since it is quite impossible to determine a real chronological "moment" in ethnological investigations, inclusive of cartographical ones, a "synchronic" map is a technical question of agreement (Bratanić in *Arbeitskonferenz* 1972:26), and leaving out some forms of phenomena which connect various parts of, say, Europe, only because they lie "diachroni-cally" apart (so that some of them can be now found only in literature or in museums), would be unfruitful and wrong.
[32]   Kroeber differentiates between "two aspects within the dynamic approach: a micro-dynamic, . . . and a macrodynamic, which alone is wide open and genuinely historic in interest (1963:187). Nevertheless, "both the microdynamic and the macrodynamic approach are justified and profitable in the field of culture, and in the end ought to supplement each other. The macrodynamic emphasizes the time factor more and deals with longer time spans" (1963:198–199).
[33]   The term has been used recently in connection with attempts to explain linguistic "micromovements" by "geographic simulation models" (Hard 1972).

notions of value. They certainly are not that, but neutral concepts, polar to each other, both of which have their definite places in scientific research, as the case under investigation may be. Also, no cultural life is conceivable without dynamics, while without statics there can be no culture at all.

In summarizing, we can say that the expanding of temporal borders of the ethnological present, so as to encompass a definite pattern of cultural phenomena, give us the possibility to draw more meaningful conclusions and better interpretations than it would be possible within any rigid chronological limits.

8. It is not the task of ethnology to catalog merely what we already know, or what we think we know. As a science, our discipline must try to come upon *new* knowledge and to find ways to do that. As a humanistic and historical science, it has specific difficulties. That which corresponds to "protocolar records" in natural sciences is not given at the beginning "but must be acquired by long and often difficult interpretative work" (Bocheński 1959:132). The relevant facts in historical sciences are never simply given. Before them come documents which only render the proper sequence possible: documents, establishing of facts, and then explaining the facts. And, as distinct from the generalizing natural scientist, the historian must *choose* from an enormous mass of documents (Bocheński 1959:132). This is a very delicate procedure which requires firm methodical principles as an indispensable basis for all preparatory work. Ethnological cartography, as it has been shown before, is a most important part of this work, and the chief general principles for it have been emphasized in the foregoing points.[34] The very selection of themes for an atlas inquiry, collecting materials and working out maps, is something like a working hypothesis which has to be tested in further research. Ethnological cartography is also a methodical tool, based on some old ideas,[35] as has been pointed out before. Now, a tool is to be judged not by what is new or fashionable about it but by its capability to serve efficaciously a definite purpose. The usefulness and necessity of a knife is not impaired by the fact that wood is better chopped by an ax, or that a screw is better turned by a screwdriver, or that it is an ancient invention, indeed; nor is its use to be renounced because some handle it ridiculously in their eating

[34] These principles constitute only the first part of the paper as it was read at the IXth ICAES in Chicago. The remaining three parts dealing with organization of the atlas work and treatment of materials, with cartographic techniques as well as with the interpretation of finished maps (the latter being extremely important but going, in the proper sense, already beyond the limits of ethnological cartography as such), could not possibly be prepared for publication in time, because of a long-lasting illness of the author. However, the Appendix to the paper, with its twelve maps, deals, although very briefly, with some of these matters.
[35] A year before his death Sigurd Erixon, speaking in a symposium about the possibilities of charting modern life said that in science we ought to proceed without egocentrism and fanaticism (1970: xiii), and that old methods still have their value, which may indicate a need to return to historical ethnology (1970:22).

manners or because it has been used, so often, alas, in killing human beings; and, of course, no anatomist would abandon his analytical knife in dissecting corpses for scientific purposes, and no conscientious surgeon would refrain from this tool in removing an inflamed appendix because the human body is such a god-given beautifully functioning whole.

APPENDIX: MAPS

Map 1 is an analytical map of the "first order" (more than 1600 research points for the whole map). By means of signs, every research point is exactly localized with an accuracy of 2.5 kilometers, which is practically more than sufficient. An orthogonal (quadratic) localization and orientation net allows not only such exact localization but also the easy finding of localities (with the help of a localities list) and, therefore, the possibility of precise documentation and control, as well as of quoting every locality in the text of a paper by means of a relatively simple and short formula — see (h), (i), and (j) in Figure 1. It also greatly facilitates and accelerates the tedious work of preparing many maps with a great number of research points, once the orthogonal frame and a permanent network of localities are established. And the "translating" of contents from one scale into another is rendered easy and mechanical. The orthogonal network is oriented geographically on longitude 15° east (the starting point of the net is the crossing of longitude 15° east with latitude 44° north). In Map 2 the data of Map 1 have been gathered together, "generalized," to fit the scale 1:4,000,000, which is the scale of the *Ethnological atlas of Europe* (i.p.). As a consequence, this is no longer a "map" in the strict geographical sense but a "cartogram." This means that no exact geographical location of every research point is possible (although the possibility of documentary control remains, in principle). The picture which is given by a cartogram shows, on the other hand, the characteristic groupings of phenomena and their spatial relations much more clearly.

Figure 1 illustrates some of the most common techniques used by some existing ethnological atlases. All the samples are reproduced in their natural sizes. They show: (a) administrative districts (of various sizes) as a basis, where the small density of data renders a smaller scale possible while retaining a clear picture — the method is applicable only to large uniform areas, and even there a greater density of data is desirable (Tolstov 1967); (b) numbering, the most simple way — applicable only for a relatively small number of data and for a large-scale map (Geiger et al. 1950); (c) wide geographic network, where, without further technical expedient, no exact localization of data is possible (*Atlas tēs Hellēnikēs laografias* 1970); (d) great density of data, where exact localization is possible, but somewhat cumbersome (Zender 1958); (e) exact localization of data easily possible with the help of a special "tracer" or "key" with a finely meshed net (supplied with the atlas) — the quadratic net is not oriented geographically, which may make comparison with other (common geographical) maps difficult (Burgstaller et al. 1959); (f) exact localization directly and easily possible from the map itself — the orthogonal net is not here oriented geographically (*Polski atlas etnograficzny* 1953–1971) applicable for a great density of data, the same system (but oriented also geographically) is used by the *Etnološki atlas Jugoslavije* (1960) — see Figure 1); (g, h, i, j) some ways of designating the position of single points on the map; (g) a rather complicated designating formula (*Polski atlas etnograficzny* 1953–1971); (i–j) the formula shorter and simpler. A comparison of some designating formulas, for the most complicated cases, reveals the following:

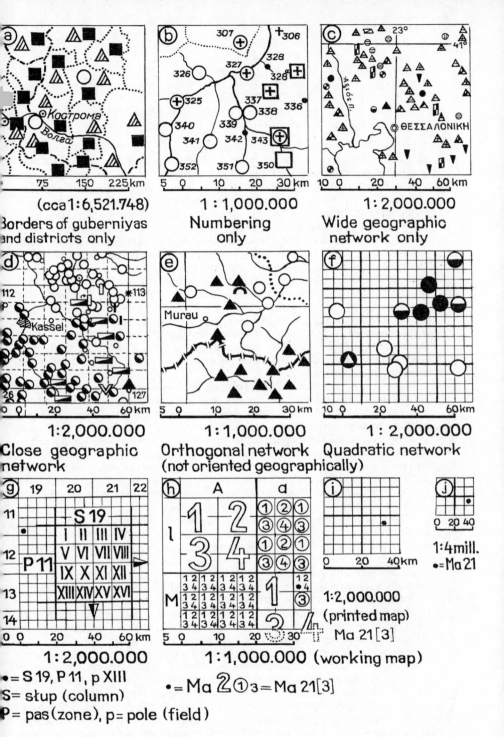

Figure 1.   The most common localization, orientation, and control techniques used by existing ethnological atlases

Zender (1958):104–30–15cu(11 characters);
Burgstaller et al. (1959):VIII E 35 y(11 characters), or even, in an extreme case:
VII/VIII E/F 35/12 y/z(22 characters!);
Polski atlas etnograficzny (1953–1971):S19, P11, pXIII(13 characters);
Etnološki atlas Jugoslavije (1960):Ma223(5 characters).

Map 3, a synthetic map of the "third order," of scale 1:4,000,000, is derived from an original documentary map in scale 1:2,000,000 (like that of Map 1). Major groupings and their spatial relations are clearly visible, but the isolated occurrence of the term *svitnjak* in the north poses an ethnological-historical problem. The map shows that it very probably belongs to the compact area of the same name far in the south. And, indeed, the people of the northern observation point have not only the same dialect as those in the south, but there are also written historical documents showing that their groups had actually migrated to the north in the seventeenth century. So this case is clear and simple. And the etymology of the word *svitnjak*, which could not be surely explained from the isolated northern evidence, becomes clear at once when compared with the southern situation. *But* if there were no written documents, as is the rule in ethnology, the pictures on the map would itself pose a legitimate problem and require its solution. The original map is based on investigations in more than 1,600 research points. If there were a smaller number of them, it may have happened that just that isolated point would be missed. Then there would be no problem and no solution of it. The distribution of the terms *oganj* and *vatra* (both having the same simple meaning "fire") is also ethnologically important.

Figure 2 is a "problem map," illustrating the occurrence of some very characteristic traits, both among Slavic and non-Slavic populations, in two widely separated areas of the Balkans and of the eastern Alps, having striking analogies also in the north and among the Basques. Map 4 illustrates two very different complexes (central and marginal), but both of Slavic origin, in the Balkan peninsula, indicating probably two different old Slavic migrations to the south. Map 5 utilizes a small number of data characteristically found among all three of the main Slavic branches, and definitely connected with the way of plowing with the *unilateral* plow, showing that this kind of plowing implement must already have been known to all Slavic branches before they parted.

Map 6 is a "problem map," illustrating the distribution of types of plow (unilateral implement) and of other kinds of plowing implements over a large area — Europe and of a part of the Near East. Map 7, however, is a "problem map" showing the distribution of some very characteristic traits in plowing implements (in this case of two-sided ards) in Europe and Anterior Asia (traces such as these are found also as far distant as Burma) whereas none such are known in western Europe or in the Mediterranean region).

Map 8 shows the distribution of numerous "Alpine" culture traits in the vast area of Europe and Asia. The details of these traits are to be found in the paper "Peasant cultures of West and East" (Bratanić, this volume).

Map 9 shows the spatial distribution of some forms of ards (symmetrical implements), showing that the intermediate forms (3 and 4) are probably younger hybrids, crosses of Types 1 and 2, not transitional forms of development. Likewise the spatial situation and intermediate forms make probable that Types 5 and 6 must be genetically connected, although they appear very different at first glance (Bratanić 1963). Finally Map 10 shows the distribution of some very small items with their occurrence fixed in percentages for several large areas, from the Atlantic to the Pacific oceans, a method which may prove very fruitful for historical investigations in ethnology.

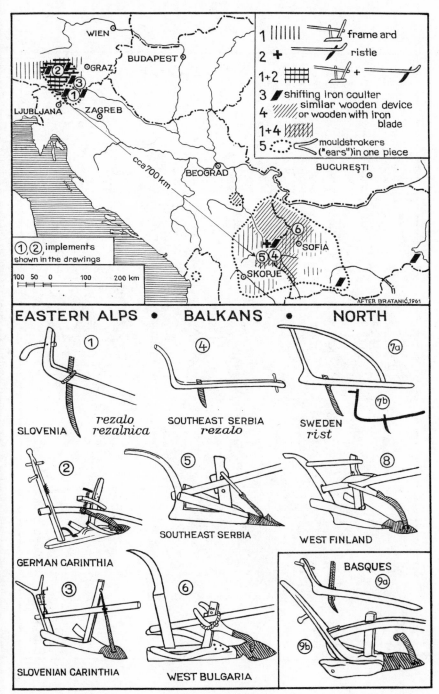

Figure 2. "Problem map": occurrence of characteristic traits in plowing instruments among Slavic and non-Slavic populations (Bratanić 1961)

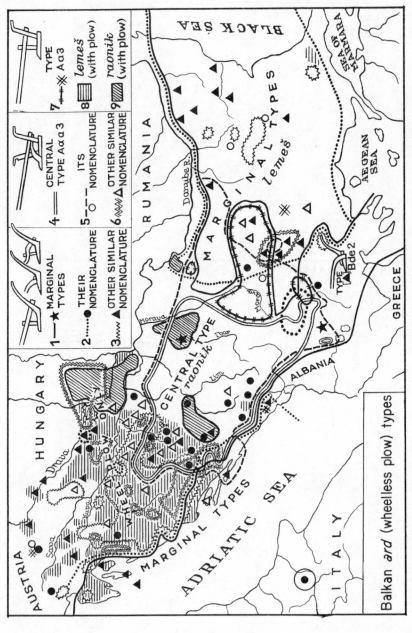

Map 4.   "Central" and "marginal" types of plowing instruments in the Balkan peninsula (Bratanić 1951: map 3)

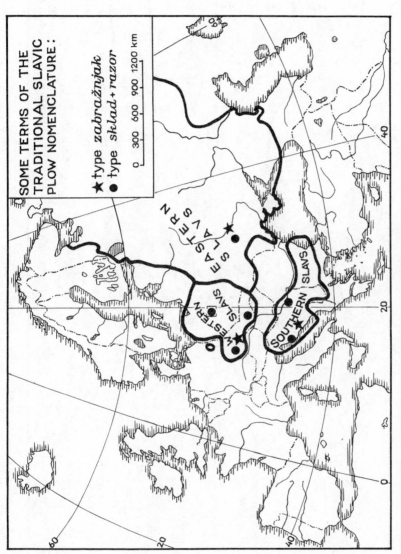

Map 5. A map illustrating data rarely occurring or not systematically collected

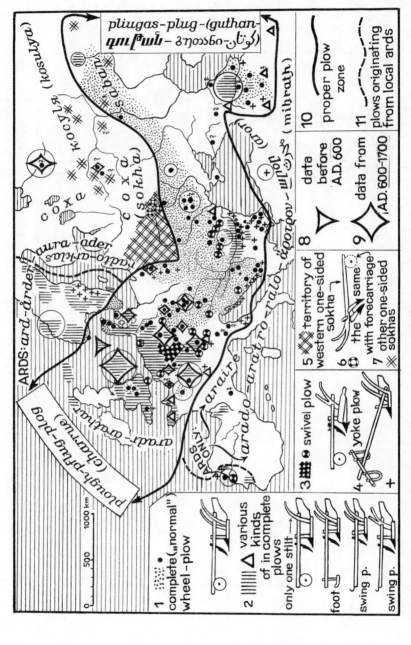

Map 6. The wheel-plow in Europe and western Asia (Bratanić 1954: maps 2 and 3)

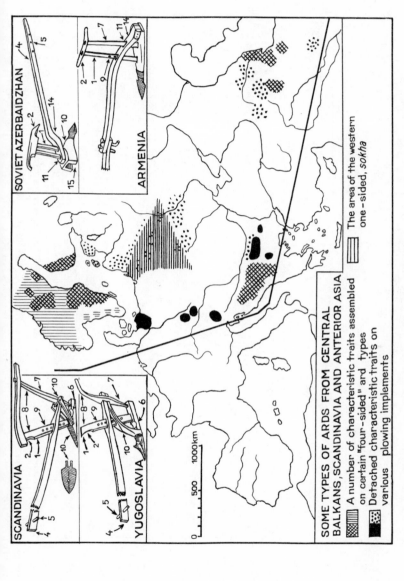

Map 7   Distribution of some characteristic traits in plowing implements (Bratanić 1960; Bdoyan 1972)

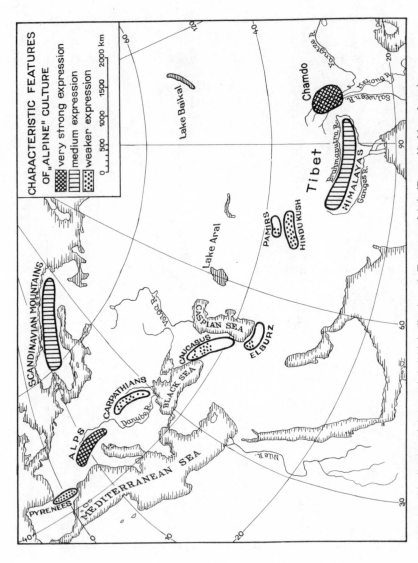

Map 8.   Distribution of characteristic "Alpine" culture in Europe and Asia (Bratanić, this volume)

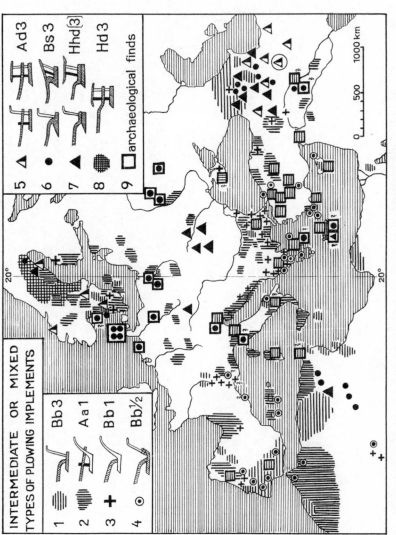

Map 9.   Spatial distribution of some types of ards in Europe and the Near East (Bratanić 1963)

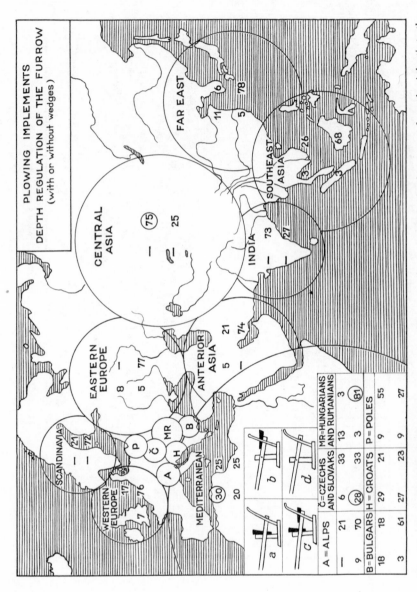

Map 10.   Percentage distributions of some very small variations in types of plowing instrument from the Atlantic to the Pacific ocean (Bratanić 1955)

REFERENCES

Arbeitskonferenz
1968 *Internationale Arbeitskonferenz über die ethnologische Kartographie, 8–10 Februar 1966: Bericht/Conference international de travail sur la cartographie ethnologique, 8–10 février 1966: compte-rendu.* Zagreb: Center of the *Etnološki atlas Jugoslavije.*
1970 *Zweite Arbeitskonferenz der Organisationskommission für den Volkskundeatlas Europas und seiner Nachbarländer 12–15 März 1968 in Bonn.* Bonn: Atlas der deutschen Volkskunde.
1972 *Dritte Arbeitskonferenz der Organisationskommission für den Volkskundeatlas Europas und seiner Nachbarländer, 11–14 Mai 1970 in Helsinki.* Bonn: Atlas der deutschen Volkskunde.
Atlas der Luxemburger Volkskunde
i.p. *Atlas der Luxemburger Volkskunde.* In preparation.
Atlas tēs Hellēnikēs laografias
1970 *Atlas tēs Hellēnikēs laografias* [Atlas of Greek ethnology], three maps, one questionnaire. Athens: Kentron Ereunēs tēs Hellēnikēs Laografias tēs Akadēmias Athēnōn. Continuing.
Atlasul etnografic al României
i.p. *Atlasul etnografic al României* [Ethnographical atlas of Rumania]. In preparation.

BARABÁS, JENO
1963 *Kartográfiai módszer a néprajzban* [Cartographic method in ethnology], with German summary. Budapest: Akadémiai Kiadó.
1970 "Die Deutung der ungleichen Entwicklung auf Grund der ethnographischen Karten," in *Actes du VIIe Congrès International des Sciences Anthropologiques et Ethnologiques*, volume eight. Edited by S. I. Bruk, 504–507. Moscow: Nauka.

BDOYAN, VARD H.
1972 *Ekragortsakan mšakujthe Hayastanum* [Agriculture in Armenia]. Erevan: Institute of Archaeology and Ethnology, Academy of Sciences of the Armenian Soviet Socialist Republic.

BOCHEŃSKI, I. M.
1959 *Die zeitgenössischen Denkmethoden.* Berne: Francke.

BRATANIĆ, BRANIMIR
1951 "Uz problem doseljenja Južnih Slavena: nekoliko etnografsko-leksičkih činjenica [On the problem of the settlement of Southern Slavs: some ethnographical-lexical facts]," in *Universitas litterarum zagrebiensis, facultas philosophica: collectanea*, volume one. Edited by A. Barac et al., 221–250. Zagreb: Nakladni zavod Hrvatske. English summary.
1954 "Nesto o starosti pluga kod Slavena" [A note on the antiquity of the unilateral wheel-plow among the Slavs], in *Universitas litterarum zagrebiensis, facultas philosophica: collectanea*, volume two. Edited by A. Barac et al., 277–306. Zagreb: Školska knjiga. German summary.
1955 "Einige Möglichkeiten zur Fortführung der Pfluggeräteforschung," in *Actes du IVe Congrès International des Sciences Anthropologiques et Ethnologiques, Vienne, 1–8 septembre 1952*, volume two, 90–98. Vienna.
1959a Etnološki atlas Jugoslavije [The ethnological atlas of Yugoslavia]. *Etnološki Pregled* 1(1):9–18.
1959b "Bericht über die volkskundliche Kartographie in Jugoslawien," in

Konferenz für volkskundliche Kartographie in Linz a/d Donau, 11–13 Dezember 1958: Tagungsbericht, Referate. Edited by B. Bratanić and E. Burgstaller, 44–49. Linz: Zentralstelle für den Volkskundeatlas in Österreich.

1960   "Some similarities between ards of the Balkans, Scandinavia, and Anterior Asia, and their methodological significance," in *Selected papers of the Fifth International Congress of Anthropological and Ethnological Sciences, Philadelphia, September 1–9, 1956*. Edited under the chairmanship of A. F. C. Wallace, 221–228. Philadelphia: University of Pennsylvania Press.

1961   "Einige unbekannte Zusammenhänge zwischen den Ostalpen und dem serbisch-mazedonisch-bulgarischen Grenzgebiet," in *3. Arbeitstagung über Fragen des Atlas der deutschen Volkskunde in Bonn vom 27 bis 29 April 1961: Protokollmanuskript*. Edited by G. Wiegelmann, 63–65. Bonn: Arbeitsstelle des Atlas der deutschen Volkskunde.

1963   "A note on the typology of ploughing instruments," in *Actes du VIme Congrès International des Sciences Anthropologiques et Ethnologiques, Paris, 30 juillet — 6 août 1960*, volume two, 511–516. Paris: Musée de l'Homme.

1965   Bericht über die Tätigkeit der ständigen internationalen Atlaskommission in den Jahren 1954–1964. *Zeitschrift für Volkskunde* 61:243–247. Stuttgart.

1967   Internationale Arbeitskonferenz über die ethnologische Kartographie, Zagreb, Februar 1966. *Ethnologia Europaea* 1:75–77. Paris.

1970   "Ethnologische Kartographie und ethnologische Atlasse," in *Actes du VIIe Congrès International des Sciences Anthropologiques et Ethnologiques*, volume eight. Edited by S. I. Bruk, 393–395. Moscow: Nauka.

BRUK, S. I.
1973   Istoriko-etnografičeskoe kartografirovanie i ego sovremennye problemy [Historical-ethnographic cartography and its present-day problems]. *Sovetskaya Etnografiya* 3:3–18. English summary.

BRUK, S. I., *editor*
1970   "Symposium: méthodes de rédaction des atlas ethnographiques," in *VIIe Congrès International des Sciences Anthropologiques et Ethnologiques*, volume eight, 511–533. Moscow: Nauka.

BURGSTALLER, ERNST, ADOLF HELBOK, R. WOLFRAM et al., *editors*
1959   *Österreichischer Volkskundeatlas*, four parts, two volumes of commentaries, six questionnaires, three volumes of special publications. Linz/Vienna/Graz/Cologne: H. Böhlau. Continuing.

CAMPBELL, ÅKE, ÅSA NYMAN, *editors*
i.p.   *Sagen, tro och hogtidssed/Popular beliefs, legends, and festival customs*. Atlas över svensk folkkultur [Atlas of Swedish folk culture] 2. In preparation.

DARWIN, CHARLES
1878   *The descent of man and selection in relation to sex*, new edition, revised and augmented. New York: D. Appleton.

DIAS, J., F. GALHANO, *editors*
1968   *Atlas etnologico de Portugal continental*. Lisbon: Centro de Estudos de Etnologia Peninsular. Continuing.

ERIXON, SIGURD
1955   Maps of folk culture: an international inquiry. *Laos* 3:79–98. Stockholm.

1970   "Address of welcome" and "Ethnological investigation of the present," in *The possibilities of charting modern life*. Edited by Sigurd Erixon with G. Arwidsson and H. Hvarfner, xiii, 1–22. Oxford: Pergamon.
ERIXON, SIGURD, *editor*
1957   *Materiell och social kultur/Material and social culture*. Atlas över svensk folkkultur [Atlas of Swedish folk culture] 1. Uddevalla: Niloe.
Ethnological atlas of Europe
i.p.   *Ethnological atlas of Europe and its bordering countries/Ethnologischer Atlas Europas und seiner Nachbarländer/Atlas ethnologique de l'Europe et des pays voisins/Etnologicheskiy atlas Evropy i sopredel'nyh stran*. In preparation.
Etnografický atlas Slovenska
i.p.   *Etnografický atlas Slovenska* [Ethnographic atlas of Slovakia]. Bratislava: Centrum Etnografického atlasu Slovenska (Národopisný ústav, Slovenská akadémia vied). In preparation.
Etnološki atlas Jugoslavije
1960   *Etnološki atlas Jugoslavije* [Ethnological atlas of Yugoslavia]. Zagreb: Center of the *Etnološki atlas Jugoslavije*. Continuing.
GAJEK, JÓZEF
1947   *Polski atlas etnograficzny* [The Polish ethnographic atlas]. Annales Universitatis Mariae Curie-Skłodowska, Section F: Philosophie et lettres, supplement one. Lublin: Unywersytetu Marii Curie-Skłodowskiej.
1958   "The Polish ethnographic atlas trial issue: preliminary remarks," in *Polski atlas etnograficzny: zeszyt próbny* [Polish ethnographic atlas: text volume]. Edited by Jósef Gajek, 16–26. Wroclaw: Wydawnictwo Polskiej Akademii Nauk.
1971   Znaczenie *Polskiego atlasu etnograficznego* dla etnografii Polski [The significance of the Polish ethnographic atlas for the ethnography of Poland]. *Etnografia Polska* 15(2):17–36.
GEIGER, PAUL, RICHARD WEISS *et al., editors*
1950   *Atlas der schweizerischen Volkskunde/Atlas de folklore suisse*, fifteen parts, with commentaries in separate volumes. Basle/Zurich: Schweizerische Gesellschaft für Volkskunde/Société Suisse des Traditions Populaires/Rentsch.
GLEASON, H. A., JR.
1955   *An introduction to descriptive linguistics*. New York: Henry Holt.
HARD, GERHARD
1972   "Ein geographisches Simulationsmodell für die rheinische Sprachgeschichte," in *Festschrift Matthias Zender: Studien zur Volkskultur, Sprache und Landesgeschichte*, volume one. Edited by E. Ennen and G. Wiegelmann, 25–58. Bonn: Röhrscheid.
HARMJANZ, HEINRICH, ERICH RÖHR, *editors*
1937–1940 *Atlas der deutschen Volkskunde*, six parts. Leipzig: Hirzel.
i.p.   *Irish ethnological atlas*. In preparation.
KROEBER, ALFRED L.
1948   *Anthropology*, revised edition. New York: Harcourt, Brace. (Originally published 1924.)
1952   *The nature of culture*. Chicago: University of Chicago Press.
1953   "Introduction," "Discussion," and "Concluding review," in *An appraisal of anthropology today*. Edited by Sol Tax, L. C. Eiseley, I. Roúse, and C. F. Voegelin, xiii, 151, 357–376. Chicago: University of Chicago Press.

1954   "Critical summary and commentary," in *Method and perspective in anthropology: papers in honor of Wilson D. Wallis*. Edited by R. F. Spencer. Minneapolis: University of Minnesota Press.

1963   *An anthropologist looks at history*. Edited by Theodora Kroeber. Berkeley: University of California Press.

Magyar néprajzi atlasz

1967   Mutatvány a *Magyar néprajzi atlasz anyagából* [Sample from the material of the Hungarian ethnological atlas]. *Néprajzi Értesítö* 49: 5–72. (Reprinted in *A Néprajzi Múzeum Füzetei* 23. Budapest.) Continuing.

MEERTENS, PIETER J., MAURITS DE MEYER *et al.*, *editors*

1959   *Volkskunde-atlas* [Ethnological atlas], four parts, four volumes of commentaries. Volkskunde-commissie der Koninklijke Nederlandse Akademie van Wetenschappen/Koninklijke Belgische Commissie voor Volkskunde. Antwerp/Amsterdam/Utrecht: Standaard.

Polski atlas etnograficzny

1953–1971 *Polski atlas etnograficzny* [Polish ethnographical atlas], four parts, one trial part, nine questionnaires. Warsaw/Wroclaw: Państwowe Wydawnictwo Naukowe/Wydawnictwo Polskiej Akademii Nauk.

REICHENBACH, HANS

1951   *The rise of scientific philosophy*. Berkeley: University of California Press.

Scottish ethnological atlas

i.p.   *Scottish ethnological atlas*. In preparation.

Suomen kansankulttuurin kartasto

i.p.   *Suomen kansankulttuurin kartasto* [Atlas of Finnish folk culture]. In preparation.

TOLSTOV, SERGEI P., *main editor*

1967   *Russkie:istoriko-etnografičeskiy atlas* [Russians: a historical-ethnographical atlas], two volumes. Moscow: Izdatel'stvo "Nauka." Continuing.

TYLOR, EDWARD B.

1929 [1871] *Primitive culture*, volume one, fifth edition. London: John Murray.

WATERMAN, JOHN T.

1963   *Perspectives in linguistics*. Chicago: University of Chicago Press.

WEIJNEN, TOON

1972   "Introduction, deuxième projet," in *Atlas linguistique de l'Europe*. Nijmegen: Nijmegse Centrale voor Dialect– en Naamkunde.

WEISS, RICHARD

1950   "Einführung," in *Atlas der schweizerischen Volkskunde/Atlas de folklore suisse*, commentary part one. Edited by Paul Geiger and Richard Weiss. Basel: Schweizerische Gesellschaft für Volkskunde/Société Suisse des Traditions Populaires.

ZENDER, MATTHIAS

1959   "Einführung," in *Atlas der deutschen Volkskunde*, new series, part one. Edited by Matthias Zender, 3–16. Marburg: N. G. Elwert.

ZENDER, MATTHIAS, *editor*

1958   *Atlas der deutschen Volkskunde*, new series, four parts, two supplementary parts. Marburg: N. G. Elwert. Continuing.

Peasant Cultures of West and East

BRANIMIR BRATANIĆ

RÉSUMÉ: LES CULTURES PAYSANNES DE L'OUEST ET DE
L'EST

Les cultures paysannes avec leurs variantes en Europe, en Afrique du Nord et
jusqu'au Japon en passant par l'Asie forment le lien véritable entre l'Occident et
l'Orient. Il s'agit de définir la signification exacte de "cultures paysannes."
　Les anthropologues et ethnologues qui s'y sont appliqués sont des américains :
d'abord Kroeber et Redfield, puis, plus près de nous, E. R. Wolf et G. Dalton.
　Des points de vue sociologique et psychologique, les communautés sont
restreintes, basées sur la parenté et le voisinage, constituant un type particulier
d'humanité, patient et enclin à la docilité. Kroeber et Redfield ne considèrent pas
leur culture comme autonome mais dépendante de la civilisation ambiante. De
même que la société paysanne est une demi-société, sa culture est une demi-
culture, une "dimension rurale des anciennes civilisations."
　Les chercheurs adoptent une version déjà formulée par Michelet : système
social composé de deux couches : l'une supérieure, l'autre inférieure . . . et même
Lenine : ". . . il y a deux cultures nationales dans toute culture nationale . . . ,"
mais, pour le croate Radić, la différence entre la culture populaire (paysanne) et
la citadine n'est pas constituée par "l'éducation, la pauvreté, le dur labeur ou le
vêtement, mais par leur contenu, leurs traditions, leurs origines; ainsi la civilisation gréco-romaine et ses variantes en Europe représente pour le peuple slavo-
croate une culture étrangère." Ceci introduit le problème de l'Histoire pour
l'origine, à la fois de la civilisation et des cultures paysannes.
　Kroeber, le premier a vu dans "l'agriculture à la charrue," qui remonte à la
période néolithique, l'élément central de toute culture paysanne, permettant de
les relier entre elles. Leser, plus tôt, en 1928, avait montré comment ce grand type
économique s'était, en réalité, différencié en formant des variétés distinctes à
partir d'une "sub-structure uniforme"; l'un de ces groupes étant la "haute culture
du monde ancien."

An earlier version of the present paper was prepared for the VIIIth ICAES in Tokyo (1968)
for a special symposium dealing with the cultures of East and West. But as this symposium
was never realized the paper was not read at the Congress nor published in its proceedings,
and the manuscript, sent in time, was somehow lost.

Jusqu'à maintenant, l'étude, du point de vue historique, ne s'intéressait qu'à l'aspect économique de la culture, mais il semble que les complexes culturels, possédant tous les aspects de la culture — comme les diverses régions de l'Europe, avec leur traditionnelle culture paysanne méditerranéenne, balkanique, alpine, scandinave, etc. ... qui chacune semblent composées de couches variées de culture, dont certaines prévalent, selon le lien, et les traces de ces complexes culturels — peuvent se retrouver aussi bien en Afrique du Nord qu'en Asie : par exemple, en zone alpine et dans l'Himalaya, les coutumes calendaires d'élevage du bétail, les occupations réservées aux femmes, le rôle du beurre dans l'alimentation, la forme des maisons et de leurs toits, les costumes masculins et féminins, les masques à cornes et jusqu'au chant "yodlé." En plus des concordances frappantes entre les éléments cités, il existe des similarités linguistiques. La connaissance détaillée de ces éléments est indispensable pour ce type de recherche, mais les informations et les documents sont rares, parfois même inexistants. Grâce à la parution du nouvel *Atlas ethnologique de l'Europe et des pays voisins* (en Asie et Afrique du Nord), on peut espérer pallier certaines des lacunes.

In a long, continuous zone across the Old World, a special kind of culture strikes us immediately: the peasant cultures found in many variants in Europe, North Africa, and in a large part of Asia, from Turkey to Japan. These cultures are "the real link between East and West" (Redfield 1956:106), and certainly they are *folk cultures* as Sumner (1907) and Kroeber (1948:265–267) understood them. But what is exactly meant by the expression "peasant" and "peasant culture"? Many writers have dealt with this question. Among anthropologists (ethnologists), the American scholars Kroeber and Redfield ought to be mentioned in the first place, and, in recent years, especially Wolf (1966) and Dalton (1972).

The most common approaches to the problem of peasants and their culture until now have been sociological and psychological. The *social approach* shows that peasant communities are small — the *Gemeinschaft* of Tönnies (1887) — based largely on kinship (especially in the form of the extended family like the South Slavic *zadruga*), but also on neighborhood and on local groupings, with all characteristics of such small societies (cf. Kroeber 1948:272), as for example their "primitive democracy" (Kroeber 1948:281), their "organic" solidarity (versus the Durkheimian "mechanic" one), the fixity of their social structure, their homogeneity, the narrowness, depth, and intensity of their cultures (Kroeber 1948: 282), their common habits of collective labor (Tokarev 1968:16), their lack of organization (Radić 1937 [1907]:83) and so on. In the *psychological approach* Sumner's *Folkways* (1907) and unconsciousness of social forces are stressed (cf. Kroeber 1948:266), their conservatism and non-revolutionary peaceful attitudes, their submissiveness and obedience (Radić 1937 [1907]:82) and their resignation, whereas about positive sides of folk mentality the French historian Jules Michelet (1846) has written (cf. Radić 1936 [1898]:104, 105, 107). Redfield (1956:106, 107) sees in all peasants "somehow a type of mankind" and quotes other authors who attributed to them "an integrated pattern of dominant attitudes" and even called them "a psycho-physiological race" in their own right. He is interested in the "ethos or value-orientation" (1956:139, 140) of peasantry, and also gives us, cautiously, a "modified statement of peasant values."

Although all these social and psychical qualities by no means wholly correspond to what Kroeber (1948:280, 611) calls "rural and urban — folk and sophisticate facets" of culture, both he and Redfield regard the peasants as "definitely rural," but primarily *as a part of large civilizations*. Therefore Kroeber could say: "They constitute part-societies with part-cultures" (1948:284). Redfield fully agrees (1956:33) and even extends this statement: "The culture of a peasant community . . . is not autonomous. It is an aspect or dimension of the civilization of which it is a part. As the peasant society is a *half-society*, so the peasant culture is a *half-culture*" (1956:68; emphasis added). And in another place he expresses himself in a most characteristic way: "I *want* to *think* about peasants as the rural dimensions of old civilizations" (1956:29; emphasis added). Similarly for Wolf (1966:8) "a peasantry always exists within a larger system" (cf. also Dalton 1972:392, fn. 17). It is understandable, then, that both Kroeber (1948:610–611) and Redfield (1956:70), who differentiates between "a great tradition" and "a little tradition," depict a series of social and psychical qualities by which peasantry is distinguishable from the civilized urban life of which it is a part. And those qualities are not in favor of civilization at all.

Everything which has been said before — and much more of what Kroeber, Redfield, and Wolf have to say about peasants — for example Redfield's definition of peasant, with his remark that the peasant does not have to "own the land or that he have any particular form of tenure or any particular form of institutional relationship to the gentry or the townsman" (1956:27–28) — may be quite right, especially if one "wants to think" in that way. But this is not the whole story. There is a very important *strictly cultural aspect*. The difference between folk culture and that "compound culture that deserves a special word, '*civilization*'"(Redfield 1956:70; emphasis added) has been noted repeatedly. Michelet (1846), writing about *le peuple* speaks of "another culture (different from our way . . .)" (quoted in Radić 1936 [1898]:109). Redfield says: "In peasant societies we see a relatively stable and very roughly typical adjustment between local and national or feudal life, a developed larger social system in which there are *two cultures* within one culture, one social system composed of upper and lower halves" (1956:65; emphasis added). Even Lenin — philosopher, politician, uncompromising revolutionary, and a vehement adversary of the "fight for every national development, for 'national culture' in general" (1948 [1913]:18) — saw in every modern national culture, besides a bourgeois one, also "elements of a democratic and socialist culture" (1948 [1913]:8) so that "there are *two* national cultures in every national culture" (1948 [1913]:16; quoted also by Tokarev 1968:7; emphasis added). From all these formulations, however, it is visible that the point of view of their authors is not a strictly cultural, but rather a sociopsychological one. And Redfield goes definitely too far when he writes: "We are looking at rural people in old civilizations, those rural people who control and cultivate their land for subsistence and as a part of a traditional way of life and who look to and are influenced by gentry or townspeople *whose way of life is like theirs* but in a more civilized form" (1956:31; emphasis added). A. Radić, the son of a true Croatian peasant family, sees on the contrary that Michelet's "other culture" is different only by its mode. Michelet, then, does not classify mankind after the essence of the culture, but only condemns the whole mode of our Greek-Roman-Christian culture (Radić 1936 [1898]:113). For Radić, the difference between the "folk" (peasants) and the townspeople is not "being uneducated, or poor, or doing heavy manual labor, or their clothing" (1936 [1897]:5), but another *culture*, different by its *contents*, its tradition and its origin (1936 [1897]:6). Therefore the civilization in its Greco-Roman and Christian variant — cf. Dalton's "Roman and Christian acculturation of parts of . . . Europe" (1972:403, fn. 37) — is for the Slavic Croatian people a *foreign culture* (Radić 1936 [1897]:8–10). Here, then, the *historical moment* appears very clearly. But if a historical problem is involved in the study of peasants — and there is no doubt about this — then it becomes *indispensable* to deal with the question *also* from the point of view of cultural history if the whole study is to be really scientific and productive. This means that we must try not only to find out and to comprehend what is the *nature* of being peasant, the nature of culture in general, the nature (or the type) of peasant culture, and the nature of civilization, but also to recognize that both peasant culture (or cultures) and civilization (or civilizations) have their concrete contents, their historical origins, and their historical past in the course of events. And as far as we are able to find out something about these historical matters, there will be less speculation, our understanding of the nature of things which interest us here will be better, more certain and, above all more scientific.

This *historical approach* has not been lacking,[1] either, in ethnology, especially in regional European ethnology (*Volkskunde*) to which also Radić's considerations belong. On a more general level it was Kroeber who delineated the core of all proper peasant cultures of which we are speaking. This is "plow agriculture" which, in Kroeber's own words:

---

[1] Dalton (1972), for example, tried to reconstruct the characteristics of three periods of economic history regarding peasantries in West European countries.

... comprises the plow itself; animals to draw it; domestication of these beasts; grains of the barley or wheat type shown by broadcast scattering, without attention to individual seed, seedling or plant; fields larger than gardens and of some length; and fertilization with dung, primarily from the draft animals [one might add *"oxen*, above all"] (1948:313).

This "Eurasian grain farming" (Wolf 1966:30) is what Kroeber calls a "systemic pattern," limited "to one aspect of culture," here to economics (Kroeber 1948:312). And for Kroeber a "systemic pattern" is largely a historical concept: "it can be diffused cross-culturally, from one people to another" (1948:312), and according to Kroeber the pattern of plow agriculture actually "originated in the Neolithic period, probably in western Asia or near it, and by A.D. 1500 had spread from Morocco to North China" (1948:313). Moreover "the peculiar interest of these systemic patterns is that, within the endless kaleidoscope of human culture, they allow us to recognize things that are *actually related in origin* as against things that appear similar but are not connected in origin" (Kroeber 1948:315; emphasis added). And further: "it is in working-out of these *real* relationships, structural and genetic relationships as against mere functional similarities, that the recognition of culture patterns of the systemic type finds one of its chief uses" (Kroeber 1948:316; emphasis added). But this is only a first step in trying to generalize our historical knowledge. The reality is much more complex. Leser (1928) has shown that within the framework of plow agriculture (Kroeber's "systemic pattern" of it) there exist several characteristic groups, from the Atlantic Ocean to the Far East; every one of them marked not only by various types of plows, but also by other characteristic agricultural tools and implements and agricultural techniques. With that, and at the same time, Leser extends on the one hand the contents of Kroeber's "plow agriculture patterns" (as quoted above), and on the other hand states some of the ways in which such an extended general economic pattern had in reality differentiated, forming distinctive units grown from a "uniform substructure" (*einheitlicher Unterbau* — Leser 1928:481). One of these groups — the oldest one according to Leser — encompasses the whole territory of the "high culture of the Old World" (*altweltliche Hochkultur*). It may be, at first glance, not quite clear whether the expression *Hochkultur* should, here, denote only the great *civilizations* of the Old World or, perhaps, simply the developed *peasant cultures* having plow agriculture as their economic basis. That the latter interpretation is correct not only follows from the context (1928:481), according to which some of Leser's groups might be older than the *Hochkultur*, but also from direct personal communication with Professor Leser.

Until now only the *economic aspect of culture* was dealt with from a historical point of view. But are there, perhaps, whole cultural complexes, comprising all aspects of culture, which belong to peasant peoples with plow agriculture? It seems so. We have in Europe, speaking very roughly, several different areas of traditional peasant culture, say Mediterranean, Balkan, Alpine, Scandinavian, West, Central, and East European. Every one of them seems to be composed of various layers, or culture complexes, one of which (or some mixture of them) prevails in a particular area in question. Although the available data are exceedingly scarce, or too generalized, we can follow the traces of such culture complexes not only to North Africa and Anterior Asia (which largely belong to the European culture characteristics found in the agricultural population two instances — it is known that in the Himalayas and in southeastern agricultural Tibet (the region of Chamdo on the border of China proper) many calendar customs are similar to European ones. Among several European culture characteristics found in the agricultural population of Tibet, especially striking is such a whole complex of concordances between that southeastern corner of Tibet mentioned (and the Himalayas) and the European Alpine area (cf. Haberlandt 1923). The highly characteristic elements of this complex, on both sides, are: Alpine-type cattle-breeding (with stables in valleys and summer pastures in mountains); women as shepherdesses and dairy workers; wooden butter-churns and the important role of butter in life and customs (even to the extent of figures being made of it); haymaking with special racks consisting of horizontal poles (sometimes added to the dwelling-house itself) for drying hay and grain; "Swiss-style" houses with low gabled roofs of boards (sometimes weighted with stones) and wooden galleries, having the first floor of masonry and one or two more of logs, with wood wainscoted inner walls (sometimes flower-painted) and flowers before the windows; knee-breeches, small felt hats, and earrings (in one ear!) in the male costume; wide plaited skirts, aprons, hats, some forms of headgear, braids put around the head, in women's costume; male weavers; plenty of highly characteristic masks (with fleece and horns) of similar type (also hobbyhorses) representing similar mythical personages; winter customs with driving-out or burning the masks; "carrying-out" a figure of Death (or Winter); "yodeling" style of singing; and "Alpine" horn in music. A number of elements of this complex of characteristics are found also elsewhere, especially in high mountains: Scandinavia, the Pyrenees, the Carpathian Mountains, northeastern Russia, the Caucasus, the Gilan and Elburz mountains of northwestern Iran, the Hindu Kush, the Pamirs (see Bratanić, this volume, Map 8). Besides such striking *formal concordances* in culture elements, even some *linguistic similarities* seem to have analogous, or very large at least, spatial range. Thus the word *yoke*, a common Indo-European term (cf. Haudricourt and Jean-Brunhes-Delamarre 1955:48), appears in Turkish and Caucasian languages and goes further southwards and eastwards as far as Burma, Thailand, Vietnam, and China, even to Peking (Haudricourt

1948:61, Figure 12). A similarly wide distribution Haudricourt shows (on the same figure) also for the word *hame/kummet* [horse-collar] which is found from the Atlantic Ocean to Manchuria, but not only among agricultural peoples it is true. Among clothing nomenclature much the same holds for the common Euro-Asian words of *juba/juban* type which appear also in Tibet and even in Japan. But there are very few of such linguistic concordances known as yet, and this field of research might be promising.

The *detailed* knowledge of the culture elements and their nomenclature is indispensable for such a type of research, and *such* data are very scarce everywhere, in many large areas almost nonexistent (cf. Leser 1928:484). It is hoped that the new *Ethnological atlas of Europe and its bordering countries* (i.p.) including Anterior Asia and North Africa, will make up for much of this shortcoming in the western part of the long zone of peasant peoples. A similar systematic action would be very important also for the remaining areas of plow agriculture in Asia.

Finally, a few more words about the relationship of peasant *cultures* to urban *civilizations*. We cannot discuss here what a "civilization" is, es-pecially not the concepts of various authors, primarily sociologists (about these see Kroeber 1952:154–157). My own views are expressed in an earlier paper (Bratanić 1956:17–18). Here it may be sufficient to say that in the present paper the word "civilization" is used for a special *kind* of culture, a *"city syndrome*, with writing, metallurgy, urbanism, and politi-cal structures" (Adams et al. 1960:227; emphasis added), which has, of course, its definite historical origin and past. This corresponds also to Kroeber's "major culture" (1952:154), and to what some writers also have called "relation to *state*," "*cities*," "civilizing others," "becoming urbane," "literate" as well as to such expressions as "Chinese civilization" versus "Eskimo culture" (cf. Kroeber and Kluckhohn 1952:16, 20). It is inter-esting what Kroeber (1948:284) says himself:

... a number of societies exhibit rather conspicuous peasantlike qualities: the Neolithic Europeans for instance . . . ; also the Indian, Greek, and other early Indo-Europeans. . . . These are all peoples who had become settled but, either from newness or from remoteness, had made little progress toward urbanization. The Near East may have gone through a similar phase on which we are less well informed because it happened two or three thousand years earlier (1948:284).

There is a possibility, then, of peasant cultures without (or before) cities. It is also interesting to see what Robert Adams, and archaeologist and specialist in Mesopotamian civilization, and anthropologist Leslie White have to say in this connection (Adams et al. 1960). Adams (Adams et al. 1960:222) stresses that in urban civilization "technological improvements" were "primarily of an organizational character," and "organization of new inventions and old techniques within a social framework," and that in agriculture (Adams et al. 1960:223) the trend was toward "the expansion and increasing capitalization." And L. White denies that V. Gordon Childe's "urban revolution" was any "revolution" at all, but "merely the culmination of the agricultural revolution" (i.e. in the Neolithic period, Adams et al. 1960:229). All this and what was said before about various, as yet not sufficiently investigated, complexes forming whole peasant cultures would mean that, from a historical point of view, these are no "part-societies with part-cultures" or mere subcultures in the frame of great civilizations. They are, originally at least, full-fledged cultures, encompassing all aspects of human life, and it is most probable that they are older than civilizations of which they are parts today.

REFERENCES

ADAMS, ROBERT M., LESLIE WHITE, GORDON R. WILLEY
1960 "Contributions in the discussion of Panel Five, Social and Cultural Evolution," in *Evolution after Darwin*, volume three: *Issues in evolution*. Edited by Sol Tax and C. Callender, 221–229. Chicago: University of Chicago Press.
BRATANIĆ, BRANIMIR
1956 "Europäische Ethnologie," in *Actes du Congrès International d'Ethnologie Régionale, Arnhem 1955*, 15–20. Arnhem: Rijksmuseum voor Volkskunde, "Het Nederlands Openluchtmuseum."
DALTON, GEORGE
1972 Peasantries in anthropology and history. *Current Anthropology* 13 (3–4): 385–415.
Ethnological atlas of Europe
i.p. *Ethnological atlas of Europe and its bordering countries/Ethnologischer Atlas Europas und seiner Nachbarländer/Atlas ethnologique de l'Europe et des pays voisins/Etnologicheskiy atlas Evropy i sopredel'nyh stran*. In preparation.
HABERLANDT, ARTUR
1923 "Die Bevölkerung Tibets," in *Völkerkunde, illustrierte*, volume two, part one: *Australien und Ozeanien; Asien*. Edited by Georg Buschan, 435–450. Stuttgart: Strecker und Schröder.
HAUDRICOURT, ANDRÉ-G.
1948 Contribution à la géographie et à l'ethnologie de la voiture. *Revue de Géographie Humaine et d'Ethnologie* 1(1): 54–64.
HAUDRICOURT, ANDRÉ-G., MARIEL JEAN-BRUNHES-DELAMARRE
1955 *L'homme et la charrue à travers le monde*. Paris: Gallimard.
KROEBER, ALFRED L.
1948 *Anthropology*, revised edition. New York: Harcourt, Brace. (Originally published 1924).
1952 *The nature of culture*. Chicago: University of Chicago Press.
KROEBER, ALFRED L., CLYDE KLUCKHOHN
1952 *Culture: a critical review of concepts and definitions*. New York: Random House. (Reprinted 1963. Vintage Books 226).
LENIN, V.I.
1948 [1913] "Kriticheskie zanetki po natsional 'nomu voprosu" [Critical

remarks concerning the national question], in *Sochineniya* [Works], fourth edition, volume twenty, 3–34. Moscow: OGIZ. (Originally published 1913. Translated 1930 in *The collected works of V. I. Lenin*, volume twenty. Edited by Alexander Tcachtenberg. London: Martin Lawrence).

LESER, PAUL
1928 "Westöstliche Landwirtschaft. Kulturbeziehungen zwischen Europa, dem Vorderen Orient und dem Fernen Osten, aufgezeigt an landwirtschaftlichen Geräten und Arbeitsvorgängen," in *Festschrift: publication d'hommage offerte au P. W. Schmidt.* Edited by Wilhelm Koppers, 416–484. Vienna: St. Gabriel-Mödling.

MICHELET, JULES
1846 *Le peuple.* Paris: Hachette (Translated 1846 by C. Cocks as *The people*. London: Longman).

RADIĆ, ANTUN
1936 [1897] "Osnova za sabiranje i proučavanje gradje o narodnom životu" [A plan for collecting and studying materials concerning folk life], in *Sabrana djela* [Collected works], volume one. Edited by Vladko Maček and Rudolf Herceg, 3–85. Zagreb: Seljačka Sloga.
1936 [1898] "Narod: J. Michelet's *Le Peuple* (1798–1898)," in *Sabrana djela* [Collected works], volume one. Edited by Vladko Maček and Rudolf Herceg, 103–124. Zagreb: Seljačka Sloga.
1937 [1907] "Seljačko pitanje" [The peasant question], in *Sabrana djela* [Collected works], volume eight. Edited by Vladko Maček and Rudolf Herceg, 74–89. Zagreb: Seljačka Sloga.

REDFIELD, ROBERT
1956 *Peasant society and culture*. Chicago: University of Chicago Press.

SUMNER, WILLIAM G.
1907 *Folkways, a study of the sociological importance of usages, manners, customs, mores, and morals*. Boston: Ginn.

TOKAREV, SERGEI A.
1968 "Vvedenie" [Introduction], in *Osnovy etnografii* [Foundations of ethnography]. Edited by S. A. Tokarev, 5–38. Moscow: Vysšaia škola.

TÖNNIES, FERDINAND
1887 *Gemeinschaft und Gesellschaft*. Leipzig: Reisland.

WOLF, ERIC R.
1966 *Peasants*. Foundations of Modern Anthropology. Englewood Cliffs, N. J.: Prentice-Hall.

PART TWO

Culture and Social Organization

The Relationship Between the System of Kinship Relations and the System of Customs

MIHAI POP

LE RAPPORT ENTRE LE SYSTÈME DES RELATIONS DE PARENTÉ ET CELUI DES COUTUMES

Au terme de recherches de terrain effectuées dans la zone de Maramures, au Nord de la Roumanie, l'auteur étudie les rapports entre les relations de parenté et les coutumes.

Les communautés ethniques roumaines sont constituées de groupes sociaux fondés sur la parenté qui, outre la famille nucléaire, comprend toutes les personnes liées par le sang, l'affinité et le parrainage. Base biologique et sociale des relations de parenté, la consanguinité est complétée sur le plan proprement social par l'affinité qui, établissant les échanges matrimonieux sur un plan social, élargit le système d'alliance. Le parrainage, intervenant à son tour dans les relations de parenté, repose sur une alliance spirituelle manifestée dans des actes sociaux et économiques. L'office de parrain/marraine présente, dans le communautés roumaines, un caractère de permanence, manifesté plus spécialement lors de tous les rites de passage (baptême, mariage, etc.), établissant ainsi un troisième mode de parenté, liant non plus seulement les individus, mais deux familles de génération en génération.

La parenté se traduisait, sur le plan économique, dans les communautés rurales de paysans libres, par des droits d'ordres divers, des actes d'entr'aide, et cette communauté se prolongeait sur le plan rituel.

Chaque membre du système de parenté a statut et un rôle inhérent à ce statut au sein des trois lignes de relation de parenté, obéissant un langage — système de comportements ritualisés et socialisés — non seulement verbal, mais encore manifesté dans les échanges de biens et de services, particulièrement dans les rites et coutumes. Ces rôles recèlent une dynamique, elle-même exprimée dans les coutumes.

Les règles d'interdiction des mariages, lois sévères, tant civiles qu'ecclésiastiques, régissent avec rigueur les mariages et jouent non seulement sur la lignée de la consanguinité et de l'affinité, mais aussi dans les relations avec la famille des parrains, ce qui permet de définir la parenté comme une unité exogame dans le cadre d'une endogamie locale. Dans le cas d'individus appelés à devenir beaux-pères, l'échange des femmes devient systématique, obéissant à une motivation économique : les biens et la fortune reviennent aux hommes, et les femmes passent dans la maison de leur mari.

Dans les communautés roumaines, les paysans libres sont divisés, depuis le Moyen-Age, en une hiérarchie de familles et de titres, donnant à la structure des villages une organisation de caste, chacune des trois catégories de la parenté respectant l'endogamie locale à des degrés variables en fonction de l'intérêt. L'évolution des nécessités économiques au cours de l'histoire aboutit à l'établissement d'un nouveau système d'alliances.

L'antique système virilocal est attesté par la terminologie des relations de parenté. Avec le processus d'industrialisation, ce système est inversé, pour céder même la place à des formes tout-à-fait modernes, telles l'établissement de relations de parenté, par correspondance, aboutissant dans certains cas à une déviation totale des coutumes traditionnelles.

Au-delà de la terminologie, les coutumes reflètent à leur tour le système des règles du mariage, leur finalité visant à conserver et consolider la structure de la parenté dans ses systèmes d'alliance.

Dans la province du Maramures, les échanges matrimoniaux s'effectuent entre parentés du même niveau, chaque mariage étant précédé de rites — tel celui de la danse dominciale — systématiques pour les hommes et les femmes, jadis réservés au groupe hiérarchique de communauté ou de voisinage, auxquels participe maintenant la totalité de la communauté rurale. Les femmes y jouent cependant un rôle prépondérant.

Puis les fiançailles, acte par lequel deux familles manifestent leur intention de se livrer à un échange matrimonial, sont suivies, la veille du mariage, par une série d'actes visant à détacher les deux partenaires de leur groupe d'âge pour leur permettre d'accéder à un autre état, jouissant d'un autre statut, et à détacher la mariée de sa famille, afin qu'elle s'intègre à celle de son époux.

Le mariage lui-même est marqué par une danse rituelle de la mariée, d'abord chez elle, après un repas cérémoniel, où elle prend congé successivement des membres de sa parenté, puis après un autre repas rituel, dans la maison du marié où, après divers rites propitiatoires, la mariée reprend la danse avec ses nouveaux alliés dans un ordre hiérarchique inverse. Quiconque danse avec la mariée doit lui faire un don en argent ; le dernier partenaire est le marié dont le don en argent doit être supérieur aux autres dons individuels. Vient ensuite une ronde collective des deux familles, danse à laquelle participent, après le départ des jeunes époux, tous les invités, en signe d'acceptation de l'échange par toute la collectivité.

This paper is an attempt to deal with certain considerations concerning the relationship between kinship relations and customs, a relationship between two systems which are interconnected in European ethnological communities. My considerations are based on observations made over two years when conducting field research in the Maramures area in northern Rumania.

KINSHIP

The basic social group in Rumanian ethnological communities is the kinship group, which, beyond the nuclear family — parents and children — includes all members related by consanguinity, affinity, and by sponsorship.

Consanguinity can be considered to be the biological and social basis of kinship relationships; and affinity the manner of establishing a wider system of alliances on a social level, by matrimonial exchanges. On the other hand, sponsorship, which plays a special role in kinship relationships, is based on a spiritual alliance demonstrated in social and economic acts. Sponsors assist someone passing from one social state to another, they assist the child when he is baptized and the young couple getting married. They are, in the sense of the passage rites, the initiators of those entering another state. This is the role, the function, they have among all European peoples. But in Rumanian ethnological communities, the office of godparent is not an occasional function: it has a permanent nature. We therefore have a third kind of kinship. The godfather of a young couple getting married will also be the godfather at the christening of all their children. Should the godfather who assisted the young married couple die, the role passes to the eldest son and then again, in his absence, to the other sons of the originator of this kinship relationship. The two families thus establish together relationships of kinship which are maintained generation after generation and are demonstrated in a series of deeds which are intended to maintain and consolidate these kinship relationships.

Kinship, the great unit which is the basis of the relationships and alliances leading to groups of interest, used to be demonstrated, economically, in rural communities of free peasants (i.e. those not in bondage) by the right to cultivate jointly their own share of the community's alpine forest and pastures; by associations for the use of fountains, mills, seats in churches, and by a series of acts of assistance, harvest and reaping jobs, housebuilding jobs, and so on. Relatives retained their cohesion not only in living reality but also beyond, in the myth on a ritual level. This cohesion is demonstrated by a series of deeds linked with funeral and postfuneral ceremonies.

In the kinship system, each member, depending on which of the three types of kinship relationships he belongs to, has his own status and must play the respective part. He must perform the functions devolving on him in the various hypostases of communication between him and the other members of the family. Kinship is a reality with its own hierarchy, and with its own language in relations between persons. This language, a system of socialized, ritualized behavior, is used not only in verbal communications and in exchanges of goods and services, but also in what this paper deals with especially, in ceremonies and customs. In the life of the kinship, certain roles are of a temporal nature, and others change with the change in status of the members involved. We can therefore speak of a dynamic factor specific to kinship relationships which is in turn expressed in customs.

The Local Endogamy and its Extension in Relation to the Castes

In the traditional Rumanian village, kinship was and still is an exogamous unit within a local endogamy. Marriages are only permitted beyond the third degree and in certain places, even beyond the fourth degree of kinship. The ban on marriage between relatives of up to the third degree is upheld both by civil law and by the Church. Furthermore it is traditionally unacceptable for in-laws to marry except when the brother and the sister of one family marry the brother and the sister of another family, and celebrate the marriages on the same day, and therefore before any relationship at that degree is established. In certain areas the rules of prohibition covering the line of consanguinity and affinity are also applicable in relationships with the family of the sponsors.

In the case of such a marriage the wives' property is exchanged on a symmetrical basis (see Figure 1).

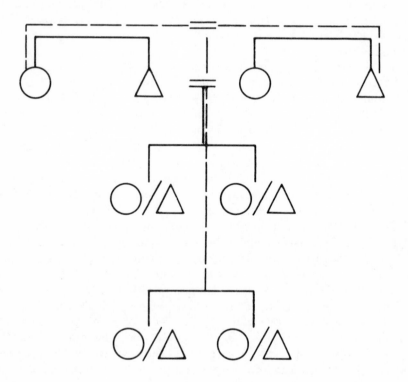

Figure 1.

This symmetrical model, frequently found today in the Maramures area, has an economic motivation. To avoid the division of the family fortune, where a family has two children of opposite sexes another family with the same structure is sought. The two marriages are celebrated the same day and for each party, after an exchange agreement profitable to both parties, ownership reverts to the men who inherit their father's houses and their parents' fortunes, while the women are accepted in the houses of their husbands.

Rumanian ethnological communities — the villages of free peasants — were not and are not today either, egalitarian associations of kinships. They developed, probably in the Middle Ages, their own hierarchic system, strengthened after feats of arms by the titles bestowed by the reigning princes of the three Rumanian principalities.

A hierarchy based on family origin and titles was therefore created among the free peasants. The village structure therefore acquired a caste organization.

The relationship between caste structure, where kinship was on a hierarchic basis with at least three categories, and the principle of local endogamy, is also interesting for the understanding of the internal mechanism of kinship, alliance, and interest group relations. The members of the more numerous lower category would find the possibility of establishing marriage relations in the village community and thus observed the local endogamy. The members of the middle category, even if they extended beyond the village limits, did not go any further than the neighboring villages; and thus, in the actual geographic conditions of Rumanian villages, no further than a distance of about twenty to thirty kilometers. The fewer members of the higher category, to avoid marrying beneath themselves, or, better still, to establish useful multilateral alliances on caste level, had to extend the system of matrimonial relations over a whole region, or a whole country.

We can thus speak, in relation to the social hierarchy, of three types of local endogamy, each with a different territorial area: the village, the nearby villages, and the country, or zone area. This situation could correspond to the kinship relationships of the feudal period and in some parts of Rumania it has lasted until today.

Later — probably toward the end of the eighteenth century — in the pastoral areas of the Carpathians, when the peasants, who became the owners of flocks of sheep which were greater than necessary for the rural self-sufficient economy, began to produce for selling on the market and had to engage shepherds not belonging to the family, they usually brought them from the villages whose frontiers were adjacent to theirs beyond the mountains — and therefore from the area outside the Carpathians. Some of these were accepted in the families of their masters, and thus extended the local endogamous area and at the same time broke the rules of marriage laid down by the caste hierarchy. The new kinship relationships led to the establishment of a new system of alliances based on economic needs.

Virilocality and its Transgression

In the case mentioned above, the social groups formerly restricted by the local endogamy brought only men from outside the endogamous area. This fact led to transgression of the virilocal system. In accordance with the marriage tradition, the woman always came into the man's house. This rule is also marked by the terminology of kinship relations. A man *gets married* and a woman *is married*. If, in accidental situations where, for instance, a family had only one child of female sex to be married, and the husband came into the wife's house — thus infringing the virilocal system — the villagers would say, in a depreciative tone of voice, that *he had been married*. So all the men brought from beyond the mountains, first being employed and then accepted in the family and married, found themselves in a special situation with regard to the traditional rules; however, they achieved a certain economic and social promotion.

The situation in the same areas is reversed today. In the industrialization process, young men leave the villages to integrate themselves into urban society, in varying ways. The girls, even if they stay in their villages, tend to marry townsmen and very often young men who have left the village. Young men who stay in their village thus have difficulty in finding wives in their home village or within the limits of local endogamy. They have to find their wives in the villages beyond the mountains, whence their parents had formerly brought their husbands. The former kinship relations are operative in these cases for the women of the same area in which they were applicable to the men.

I recently observed among the Szeklers that modern forms had gone beyond the traditional ways of establishing kinship relations, for instance the establishing of kinship relations by correspondence. The young man who cannot find a wife in his own village, following the direction of certain persons who found marriage partners in a village beyond the mountains, writes to a specific girl he does not know. He encloses with the letter a photograph of himself and the money necessary for the girl to be able to travel to his village.

In the one case, kinship relations are established in addition to the previously existing relations between the two social groups. The girl comes with her parents and she is given a house where she gets ready for the marriage, so that everything obeys the rules of the traditional customs. Kinship relations between the two families are thus established in accordance with custom. In the other case, the girl comes over with a girlfriend and the marriage is celebrated in the house and by the family of the young man, without the participation of the girl's family. Whereas in the first case the kinship relations concern both families, in the second case they are restricted to the close family and denote a total deviation from traditional customs.

The rules of kinship relations are expressed by the terminology of these relations and by the complex socialized and ritualized language of these customs.

The Terminology of Kinship Relations

Rumanian terminology of kinship relations is generally similar to that of the other Romance peoples both in structure and in linguistic expression.

The petty or close family consists of: *tată* [father], *mamă* [mother], *soţ* [spouse], *soţie* [spouse], *bărbat* [husband], *femeie-nevastă* [wife], *copii* [children], *unchi* [uncle], and *mătusă* [aunt], both for the father's brother or sister and for the mother's brother or sister.

In ascending line there are *bunic-moş* [grandfather], *bunică-moaşă* [grandmother], or *străbunic* [great-grandfather], *străbunică* [great-grandmother]; and in descending line, *nepot* [grandson], and *nepoată* [granddaughter], *strănepot* [great-grandson], and *strănepoată* [great-granddaughter].

The children of the same parents are *fraţi* [brothers] — the same name is used for both sexes. But *fraţi* [brothers] in the restricted sense are only male children. Female children are called *surori* [sisters].

In relations with uncles and aunts they are *nepoţi* — *nepot* and *nepoată* [nephews — nephew and niece], the same terms as used in relations with the grandfathers. On the same level, children amongst themselves are *veri* [cousins], *văr* [male cousin] and *vară* [female cousin] and according to the degree of kinship, first cousins or "soft" cousins, cousins of brother or sister, or cousins twice, three times or four times removed, and so on.

Families related by marriage (*se incuscresc*) are termed as follows: the parents of the newly married couple become, amongst themselves, *cuscri*, *cuscră*, *cuscru* [parents by marriage] and thë brothers *cumnaţi*, *cumnat*, and *cumnată* [brothers-in-law, brother-in-law, sister-in-law]. The parents of the young couple are *socri*, *socru*, and *soacră* [parents-in-law, father-in-law, mother-in-law] and the young couple in relation to the parents are *ginere* [son-in-law] and *noră* [daughter-in-law]. Sponsorship relations are known as *naş* and *naşă* [godfather and godmother] and *fini*, *fin*, and *fina* [godsons, godson, and goddaughter].

Thus, apart from *tată*, *mamă*, *soţie*, *bărbat*, *femeie-nevastă*, *fraţe*, *soră*, *unchi*, *matusă*, *ginere*, and *noră*, the difference between sexes is made at all degrees on the basis of the masculine form to which is applied the feminine ending, as: *bunic* and *bunică*, *naş* and *naşă*, *nepot* and *nepoată*, *cumnat* and *cumnată*, *cuscru* and *cuscră*. In the area studied there are no separate terms denoting age differences in the same category levels. But in southern Rumania younger brothers call their elder brothers *nene* [big brother] and the elder sisters are called *tată*.

There is, however, a hierarchic difference between the parents of the bridegroom and those of the bride during the marriage ceremony. The bridegroom's parents are *socri mari* [great parents-in-law] and the bride's parents are *socri mici* [small parents-in-law].

Terms of kinship relations are not transferred to age categories of the community framework beyond the real kinship relations except for *unchi-matuşă* [uncle-aunt] and *nepot-nepoată* [nephew-niece] whereby one can call persons of corresponding age, who do not have any real kinship relationship, relatives.

CUSTOMS

The system of rules is expressed by customs, or rather, ceremonies and nonceremonial behavior, and is found in verbal form in the ceremonial chants, in the proverbs and sayings and in other oral literature texts.

Arnold van Gennep (1909) drew up a model of the customs of family life which can be traced in the passing of a man from one state to another, from one status within a family and a community to another, in the Rumanian customs to which this paper will refer. The full meaning of these customs can only be understood if we establish correlations with the rules of kinship relations, and if we consider them directly in relation to the needs for conservation and consolidation of the structure of the alliance system of kinship. It is not possible here to give a full description of these customs, but the moments when these correlations become obvious will be emphasized.

In the Maramures, where several research projects are in progress at the moment, and where the peasant communities still retain obvious traces of the former caste hierarchy, marriages are made between kinships on the same level.

The establishing of kinship relations by marriage is preceded by a series of deeds whose intention can be implicit but is also explicit. Among the deeds of explicit intention one can mention two customs, one of them performed by men and the other by women. These are the Sunday dance organized by the young men and the watches organized by the girls. The two age groups have two customs here which are symmetrical in the premarital stage. Those of the opposite group take part in each custom as guests and partners.

The dance usually belonged to the community or neighborhood

hierarchic group. If young men of another social group wanted to take part in the dance they could only do so by invitation, which often had to be made by the organizing group. In this case, before participating in the custom, they had to undergo an acceptance ceremony. They had to be received and entertained in the home of a member of the inviting group. In the same situation, the girls could only participate if they were introduced by a family of the respective community to which they were related. Today the dance belongs entirely to the whole rural community.

The whole community and the representatives of the two social groups participate with great interest, respectively as actor-spectators and as assistants, in the explicit deeds preceding the establishing of matrimonial relations. Particularly the women of the kinship are very active, not only to look but also to comment and to act subversively, as the case may be, either for or against the relations which the young people establish more or less spontaneously.

As, in fact, in the whole of the Rumanian ethnic territory, marriage is preceded by a betrothal, there is a preliminary act by which two families demonstrate the decision to make matrimonial exchanges. The marriage begins by the detachment from a state and from a status, to be able to pass into another state, to enter a category with another status.

The act of detachment from the age group is compulsory for both partners. It takes place on the eve of the wedding day when the girls prepare the bride's wreath and the young men, the bridegroom's flag. The separation of the bride from her age group is marked by a song, a poetic and musical act. In certain areas this separation is performed for the bride when she puts on the ceremonial apparel and for the bridegroom when he is ceremonially shaved. In the marriage ceremony the bride is accompanied by two to four representatives of her age group — *druste* [bridesmaids] and the bridegroom by the *stegar* [flag-bearer] who is also the master of ceremonies.

The detachment is made not only from the age group but from the family too. While the separations are symmetrical for the age group on the bride's and on the bridegroom's side, the separation from the family only occurs for the bride, because in the virilocal system only the bride leaves her family and passes into and joins the family of her husband. However, there is not a total lack of symmetry. It is made up for by an act which has been preserved in an area of northwestern Rumania, in the Bihor area. When the bridegroom comes to collect the bride and take her to the wedding, he has to undergo a number of tests. He is asked, in the form of riddles which are now ritualized, a series of questions where he has to show the quick-wittedness and standard of knowledge necessary for his new status. This is perhaps a compensating act, a moment marking his acceptance by the bride's family. The bride's family really loses a member and therefore loses its balance but ceremonially and metaphorically accepts another, and reestablishes its balance, as often happens in the world's ethnological order, by a metaphorical jump.

In the area where the research was conducted, marriage takes place at the same time in the two families; and the transfer from one family to the other is marked by moments where the effective exchange is made by the language of customs. The bridegroom does not come into the bride's house to lead her to the wedding as in most Rumanian ethnic areas. The bridegroom's procession, consisting of his parents, friends, and neighbors, leaves for the church first, where it waits for the bride to arrive. After the wedding, the bridegroom and the sponsors, and the closest members of the family — but not the parents — leave with the bride's whole procession for her home. Here a ceremonial meal is served and the places are set according to a traditional protocol.

After the meal comes the first part of the passage ceremonial, marked by a two-step dance, called "the bride's dance" because the bride is the main actor and the subject of the exchange. The order of the persons who dance with the bride marks her departure from her father's house, the moment when she leaves her kinship. The flag-bearer dances with the bride to open the dance, and he is followed by the bridesmaids, the uncles, the aunts, and then the brothers and sisters, and finally the parents. Everybody makes a gift of money to be allowed to dance with the bride.

At the end of the dance the bridegroom and his guests, together with the bride and her bridesmaids, her parents, her sponsors, and a few of the closest guests, leave for the bridegroom's house. Here, after the ritual acts of reception, the prophylactic sprinkling of water to the four horizons to drive away the maleficent forces, and the beneficial throwing of wheat, comes the reception of the bride by embraces from the bridegroom's mother, the great mother-in-law. A meal is again served with a similar protocol. Then, to mark the entry into the new house, into the new kinship, the bride's dance is repeated in reverse hierarchic order. The flag-bearer opens the dance, then the bride dances with the sponsors, the relatives closest to the bridegroom, the uncles and aunts, and then the brothers and sisters; and finally with the bridegroom's parents. The last person to dance with the bride is the bridegroom, whose gift of money must be more than any individual gift donated by the others.

As can be seen, the dance is not just a party, but a well-organized ceremonial act. It reproduces in the order of hierarchic acts the family structure of the two kinships involved in the wedding. Without correlating this with the structure of kinship and with the rules of family relations, the meaning of the dance would be incomprehensible. By the language of the dance, the community expresses in the system of the rules of kinship the execution of the exchange — the cession of the bride by her family and her reception in the bridegroom's family.

After the bridegroom's dance with the bride, the young couple join in a ring dance in which all those who have been dancing until then take part. This is in fact the seal that is affixed to the unwritten contractual deed between the two families, expressed with such strict protocol in the dance where the bride was offered and accepted. Then the bridegroom and the bride withdraw and this is followed by a general dance in which all the guests take part, a sign of the acceptance of the exchange by the whole community.

The presentation of factual data on marriage customs, intended to demonstrate the close relationship they hold with regard to kinship customs and rules, stops here, but it should also be noted that what can be observed in the real marriage ceremony for marriage exchanges between parents can be observed on the ceremonial and rite level in connection with mythology, in funeral ceremonies concerning the detachment of the deceased from the living part of the kinship and his integration in the dead part. The myth of the great passage, expressed in Rumanian popular culture by a ceremonial chant, is only the second part of a unique ceremonial, the first part of which takes place in real life whereas the second can only be considered on the mythic level. The life of rural communities is organized on a system of rules which ensure its balance. Any exchanges marked by the above-mentioned customs interfere with this balance and, for the age group, any detachment of a member produces a state of unbalance. In the rank of the living, any dead person is a loss which produces an unbalance. For the bride's family, marriage means, in turn, a loss and an unbalance, but the proper order of the ethnological communities needs the return of the state of balance. When this has been achieved, the compensating system plays a special part. The compensation is expressed in the above-mentioned cases by the complex language of the ceremonial, as an expression of the rules of kinship. If each of the two parallel levels did not have its own tongue and its own language, we could say that the grammar of the rules of kinship finds its expression in the complex multilingual language of customs. We cannot decode a message without knowing its code, its grammar and its lexicon. Similarly, we cannot decode the message of customs without knowing the code of the rules of kinship — the family's structure — the manner of establishing the systems of alliances. The two systems, the kinship relationships and the customs system, are interconnected. The rules of the former are not only expressed by its own terminology, but also by the language of customs. It is therefore natural that in actual ethnological research, they should be studied on a closely interdependent basis, since the data of the direct observation of customs cannot be explained if the rules of kinship relations are not known.

REFERENCE

GENNEP, ARNOLD VAN
1909   *Les rites de passage*. Paris: É. Nourry. (Translated 1960 as *The rites of passage* by Monika B. Vizedom and Gabrielle L. Caffee. London: Routledge and Kegan Paul.)

Mating in French Preindustrial Rural Areas

MARTINE SEGALEN

RÉSUMÉ: LE CHOIX DU CONJOINT DANS LES COMMUNAUTÉS RURALES FRANÇAISES

Pour les anthropologues cherchant à connaître le système d'alliance des sociétés pré-industrielles européennes, le concept démographique d'isolat peut se révéler très fécond. Comme dans les sociétés primitives, la parenté joue un rôle majeur dans le choix du conjoint. Mais, tandis que dans ces dernières, le réseau de parenté segmente la population entre épouses prescrites et épouses prohibées, dans les sociétés européennes pré-industrielles nous formulons l'hypothèse que cette segmentation résulte de caractéristiques allogènes: groupes socio-professionnels ou artisanaux, religion, politique, etc. . . .

Nous analysons dans cet article, à travers les données de deux villages français, les causes sociales de la constitution des isolats, leurs conséquences et l'ouverture de l'isolat. Nous essayons ainsi de montrer l'interaction entre structure démographique et structure sociale.

Mating in European preindustrial rural areas has been largely overlooked in anthropological terms. We find many studies devoted to its purely demographical aspects (age at marriage, nuptiality rate, widowhood and remarriage rate, and so on), juridical aspects, or "folkloristic" aspects. But no study attempts to build a model that can account for the country in its entirety as well as its local varieties. Authors refer to the classical distinction, according to Lévi-Strauss (1949), between simple and complex societies, ranging among the latter the European preindustrial areas. Thus the choice would be totally free and only marriage between a few close kin would be prohibited.

Yet we have to consider that European preindustrial rural areas were very segmented. They were isolated not only by geographical barriers — created more by difficulty of transportation than by real isolation — but also by mental barriers dividing the population into closed groups. Thus we arrive at the concept of "isolate," used in its specifically demographic meaning: areas of population inside which intermarriage is possible. This concept was elaborated by two Swedish demographers, G. Dahlberg and S. Walhund, and applied in France by Sutter and Tabah (1951, 1955) who endeavored to compute the size of the isolates and their numbers in France. Intermarriage inside a closed group leads to inbreeding, hence the interest of demographers and geneticists in this concept. Isolates are also a very rich subject for the anthropologist who is trying to understand what marriage meant in rural areas, and what were its consequences, as concepts of neither "complex" nor "simple" societies account for the configurations of alliance networks. Two anthropological levels can be elaborated: the normative model and the actual model. The first one is how people think they marry or they should marry. This level is the conscious, indigenous representation of the alliance rule, as it is revealed in interviews, or found in written sources such as proverbs, oral literature, folklorists' works, and so on. The actual model brings us directly to a reality we can grasp through the accumulation of various data: oral genealogies collected directly among today's villagers and civil and religious records. Thus the anthropologist's work lies in accounting for the distortion — if there is one — between the two levels. As Leach said (1962:153): "The literature seldom reports the statistical incidence of the preferred type of unions . . . , but where figures are given, they are usually low. In some cases, the 'preference' is merely a verbal formula which does not correspond to the facts at all — e.g. Powell's discovery that out of eighty-five Trobriand marriages only one was with the supposedly preferred father's sister's daughter." The demographic incidence is primary to the explanation of marriage and alliance systems in exotic societies, but may be even more important in European groups. As Kunstadter et al. state (1963:511–519): "No description of a marriage system, even in ideal terms, is complete without a statement of the demographic conditions within which that system operates."

If traditional methods, successfully used in exotic societies, fail in European societies, we might try a step in a new direction through the construction of a third anthropological level, combining the model of the "official" rule, and the observed attitudes, as suggested by Cuisenier et al. (1970:31).

I wish to present here two field studies conducted in two different areas of Normandy, observing the causes of the formation of the isolate, the way it worked, its consequences, and how it was ruptured. It will be attempted thus to show (a) the interaction between structure and ideology; and (b) the mental barriers that hamper easy circulation among men. Marriage appears then as a mental construction which is more powerful than mountains or forests in causing the segmentation of the population.

Did the knowledge of all these mental barriers help toward building the alliance system of European preindustrial rural societies?

Vraiville, situated 120 kilometers west of Paris in the department of Eure, today has 300 inhabitants.[1] Half of its population is presently employed in the big factories on the River Seine, and the other half works in agriculture. This factory-in-the-country tradition is quite ancient: as far back as the seventeeth century we find spinners working at home to complement their agricultural resources, and at the beginning of the eighteenth century there were home weavers. The population was over 500 in the nineteenth century and sharply declined as these home weavers had to leave their looms at the end of the century to work in the factories. The main characteristic of the population of Vraiville in the nineteenth century is thus the presence of this large group of specialized craftsmen who led a different life from that of their farmer covillagers: in contrast to spinning, weaving was a fulltime job and rarely did weavers participate in communal work or mix with the rest of the population.

Sainte-Honorine-la-Chardonne is 250 kilometers southwest of Paris in the Orne, a somewhat traditional *département* of France.[2] Its present population, 700, has also declined by half since the last century. Here the segmentation of the population is not related to a socioprofessional variable but to religion: we find there a strongly structured group of Protestants, whose origin dates back to 1560. In 1876, according to the census, there were 123 Protestants in a total population of 1,519: now only 56 remain out of a total of 700. The Protestant group is not limited to Sainte-Honorine, for it is scattered over a distance of 20 kilometers in the area of the "Église du Bocage," but the main group lives in Sainte-Honorine and the adjacent town of Athis, which now has a population of 2000. Caen, the closest city with Protestants, is 60 kilometers to the north, which, in terms of nineteenth-century transportation, was quite remote. The isolate coincides geographically and demographically.

In both field studies similar data were collected: marriage records from 1706 to 1969 in Vraiville — 935 records (the long-range information was also used — for information on nuptiality, see Segalen 1972); and from 1840 to 1971 in Sainte-Honorine — 1,025 records; birth and death records in Vraiville, and only for Protestants of Sainte-Honorine;[3] the

---

[1] The Vraiville fieldwork, conducted from 1968 to 1970, was intended for a doctoral thesis (see Segalen 1972).

[2] The Sainte-Honorine-la-Chardonne fieldwork is part of a study of the *Centre d'Ethnologie Française* where a team of researchers works on the subject of "transmission within the family." Under the guidance of Jean Cuisenier, head of the *Centre* and head of the *Musée des arts et traditions populaires* in Paris, the results of the research were published with the fictitious title of "Chardonneret" in 1974 (*Ethnologie Française* 1974).

[3] In contrast to Vraiville, where we used only the civil records, we had to work on the parish registers of the Protestant church of Sainte-Honorine. These registers were used mainly to track down Protestant weddings in the civil records, to which we went back for information, as parish registers are very laconic.

number of dispensations bestowed by the Catholic church for consanguineous marriages.[4] Also collected orally were a number of
genealogies, primarily among the Protestants. In Vraiville a few of them
enabled us to control the validity of the reconstituted pedigrees.

A SOCIOPROFESSIONAL ISOLATE: VRAIVILLE

The marriage records do not mention regularly the spouses' profession
during the eighteenth century. Besides, economic history shows that the
home weavers' class developed during the nineteenth, with the expansion
of drapery mills at Elbeuf, on the Seine, and at Louviers, on the Eure
River, both cities located approximately ten kilometers from Vraiville.
Hence the analysis bears on the years 1800–1969. From the indications of
the spouses' professions or those of their parents, we can open five
socioprofessional categories and study the distribution of marriages
according to the profession of the spouses (see Table 1).

On the main diagonal of these matrices are the higher figures, which
show that a strong mate selection ran through the nineteenth century.
Socioprofessional homogamy was very strong among two classes: farmers
and weavers. Together with Albert Jacquard, we have given a mathematical measure of the phenomenon by situating these data between two
theoretical models: a model of random mating, "panmictic model",
where marriages are all contracted at random, and a model of total
homogamy (see Jacquard and Segalen 1971:494), where farmers marry
only farmers' daughters, craftsmen marry craftsmen's daughters, and so
on. This "homogamy index" shows that homogamy was very strong until
1920 and then declined, but is still not negligible. In terms of mating it
means that during the nineteenth century farmers married farmers'
daughters and weavers married weavers' daughters. The Vraiville population of 500 was divided into two subgroups. And yet the pressure of the
population structure was such that these isolates were not one hundred
percent hermetical. The lack of balance between sexes made marriage
necessary in the "forbidden" category. What is remarkable is that only
girls "suffered" these misalliances. As a French saying goes: *Marie ton fils
comme tu veux, ta fille comme tu peux* [Marry off your son as you wish,
your daughter as you can]. In other words the marriage rule was abided by
for boys, but not always for girls.

In spite of this important homogamy, the consanguinity rate (measured
by the percentage of all consanguineous marriages) was low. Homogamy

---

[4] The Catholic church forbids marriage with a niece, first cousin or second cousin.
However, when required, it grants dispensations for such marriages. The diocesan archives
communicate this information. The Protestant church does not forbid such unions; thus
consanguineous marriages have to be traced through genealogies.

was so strong that people preferred to choose a mate of the same professional category from another village, rather than a covillager with whom marriage was forbidden. During the nineteenth century the geographic area of mate choice, as shown in the records, was 90 percent restricted to the adjacent villages; the proportion still runs high nowadays (40 percent of all spouses either were born in the village or in those surrounding it). Working on the genealogies gives us a different insight into the question. According to Sutter's method (1956) we have built "downward pedigrees," showing all the descendants of a common ancestor. Besides showing those consanguineous marriages whose blood links are not controlled by the Church, they shed light on what might be, in this area, a structural principle of kinship: solidarity of siblings with its corollary "relinking of marriages." In other words, the endogamy rule is so strong that it supposes, as much as possible, that two siblings or two cousins will marry two siblings of another family. We observe a highly significant number of this type of marriage. They are the expression of the same rule: that of marrying within one's class. The demographical difficulty of this rule encourages the families who have found an acceptable mate for their child to look in the same family to find another mate for another child.

Marriage, particularly endogamous marriage, is not an individual act, but rather is one incident on the longer trajectory of economic family policy. Forced by Napoleon's Civil Code to share their lands equally among all heirs, farmers of Vraiville have tried to fight this obligation by having their children marry children of other farmers. Both parties thus receive by marriage, and later by inheritance, an amount of land large enough to reconstitute the whole property.

Weavers' endogamy is harder to explain in terms of landholding. They were not landholders, generally only tenants, but they owned their looms. Their endogamy stemmed from an economic necessity: two looms were better than one for the diversification of the production. Women were more skilled at weaving with fine threads, whereas men would make the "Elbeuf drapery," the weaving of which required physical strength. Thus the couple was a production unit, in which even children were associated: they unwound the bobbins of the weft. At marriage, bride and groom brought, as a dowry, their weaving looms.

The isolate was ruptured by the demographic unbalance caused by the weavers' departure and the transformations that affected the land (price crises and so on) after World War I. Somehow the socioprofessional endogamy of farmers still lingers, but on a geographically wider and different basis. By choice, only one child remains a farmer; the other children find employment in the industrial area of the Seine. The geographical basis of choice is no longer limited to the adjacent villages, but extended to the whole *département*, where farmers meet in the markets, at local unions, and so forth.

Table 1. Distribution of marriages according to the spouses' profession

♀ \ ♂	1803–1842						1843–1882					
	Farmers	Weavers	Craftsmen	Farm-laborers	Others	Total	Farmers	Weavers	Craftsmen	Farm-laborers	Others	Total
Observed marriages n_j^i												
Farmers	28	14	2	1	1	46	18	6	2	–	8	34
Weavers	–	17	2	2	1	22	4	60	14	13	1	92
Craftsmen	5	8	5	3	3	24	3	7	2	–	2	14
Farm-laborers	–	3	3	1	3	10	1	4	3	6	1	15
Others	1	2	1	2	6	12	1	1	–	–	2	4
Total	34	44	13	9	14	114	27	78	21	19	14	159
Panmictic model p_j^i (%)												
Farmers	13.6	17.7	5.1	4.5	5.1		5.8	16.6	4.5	4.1	3.0	
Weavers	6.6	8.5	2.5	1.7	2.7		15.6	45.1	12.2	11.0	8.1	
Craftsmen	7.2	9.3	2.7	1.9	2.9		2.4	6.9	1.8	1.7	1.2	
Farm-laborers	3.0	3.9	1.1	0.8	1.2		2.6	7.3	2.0	1.8	1.3	
Others	3.6	4.7	1.4	0.9	1.4		0.6	2.0	0.5	0.5	0.4	
Homogamous model h_j^i (%)												
Farmers	34	11	–	–	1		27	–	2.4	1.3	3.3	
Weavers	–	22	–	–	–		–	78	4.6	2.7	6.7	
Craftsmen	–	10	13	–	1		–	–	14	–	–	
Farm-laborers	–	1	–	9	–		–	–	–	15	–	
Others	–	–	–	–	12		–	–	–	–	4	

Table 1. *(continued)*

Weighted model $\lambda h_j^i+(1-\lambda) p_j^i$ (%)

1883–1922, $\lambda=0.555$

♀ \ ♂	Farmers	Weavers	Craftsmen	Farm-laborers	Others
Farmers	24.8	14.1	2.3	2.0	2.8
Weavers	3.0	15.9	1.1	0.8	1.2
Craftsmen	3.2	9.7	7.1	0.9	1.7
Farm-laborers	1.4	2.3	0.5	5.3	0.5
Others	1.6	2.1	0.6	0.4	7.2

1923–1962, $\lambda=0.494$

♀ \ ♂	Farmers	Weavers	Craftsmen	Farm-laborers	Others
Farmers	15.9	8.5	3.5	2.7	3.1
Weavers	8.0	61.2	8.5	6.9	7.4
Craftsmen	1.2	3.5	7.8	0.9	0.6
Farm-laborers	1.3	3.7	1.0	8.1	0.7
Others	0.3	1.0	0.3	0.3	2.0

Observed marriages n_j^i

1883–1922

♀ \ ♂	Farmers	Weavers	Craftsmen	Farm-laborers	Others	Total
Farmers	8	2	4	2	12	28
Weavers	1	3	5	4	2	15
Craftsmen	1	1	10	2	8	22
Farm-laborers	–	2	6	19	2	29
Others	2	–	2	–	1	5
Total	12	8	27	27	25	99

1923–1962

♀ \ ♂	Farmers	Weavers	Craftsmen	Farm-laborers	Others	Total
Farmers	9	–	1	2	6	18
Weavers	–	–	1	–	1	2
Craftsmen	4	–	3	1	4	12
Farm-laborers	2	–	5	8	10	25
Others	1	–	7	8	30	46
Total	16	–	17	19	51	103

Panmictic model p_j^i

1883–1922

♀ \ ♂	Farmers	Weavers	Craftsmen	Farm-laborers	Others
Farmers	3.5	2.2	7.6	7.6	7.1
Weavers	1.8	1.2	4.1	4.1	3.8
Craftsmen	2.6	1.8	6.0	6.0	5.6
Farm-laborers	3.5	2.4	7.9	7.9	7.3
Others	0.6	0.4	1.4	1.4	1.2

1923–1962

♀ \ ♂	Farmers	Weavers	Craftsmen	Farm-laborers	Others
Farmers	2.8	–	3.0	3.3	8.9
Weavers	0.3	–	0.3	0.4	1.0
Craftsmen	2.0	–	2.0	2.1	5.9
Farm-laborers	3.8	–	4.1	4.7	12.4
Others	7.1	–	7.6	8.5	22.8

Table 1. (continued)

♀ \ ♂	Farmers	Weavers	Craftsmen	Farm-laborers	Others	Total	Farmers	Weavers	Craftsmen	Farm-laborers	Others	Total
Homogamous model h_j^i												
Farmers	12	–	3.2	–	12.8		16	–	1	–	1	
Weavers	–	8	1.4	–	5.6		–	–	1	–	1	
Craftsmen	–	–	22	–	–		–	–	12	–	–	
Farm-laborers	–	–	0.4	27	1.6		–	–	3	19	3	
Others	–	–	–	–	5		–	–	–	–	46	
Weighted model $\lambda h_j^i+(1-\lambda)p_j^i$ (%), $\lambda=0.493$ (right: $\lambda=0.259$)												
Farmers	7.5	1.1	5.5	3.9	10.0		6.2	–	2.5	2.5	6.8	
Weavers	0.9	4.6	2.8	2.1	4.6		0.2	–	0.5	0.3	1.0	
Craftsmen	1.5	0.9	13.8	3.0	2.8		1.5	–	4.5	1.6	4.4	
Farm-laborers	1.8	2.1	4.2	17.3	4.5		2.8	–	3.8	8.3	10.1	
Others	0.3	0.2	6.7	0.7	3.1		5.3	–	5.7	6.3	28.7	

A RELIGIOUS ISOLATE:
SAINTE-HONORINE-LA-CHARDONNE

The conscious norm of marriage of this community is very clear in defining those spouses eligible for marriage and those not: marriage with a Catholic is forbidden to Protestants and vice versa. This rule has been obeyed until recently. What then, are the consequences of such an interdiction when the demographical balance is precarious?

We have observed the way this isolate worked over a period of a hundred years but due to lack of data, it was impossible to go back further.[5] The spouses' pool that was tapped by Protestants was mainly that of Athis, the nearby town, but also that of the villages located twenty kilometers around Sainte-Honorine, where small Protestant groups were scattered. As with the farmers of Vraiville, the Protestants of Sainte-Honorine preferred to marry outside their native village rather than with a person of a forbidden category. The data of Table 2 show that the number of Protestants declined sharply during the nineteenth century and reached the "minimum population", the level below which a population cannot survive, according to Livi (cited by Sutter and Tabah 1951).

What are the characteristics of marriage in this group? We can summarize them by saying that marriage was difficult. Mean age at marriage for Protestants is, overall, higher than for Catholics and Protestants together. There is a high celibacy rate among girls. Nuptiality rates are generally lower. The strict religious homogamy, in a numerically small group, leads naturally to a heavy percentage of consanguineous marriages, especially during the last fifteen years, as population dwindled (see Table 2). A program used by Jacquard to calculate the genetic weight of known ancestors in closed populations has been used here (Jacquard and Segalen 1973). All Protestants now living in Sainte-Honorine have at least four pairs of ancestors in common, with genetic weight fairly important. This has consequences not only for the genetic patrimony, but also for land patrimony. It partially explains why Protestants emerged as the richest class, out of which a bourgeoisie landowner (but no longer a farmer) emigrated toward the regional towns. The weight of these ancestors is due to the combination of two factors: decrease in the size of the population and differential fecundity rate. Heavy consanguinity is thus the most characteristic feature of the marriages of the group. Eventually the demographic structure explains why the rule was broken: a few mixed marriages did occur. Since 1880, nine Protestants have taken Catholic

---

[5] After the Edict of Nantes was revoked (1685), the Protestants kept their vital records secret as Catholics would try to take the young children away and have them brought up in Catholic institutions. In 1787, Louis XVI ordered the Protestants to register their families. After the Revolution secularized the keeping of vital records, Protestants, like Catholics, reported to the mayor.

mates with the provision that no Catholic wedding ceremony would be performed and that the children would be raised as Protestants. Only three Protestants married as Catholics.

With the decrease of population, mating was becoming a dramatic problem: marrying in Sainte-Honorine meant marrying a relative; only outside the isolate would one find Protestants who were not next of kin, such as the farmer who met his wife at a regional Protestant meeting. Very recently the new trend toward ecumenism has eased the situation, enabling covillagers to marry each other. Since both churches now accept mixed marriages and no longer require that the children be raised in one of the religions, 50 percent of all Protestants marry Catholics, according to the local priest. Thus the isolate is opened.

Table 2. Decrease of population among Protestants of the Church of the Bocage

Year	Total Church of the Bocage	Athis	Sainte-Honorine
1674	700 (estimate)		
1686	3 000 (estimate)		
1690		239	
1742	1 300	200	200
1849		170	275
1868	425		
1874		106	132
1920		150	
1966	380		
1971		180	58

Sources: Abbé Macé, Histoire de l'Église du Bocage; census of Protestant parish registers; oral information; local brochure published for the centennial of the Church of Athis.

SUMMARY AND CONCLUSIONS

It has been shown through the study of two local communities in Normandy how the population was segmented according to a socioprofessional distinction in the first case, and a strict religious criterion in the second case. Preferential marriages reinforced considerably this segmentation to an extent that endangered social mobility. Weavers had a lower social status than farmers. When, after 1870, they were hit by the textile crisis, there was no possibility for them of finding other employment locally. The segmentation between Protestants and Catholics was so strong that the two communities were hardly on speaking terms until the early years of the twentieth century. Besides, the endogamous marriages accelerated the process of land property accumulation among the Protestants. The separation between the two groups was then accentuated: not only were they Protestants, but also much richer. In 1876, nearly 50 percent of all Protestants were landowners. Today all the Protestants are landowners, or rent their land from members of their kinship network. The disappearance of the isolates is mostly the result of demographic pressure. The choice of the mate is still not free but it is less rigid. A step has been made toward a complex society: "A complex society becomes such not so much because of an expansion of the isolate itself as on account of an expansion of other types of social links (economic, political, intellectual)" (Lévi-Strauss 1953:535). In European preindustrial rural societies, family weight, as in primitive societies, is preeminent in the choice of a mate for their children. In complex societies, however, the categories of marriageables do not seem to be determined within the kinship network itself, but by allogenous elements such as socioprofessional class, religion, or politics.

Needham and Leach have challenged the traditional ways of studying kinship and alliance (Needham and Leach 1971). We have endeavored here to suggest a new approach to the understanding of European marriage and kinship systems, definitely different from formal analysis, but based on the demographic data.

REFERENCES

CUISENIER, J., M. SEGALEN, M. DE VIRVILLE
　　1970　Pour l'étude de la parenté dans les sociétés européennes le programme d'ordinateur ARCHIV. *L'Homme* 10(3):27–74.
Ethnologie Française
　　1974　Chardonneret. *Ethnologie Française* 1–2.
JACQUARD, A., M. SEGALEN
　　1971　Choix du conjoint et homogamie. *Population* 26(3):487–498.
　　1973　Isolement sociologique et isolement génétique. *Population* 28(3): 551–570.
KUNSTADTER, P., R. BUHLER, F. STEPHAN, C. WESTOFF
　　1963　Demographic variability and preferential marriage patterns. *American Journal of Physical Anthropology* 21(4):511–519.
LEACH, E.
　　1962　The determinants of differential cross-cousin marriage. *Man* 62(238): 153.
LÉVI-STRAUSS, C.
　　1949　*Les structures élémentaires de la parenté*. Paris: Presses Universitaires de France. (Revised edition translated 1968 as *The elementary structures of kinship* by J. H. Bell, J. R. von Sturmer, and R. Needham. London: Eyre and Spottiswood.)
　　1953　"Social structure," in *Anthropology today*. Edited by A. L. Kroeber, 511–519. Chicago: University of Chicago Press.
NEEDHAM, R.
　　1971　"Remarks on the analysis of kinship and marriage," in *Rethinking kinship and marriage*. Edited by R. Needham, 1–34. London: Tavistock.

SEGALEN, M.
1972   *Nuptialité et alliance: le choix du conjoint dans une commune de l'Eure.*
       Mémoires d'Anthropologie Française 1. Paris: G. -P. Maisonneuve et
       Larose.
SUTTER, J.
1956   Méthode mécanographique pour établir la généalogie d'une popu-
       lation. *Population* 11(5):507–530.
SUTTER, J., L. TABAH
1951   Les notions d'isolat et de population minimum. *Population* 6(3):481–
       498.
1955   Evolution des isolats de deux départements français: Loir-et-Cher
       1870–1954, Finistère 1911–1953. *Population* 10(2):227–258.

Changing Perceptions of Roles as Husbands and Wives in Five Yugoslav Villages

JOEL M. HALPERN and BARBARA K. HALPERN

RÉSUMÉ: CHANGEMENTS DANS LA PERCEPTION DES RÔLES D'ÉPOUX ET D'ÉPOUSE DANS CINQ VILLAGES YOUGOSLAVES

Cinq villages représentatifs des diverses aires culturelles de la Yougoslavie ont servi à l'étude des modifications dans la perception des rôles des époux au sein du couple et dans la famille élargie.

Le passage du régime patriarcal sévère à un système où l'autorité du mari decroît face à l'autonomie croissante de la femme n'est qu'un aspect du changement qui affecte le couple, principalement dans ses sphères d'activités.

La structure traditionnelle de la famille serbe, la *zadruga*, est caractérisée par la séparation des activités masculines et féminines, celles-ci vaquant aux soins domestiques, ceux-là allant aux champs ou à l'usine, ou s'occupant du bétail.

Conséquence de la guerre, l'interchangeabilité des tâches devient la règle en même temps que s'accroît la fréquence du travail non-domestique pour la mère de famille, soumise ainsi à des travaux physiques éprouvants, ce qui contribue à saper l'antique organisation patriarcale. Une sensation de malaise s'instaure, due à la nouvelle idéologie et à l'impact des nouvelles valeurs sur la vie quotidienne confrontées aux patterns anciens dont ni hommes ni femmes n'arrivent à se défaire.

A l'antique relation fondamentale père–fils se substitue progressivement la dyade mari–femme, où cette dernière participe davantage aux prises de décisions — et où les partenaires vivent sur un mode d'interdépendance mutuelle dans le cadre d'une vie au niveau amélioré.

This article takes a look at change in the husband–wife relationship in the context of the ethnically diverse village cultures of Yugoslavia. Traditional values pertaining to this relationship are presented and compared with contemporary ideal points of view. Factors prompting change and conditions inhibiting altered relationships are mentioned, in an attempt to relate cultural ideals to actual behavior.

Household structure and extended kin groups in the various cultural regions of Yugoslavia are being studied increasingly from the perspective of cultural-social anthropology as well as from the viewpoints of Yugoslav ethnologists and sociologists.[1] The present narrowly restricted analysis is part of a larger study concerned with authority and decision making as these relate to household social structure. Our findings are based on data collected in individual villages during the decade 1961–1970. These include survey interviews in selected villages, solicited autobiographical materials and data derived from participant observation on the part of student assistants and the authors.[2]

The special culture regions investigated are located in Slovenia, central Serbia, the Vojvodina, Bosnia, and Montenegro. The Slovene village is represented by Šenčur in north central Slovenia, on a plain at the foothills of the Slovenian Alps and near the industrial town of Kranj. The community is Catholic. This farming region has a comparatively old industrial tradition, and many village men commute to town daily. In terms of per capita income the area is one of the most prosperous in Yugoslavia.

The Serbian materials were obtained from several culturally similar villages in Šumadija, the Serbian heartland, clustered near the market town of Arandjelovac. This region of rolling hills has long had a mixed economy of livestock-raising and cultivation. In recent years increasing numbers of village men have become peasant-workers, commuting to jobs in new factories in the town. This homogeneous area is Serbian Orthodox.[3]

The Vojvodina, an autonomous province north of the Danube, is a fertile plain containing the richest wheat and corn land in Yugoslavia. The village of Indjija, unlike the other villages in the sample, is ethnically diverse. The majority population is Serbian Orthodox, including postwar immigrants resettled from the Montenegrin uplands and elsewhere, who replaced the prewar German population. Other ethnic minorities are present. Indjija is about four times larger than the other communities in the sample, possesses some small industries, and is a railroad junction.

The Bosnian village, Župča, is in a hilly region north of Sarajevo. Its population is Muslim. Many of the men work in nearby coal mines. The general area is becoming industrialized, with steel mills in the vicinity, but

---

[1] For a basic annotated bibliography see Halpern (1969a, 1969b). A more general listing is in Halpern (1969c), with sections on peasant life and social structure. Concerning research by Yugoslav scholars see *East European Quarterly* (1970) and Salzmann (1970).

[2] Most of the fieldwork was carried out during 1961–1962, with subsequent field visits in 1964, 1966, and 1970. Research was sponsored by the National Science Foundation and later by the National Institute of Mental Health. Cooperating were faculty members of the sociology and ethnology seminars of the universities of Belgrade, Ljubljana and Sarajevo. The field questionnaire interviewing was carried out by students from these institutions. In the United States Carol and Joseph Pessah helped with translating, Vida Taranovski and Tina Pribicevich assisted in the coding and Carole Allen undertook selected compilations.

[3] Orašac, a village in this area, is the subject of monographs by Halpern (1967) and Halpern and Halpern (1972).

Župča itself, like the villages near Arandjelovac, sustains semisubsistence agriculture as a supplement to wage income.

Bukovica, the Montenegrin village, is the smallest in the sample. Located in the mountainous uplands, here sheep pastoralism is supplemented by limited cultivation on the rocky slopes. The area is sparsely populated, and there is no industry in the region. Many village men, especially younger ones, seek employment elsewhere. Like the Serbs the Montenegrins are Orthodox.

In no sense are these five diverse villages meant to represent the total range of ethnic and economic variation within Yugoslavia. The country consists of six republics, of which the largest, Serbia, has two autonomous provinces. Not represented here are two of these republics (Croatia and Macedonia) nor the predominantly Albanian province of Kosovo, which is actually an autonomous region in the Serbian republic. The 375 households in the survey (81 in Slovenia, 80 in Serbia, 72 in the Vojvodina, 119 in Bosnia, and 23 in Montenegro) do, however, represent a sampling of ethnic groups, including the three major religions: Serbian Orthodox, Catholic and Muslim.

Notwithstanding the obvious ethnic, religious, and economic differences among the five regions, there is in addition an important social distinction that sets Slovene villages apart from other South Slav communities: in Slovenia the *zadruga*, the South Slav extended household kin unit, has not existed in recent historic times. In all other regions discussed here the institution has been important and still exists in modified form.

We wish to present a sense of changing relationships as perceived by informants themselves. This account is not intended as definitive, but as an indication of something of the range which persists in the husband–wife relationship. Change in this important tie can hardly be seen as a direct alteration of relative status between the sexes in terms of a simple progression from strong patriarchal authority to decreased male authority and greater autonomy for women. These alterations do exist, but only as one aspect of change.

In considering the relationship between husband and wife in rural Yugoslavia it should be kept in mind that it has always existed not as an independent dyad but within a nexus of surrounding kin. Both spouses have important responsibilities within the larger context of extended family relationships. This is true even in Slovenia, although to a lesser degree — it is also true in urban areas, outside the scope of this paper, and has been a fruitful subject of study. The fact that focus is on the husband–wife relationship is in itself a modern concept — in terms of traditional *zadruga* structure overtly the most significant ties were between father and sons or between brothers.

A point of departure for defining traditional family structure in Yugoslavia is a description of the Serbian *zadruga* in the early nineteenth century by the Serbian historian-ethnographer Vuk Karadžić:

The Serbs live mainly in zadrugas. In some houses there are four or five married men, and one-family households are rare. There are as many *vajats* [sleeping quarters for individual couples] as there are married men, and the house itself is only for communal eating and the place in which the old women and men sleep; all others sleep each with his own wife and children in his own vajat, without fire both in summer and winter. Around some prosperous houses are groups of vajats and other outbuildings (for example, corn cribs, grain storage sheds and buildings with overhanging eaves) like a small settlement.

Every household has a *starešina* [headman] who governs and guides the household and all its property; he directs the adults and young men as to where they will go and what work they will do; he deals with the Turks and attends village and district meetings and conducts business; with the assent of the household he sells what is to be sold and buys what is to be bought; he keeps the moneybag and worries about paying the head-tax and other taxes and fines. When prayers are said, he begins and ends them; when guests come to the house (in the larger households scarcely a day passes when there are none) he talks with them and takes meals with them (in the larger households, where there are many members, first the starešina and the guests are served at one *sofra* [low, round Turkish-style table], then the men and young men who work in the fields, and afterwards the women and children eat). The starešina is not always the oldest male: when a father becomes old, he turns over the headship to the most able son (or brother, or nephew), even if he is the youngest. If it happens that a starešina does not guide the household well, the household members choose another. In zadruga households each woman spins, weaves, and prepares clothing for herself and her children; as for food preparation, each in turn does the job a week at a time. . . . Usually the wife of the starešina is the woman who all summer supervises preparation of food for the winter (Djurić 1967:63–64).[4]

One of the most significant points in this description is the division of household life into men's and women's spheres of activities. Against the background of this historical tradition it is pertinent to note here that where interviewing was done in a family context, the responses were invariably made by men. This was often the case even when certain questions were directed specifically at women. Under some circumstances women were interviewed separately, and despite some difficulties considerable information was gathered formally and informally from women.

Regarding comments on general patterns, responses in large part appear to represent the formal accepted wisdom of the household head. Concerning questions relating to actual behavior, the responses appear to have considerable validity: there is a high degree of continuity in each community.

Even informal behavior patterns of day-to-day household life traditionally were not based on a model of masculine authority founded on orders unquestioningly carried out; instead, as indicated above, the division of labor and establishment of roles based on allocation of tasks tended to create separate arenas of authority.

---

[4] Excerpt translated by the authors. Not all Serbs spent all their lives in *zadruga* households, but this institution did provide an ideal prototype.

An extensive questionnaire was used which covered many aspects of village life. Pertinent to our topic was a formal question, "What do you think is the ideal division of labor?" and the unstructured responses it stimulated. Related questions included, "How are tasks in your household divided?" "Who works more, men or women?" "Do you think women are as intelligent as men?" "Do you think women should have the same education as men?" "Who makes decisions in your family?" The main purpose of such questions was to encourage a trend of thought and to verify its consistency.

Responses from all villages can be tentatively divided into two sets of values. One set holds that traditional values, based on "a natural founddation" which recognizes physical and intellectual differences between men and women, result in clear patterns of labor division and decision making. A more contemporary point of view expresses the idea that men and women are equal in mental and (perhaps) physical capabilities and the decision making and formely sex-allocated tasks can and should be shared.

A Serbian folk saying typifies the traditional ideal: "In the house the woman is the head and the husband the guest." Following are actual responses from Serbia which express this notion.

Women should keep house and take care of the children. Men should work in the fields, care for the livestock and deal with the government.
A woman works at home and obeys her husband. The husband should protect her from difficult physical tasks.
Women should do the household chores and men the harder physical work, since they are stronger.

From Slovenia similar ideas are expressed: "Men can plow and sow, women can weed" [weeding is regarded as a housekeeping chore]. From the Vojvodina, Bosnia, and Montenegrin communities respectively:

Men should provide for the family, women should take care of the house.
Women belong at home taking care of the house, the children and the livestock. Men work on the land or in the mine or factory.
Women's job is to do the housework and take care of the livestock. Men do the marketing and give the orders.

There is a marked consistency in mentioning household tasks as women's work. Over 90 percent of the replies from Bosnia, Serbia, and Montenegro and over 70 percent from the Vojvodina and Slovenia agree on this point. Agreement is only somewhat less for male work with respect to agricultural tasks: over 80 percent of the responses from Bosnia, Serbia, and Montenegro. In the Vojvodina and Slovenia, where wage employment is more usual, over 40 percent fit this category. Regarding off-the-farm occupations for men, consciousness of this situation is particularly high in newly industrializing Bosnia (55 percent) but only about a third of the respondents in the generally more industrialized areas of the Vojvodina and Slovenia are aware of it.

Caring for livestock is seen as an important subsidiary task for men and women, especially in Montenegro where sheep-raising is significant, and also in Serbia. In Bosnia caring for livestock is mentioned more frequently as women's work. Agricultural field and garden tasks are seen as important for women in almost two thirds of the replies from Serbia and over half those from Montenegro but mentioned by a fourth to a fifth of the respondents in the other areas — generally the Vojvodina and Slovenia do not seem to conceive of tasks as too rigidly defined, and these two areas evidence some other similarities in outlook.

The traditional view revolves around what are felt to be natural physical differences in capabilities between men and women, with predictable results. The man is recognized as the giver of orders, along with having responsibility for dealing with the government, marketing, and acting as protector of his woman. There is also the notion that women are responsible for supplementing, in subsidiary agricultural tasks, the work of the men, all within a framework of mutual sex limitations: "Women can't do everything men can, just as men can't do everything women can."

The formal embodiment of the man as household protector, organizer, accountant, and intermediary in dealings with officials is particularly strong in areas of Yugoslavia formerly under Turkish rule and is illustrated in the Karadžić description. The traditional system depends for its functioning not only on explicit belief in the mutual physical limitations of man's strength and woman's childbearing but also on the formal demarcation of sectors of responsibility. This is related to the Serb idea that a man is a guest at home and should not be responsible for any inside work which might demean his outside role. In Bukovica in Montenegro many homes still reserve a special carved chair for use only by the household head. In Slovenia the idea of man as heroic household protector and representative to the outside world is not so strongly felt, but there does exist the related notion that woman should dedicate herself to home and family.

Following are responses from Serbia to conversational queries about changes in formal relationships between husbands and wives in the postwar period. The first is from a woman and the second from a man.

It used to be quite different. The wife really respected her husband more then. If they walked together to market she always walked behind. This doesn't happen any more, at least not in our area. The wife used to have to help her husband off with his boots or sandals at the end of the day and then wash his feet. But this really wasn't so bad. It was bad only if she had been working the whole day and then had to sit up until late at night waiting for him to come home so she could

wash his feet. I remember plenty of cases where a wife had to wait up for her husband in order to accomplish this task. She couldn't go to bed even if he had gone out to the *kafana*.
Relations between husband and wife have really changed. It used to be that a husband and wife couldn't fight when they lived together in the same household with his parents. They had to get along. Wives were more afraid of their husbands than they are today. These good relations have been spoiled by schooling. Now a girl finishes eight years of school, so when she gets married and gets angry she says "I can earn my own piece of bread." Formerly a wife never would have dared to say that!

The first comment gives examples of formalized behavior associated with traditional patterns and the second an instance of the contemporary potential for conflict now that "equality" is recognized. Patterned subservience is not necessarily formal subordination. Rather, the woman's behavior, which was not regarded by men or women as personal abasement, was behavior which lent support to the role of her husband as household head. Understandably her role was beset with contradictions within an extended family where one man was respected above all other males in the household.

Answers to questions about alterations in the traditional pattern reflect an idealization of the mental and physical equality of women and the abstract notion that this is both modern and good.

A wife can do everything her husband can do (Vojvodina).
Everyone should work together, and all should do as much as they can (Serbia).
Tasks shouldn't be divided strictly for men and women. Today a husband and wife help each other so that all the work can be done quickly and well (Serbia).
Some women now work in factories. If they are lucky and have good husbands the husbands help them with the housekeeping. This is as it should be (Slovenia).
If a man and wife are both employed, then they should share the housework. If only the husband goes out to work then the wife should take care of the house (Bosnia).

With the exception of the Montenegrin village, in all other areas the notion of the possibility of the interchangeability of tasks is increasing. One of the Serbian responses says that this is also more efficient. The idea of interchangeability holds for a large variety of activities and seemingly explicitly rejects the old idea about the natural division of labor. In the Slovenian quote, male help with household chores is seen as depending on the goodwill of the husband. Most responses, however, give no qualifications.

The possibility of village women working outside the home, for example, as part-time factory workers, increases the potential for conflict at home. It also brings about new kinds of social problems such as child care when there is no nursery school or mother-in-law or other relative available.

A further result of the times and the attitude is that women today are no longer protected from difficult physical labor. For example the traditional system of reaping wheat in most parts of Yugoslavia was for the men to proceed along the rows cutting down the ripe wheat with scythes, while the women followed behind gathering the fallen stalks and binding them into sheaves. For a variety of reasons including war and the dissolution of extended fraternal *zadrugas* with ample availability of able-bodied men for heavy work, plus the general atmosphere created by the government's stress on political and legal equal rights for women, it is today possible to see women engaged in the arduous task of reaping while their men are in town at factory jobs. The difficult work of plowing, harrowing, and haying is also being done increasingly by women and girls. Formerly women performed these tasks only in a wartime situation.

Women's growing role in agriculture today reflects the exodus of youth, especially boys, from the village, and the situation of the peasant-worker with one foot in the factory in town and the other as part-time farmer on his own land. The relatively smaller-sized families and the transitional state of the modernizing economy places stress on both men and women. The resulting changing roles generate new kinds of stress and tend to render old patterns of patriarchal authority untenable.

In all areas villagers sense tension between traditional ideals and the new values of the postwar period, especially those propagated by the political ideology of the Yugoslav socialist state. These include emphasis on the importance of the role of the industrial worker in helping to build a modern state, on universal education, and on formal legal equality without respect to sex. However the ways in which the new values impact on everyday life and the means by which old patterns are replaced cannot be so easily defined. In part new values are held back by the immediate needs of peasant life and child care requirements as well as by the reluctance of some people, men as well as women, to abandon old ways.

The comments below give an idea of the ambiguities and tensions in contemporary relationships as perceived by villagers:

Formerly women were really exploited. Men could beat them. But today women are men's equals, and a woman with schooling is equal to a man with the same education. However, women have to work more, from morning until night (Slovenia).

Women used to be treated as inferiors. They could not be trusted with decisions. We have a saying, "A woman supports three corners of the house and a man supports only one." The wife always works more than her husband, but his work is harder (Slovenia).

Formerly women were kept in place by their husbands. Marriages were more stable, and the children were more obedient and honest. Today women are equal to men, and this is a great evil. Today one doesn't know who is the head of the household (Serbia).

The relationship between a man and his wife is completely different today. A woman is socially a man's equal. She can do everything a man can. This sounds fine, but it only works in practice in places where there are job opportunities. Here in the village there are great differences between what a man and his wife do. The conditions of village life require a woman to be home, while her husband is able to work away from the house (Vojvodina).

The following statement is by an educated young Serbian woman who grew up in a village but now leads an urban life:

Well, you know, some men are for beating their wives, and some are not. I know men in the village who are 30 or 35 now who think they should. Younger men about 25 are perhaps a little changed. But my cousin Vlado — he's my age and has worked abroad — he beats his wife, believe it or not. This business of wife-beating was not so common earlier when there were large zadrugas. The husband didn't do it, the father-in-law did. My mother told me about one of my aunts when they were all living together in one household. One time my aunt replied to her father-in-law, "Excuse me, but I can't do such and such." That's all she said, and for this he beat her really badly. Her husband was sitting there just looking and couldn't do anything. There was nothing he could do because if he reacted his father might beat him too, even though he was already a man, married and a father himself. Even today in a smaller household where just the old father and mother and their son and daughter-in-law live together, you still find cases where the father-in-law gets angry and takes it out on the daughter-in-law. The son doesn't say anything to his father, unless maybe to agree that the father is right.

But I can think of one way, though, that relations between husband and wives are changing. This has to do with the use of names. My own mother and father, like all village couples of their generation, never addressed each other by name. My father refers to my mother as "she" and she refers to him as "he." When they address each other directly my father says, "Wife, come here!" and my mother replies, *"eh bre, eh bre,"* to let him know that she heard and is coming. I have never heard my parents call each other by name. Of course among younger couples in the village this is not the case.

When people lived together in large households it was felt to be embarrassing to refer to your wife by name in front of other people. Referring to a wife as "she" was almost the same as ignoring her in front of your father or brothers. A young husband would feel ashamed, you know, to show a close relationship with his wife before the other members of the household. Even if he went away to serve in the army his letters home were always to his father and not his wife. But this is changing now too.

In a formal sense the greatest changes have occurred in the Muslim community in Bosnia. A feeling of transformation appears to be greatest among those who matured in the prewar period. This is reflected in the comments of a man from Župča, below:

Most of us agree that woman's position has changed since 1945. Up until then all married women were veiled, of course. They had no schooling, and they did not step outside the household compound and they were thought of as very obedient tools, child-producing machines. Today girls go to school, although here in the village not as long as boys. In many families women now share as equals in making household decisions. They also now go out of the house from time to time.

A woman has to take care of the house while the husband is out working. Women would be able to work in an office, for example, but this is a problem in the village because there are no places to take care of the children. We recognize that women are as smart as men. This can be seen because there are some women doctors, lawyers, teachers and so forth, but still in the village women do not have as much schooling as men, and that is why people have different opinions on this subject.

Whether or not most Muslim men regard their women as obedient tools, the above view is too simplistic, even within veiled and cloistered Muslim village society as it existed in the prewar period. Then as today women were individuals, and some of the more forceful among them tested the limits of traditional restraints. Aspects of this testing are revealed in excerpts from recorded biographies of three Župča women of old age, middle age, and young womanhood. The eldest recalls the time of her marriage:

I remember clearly when I was given in marriage. All was arranged in three days. One evening the man who was to be my husband came to my father's house and he saw me. The next day he came to ask my father for me. Then my mother came to me, kissed me and told me that I had been spoken for. I did not mind the idea of marrying, I did not hesitate. Even though he was a stranger I loved him.

The next day everything was made ready. I was dressed in a most beautiful *dimija* [voluminous silk pants] and blouse. A silk scarf and cap were fastened on my head. Around my neck my mother put a string of gold coins and a string of beads. At midday carts were sent. My parents did not accompany me but my brothers and uncles did. And thus I arrived in Župča at the home of my father-in-law. The wedding party went on for several days.

In the beginning married life was very sad for me. They immediately covered [veiled] me. This was the worst part of it. Here I am an old woman, but I still remember how I tried to resist being covered. I lived together with my father-in-law, mother-in-law, two brothers-in-law and their wives. I would not say that they didn't like me but only that they didn't like me very much.

Those first years were the hardest. But after a while my husband separated from his father. Slowly we built our own house and then left my father-in-law's household. Then it was easier because I was by myself. The children started to arrive. I gave birth to nine. Three of them died and six are alive, three sons and three daughters. With my husband I spent a nice life, and even today he is in my memory. If he were alive I could pour out my heart to him, and that would ease things for me. I can't complain to my children as I would to my husband. I have become old. I have lived a long time, my children are all married and settled, and I would like to close my eyes. I would not like to become a burden to anyone.

The woman of middle age describes childhood unhappiness and her forms of rebellion:

Like other little girls in the village I spent my childhood caring for the cows and sheep and playing in the pastures. I was only ten when my father died, and from that day my life became different. My mother soon remarried. My older brother left the house and went off on his own. I stayed with mother, and it seems to me that I did the hardest housework. My stepfather did not like me and beat me whenever he had a chance. My mother seemed not to notice, and this is what hurt me most.

When I was 15, one morning I got up very early, prepared some clothes in a bundle and left home for the wide world. For the whole day I wandered near the village but could not bear to go further. At nightfall I became frightened and must have fallen asleep in the grass. I woke up the next morning in my home. They had been looking for me and brought me home. I thought they were going to beat me but nobody touched me. They just did not talk to me, and again I was working and working.

When my mother gave birth to a baby girl it got even worse for me. My life became unbearable. About this time a letter arrived from my brother, saying he was settled in Sarajevo and inviting me to come and join him. But they would not let me. I went to the *hodja* [Muslim priest] in the village and told him everything. He wrote to my brother and asked him to come and take me.

When my brother arrived he did not even enter the house but from the threshold ordered me to get ready and come with him. In Sarajevo he worked for a man who had a shop and lived there, and he arranged for me to stay with a woman nearby. I lived among the walls, but still it was better than before. This is the way I spent two years. Then one day a letter came from my mother saying that the stepfather had died and asking me to come home. I could hardly wait, prepared myself and went home. My mother was very glad to see me. My little half sister was already big, three years old. So the three of us lived together until my marriage was arranged.

I married here in the village. My husband was good but my father-in-law never liked me. I lived with my husband for a month and went through hell. One day my father-in-law convinced my husband to get rid of me, and they chased me out of the house. Here's what he said: "You are not good for my father so you are not good for me." I took my things and went back to my mother. Later we were even divorced in court.

In the meantime the war came. I joined the Partisans. You are probably surprised, but I felt I had no other choice. I spent two years cooking and taking care of fighters in the woods. Then I returned to the village, where I stayed until the Liberation.

Seven years passed since my husband divorced me. I had not forgotten him nor he me. One evening I made a *sijelo* [social gathering and sewing bee]. Many people came, including my former husband. He said "Enough, enough, I want to marry you again." So we remarried. He works as a truck driver and we live nicely. We have built a nice house, too. He earns enough and he brings home every dinar. I myself have a veteran's pension. We have two sons, alive and healthy.

Women in the village say, "A good woman does not marry twice." My answer to them is, "If I were not a good woman the same man would not marry me twice."

The third excerpt expresses the sense of change and frustrations felt by a girl not yet married:

Things used to be very different. Girls were not free. They had to hide. The fathers of the young people made all the decisions. Today a girl is free, she can choose whom she wants to be with and where she wants to go. She can go to *sijelo* or *teferica* [picnic] with her friends. Formerly a girl was always chaperoned by her mother or aunt.

When I cut off my braids and got a permanent wave there was a lot of disapproval and gossip. I was one of the first girls in the village to stop wearing *dimija* and put on a dress. It is interesting that although many disapproved, slowly they started to imitate. And today almost every girl in Župča has modern clothes in addition to her *dimija*. As for women, their position is much better than before. As for housework, it seems to me they work as much as before. No changes here! In fact they work even harder. Since many men now work in the mine and don't have time for farming as they used to, the women and girls have to work in the fields as well. Tasks such as sowing, reaping, and harvesting now fall on their shoulders.

Life in the village seems to me to be changing every day. I would like to leave even though I was born here. I would like to marry and live in a city, in Sarajevo, because I would like to change my way of life completely. This is my great wish, but unfortunately it is not realizable. If I were born again I would only study and not live in a village.

As the responses indicate, changes in the relationship between husband and wife and especially changes perceived by villagers themselves do not represent mere progression from a formerly repressed to a presently liberated condition. In the traditional context everyone was locked into an ordered system, each performing a specific role in the social hierarchy. Within that system conflict often occurred when individuals tried to test the limits or break through rigidly set controls. Presently people are achieving a greater sense of individuality, with roles now played out against a more flexible framework, ideally based on mutual consent. With boundaries no longer defined as rigidly as in the past, there is now a need for more conscious accommodation. A problem today is often one of defining limits.

Since the war the Yugoslav socialist revolution, with its accompanying legislation and industrialization efforts, and the general process of modernization have greatly affected relations between men and women, and specifically between husbands and wives. In the villages surveyed, absolute and formalistic assertions of male authority are unusual, but there is a general self-conscious acknowledgement that the village remains more conservative than the city. With the exception of Slovenia, the extended family is still important in modified form, although the ties that bind have definitely loosened. A vital change has been the increasing importance of the husband–wife dyad as opposed to that of father–son, even in the context of the extended family household.

A general view among observers of social change in Yugoslavia has been that patriarchal power has declined, and that women participate in decisions in an atmosphere of some equality. This is an aspect of the situation, surely, but attitudes of male superiority remain (while not always expressed as such). The notion of marriage as a working partnership, while not absent formerly, becomes more important as people begin to think of each other more as individuals and less as occupants of a specific kin status. Illustrative of restricted role playing is the example of village couples not addressing or referring to one another by name.

An important trend derived from the data appears to be that of the ambiguous liberation of self from a series of well-defined roles and duties. Some of these still exist in somewhat altered form. Thus, while a husband may be less tempted to beat his wife, he is also less likely to feel a need to shield her protectively from the outside world. The woman, for her part, no longer performs many of the minor ritual activities designed to invest her husband with status as head of the household, and she is also less likely to see a need for bolstering his self-confidence in dealing with the world beyond the household. This may be replaced in part by a voluntary sense of partnership which, while reducing the forces of compulsion in the relationship, also tends to render the relationship and the household potentially less cohesive.

In any case, it would seem more productive to think of the changing relationships between husbands and wives in the context of the functioning of the household as variations on a theme of mutual interdependence and not in any unilineal framework of evolvement toward equality. While the changes which are occurring are real and readily identifiable, their overall meaning in the context of the complex ties existing between husband and wives is not easy to define. Less formal subordination for the wife, less rigid obligations for the husband, greater personal identity for both, and overlap of areas of work and decision making, perhaps greater conflict of authority, apparently less use of force as a sanction by the husband — these aspects now exist against a background of economic development, a higher standard of living, more education, and more alternatives in crucial life choices. These result in a diminution of the theme of natural differences between the sexes. They are effecting a different kind of life but not necessarily a totally more satisfying one.

REFERENCES

DJURIĆ, V. *editor*
  1967   *Vukovi zapisi* [Vuk's notes]. Belgrade: Srpska književna zadruga. (Originally published 1827.)
East European Quarterly
  1970   Ethnology in Yugoslavia since World War II: a review of research and publications. *East European Quarterly* 4(3):328–342.
HALPERN, JOEL M.,
  1967   *A Serbian Village*, revised edition. Colophon Books. New York: Harper and Row. (Originally published 1958. New York: Columbia University Press.)
  1969a   "The people," in *Southeast Europe, a guide to basic publications*. Edited by Paul L. Horecky, 493–550. Chicago: University of Chicago Press.
  1969b   "The society," in *Southeast Europe, a guide to basic publications*. Edited by Paul L. Horecky, 571–581. Chicago: University of Chicago Press.

1969c *Bibliography of English language sources on Yugoslavia*, revised edition. Research Reports 3. Amherst: University of Massachusetts Department of Anthropology.

HALPERN, JOEL M., BARBARA K. HALPERN
1972 *A Serbian village in historical perspective*. New York: Holt, Rinehart and Winston.

SALZMANN, ZDENEK
1970 "English language publications on Yugoslavia since World War II," in *East European anthropology*. Edited by Zdenek Salzmann, 1–42. Research Reports 5. Amherst: University of Massachusetts Department of Anthropology.

Kinship and Politics in a Village of Lorraine: The Impossible Democracy

CLAUDE KARNOOUH

RÉSUMÉ: LA DÉMOCRATIE IMPOSSIBLE: PARENTÉ ET
POLITIQUE DANS UN VILLAGE LORRAIN

S'il est difficile de donner une définition du politique — concept éminemment variable — on s'aperçoit que, loin d'être limité à la Cité ou à l'État, il subsiste, caché et en partie distinct de la politique nationale, dans les villages, sous des formes différentes et autonomes,
   A la question de savoir si État et Politique sont inséparables, l'ethnologie contemporaine apporte une reponse négative : nombre de sociétes sans État, marquées par l'importance structurale et fonctionnelle des liens de parenté, sont le théâtre de luttes politiques intenses.
   Le politique pourrait être défini comme étant l'ensemble des moyens — contraintes institutionnelles, valeurs idéologiques — qui permettent l'existence et l'exercice du pouvoir en un lieu et à une époque donnés. Au terme de cette analyse, toute relation sociale peut être conçue comme une relation politique.
   Dans nos sociétés occidentales, les relations entre les communautés paysannes et les États qui les régissent se limitent à un contôle par l'État de la compétition entre groupes locaux, à condition de voir respecter sa souveraineté globale. Seuls lui sont étroitement soumis les associations, cliques, groupements ou partis qui, se situant dans le temps et l'espace de l'État, peuvent constituer un péril pour son intégrité. Ainsi l'État est souverain parce qu'il laisse opérer des régulations internes sur le mode traditionnel, donc intégrateur. Il faut donc établir un écart qualitatif entre les réseaux de pouvoir de l'État, et ceux élaborés par le pouvoir local, ces derniers procédant d'une logique particulière et différente. Les sociétés locales forment des entités politiques originales, maintenant le cours de leur propre destin tout en s'accommodant d'une règle institutionnelle unique.
   La présente recherche vise à comparer des séries de systèmes locaux ou des sous-systèmes, selon le point de référence, de manière à dégager ensuite les divers modèles indigènes du pouvoir local, le Politique étant considéré comme un fait universel, immanent à toutes les manifestations de la vie sociale. L'exemple choisi se situe en France, où la plus petite collectivité institutionnellement organisée est la commune, recouvrant un espace social légué, à travers divers avatars, par l'aurore de l'histoire nationale. Mais dans ce pays centralisé à l'extrême, ce sont

moins les transformations législatives ou économiques qui renversent l'organisa-tion sociale locale que leurs effets sur la démographie.

Le phénomène électoral — apparemment manifestation tangible de l'emprise de l'État sur le monde paysan — révèle, une fois encore, les spécificités du conflit local, où les acteurs parviennent à conserver la maîtrise des règles du jeu interne, l'autonomie locale se bornant, pour survivre, à se dissimuler sous le formalisme légal.

La "petite politique" à l'échelle villageoise n'a pas moins de violence que la politique à l'échelle nationale. Elle se révèle dans toute son intensité au cours de la période préélectorale, où les conflits, auxquels tous les villageois participent selon des règles fixes, atteignent leur paroxysme. Les concepts traditionnels de la science politique perdent leur validité dans l'étude du pouvoir municipal où les luttes ancestrales se substituent, au profit de catégories parentales et familiales, à des prééminences de partis ou de catégories sociales.

Au terme de cette analyse de l'interaction entre parenté et politique, et de la valeur attribuée au terme "famille," on peut affirmer que, pour la pensée indi-gène, le modèle idéal des comportements et des attitudes au sein de la parentèle — donc dans les rapports politiques — devrait relever d'une force affective analogue à celle qui règle les relations au sein de la famille conjugale : le terme de "famille" marque tous les membres d'une parentèle de signes sociologiques identiques à ceux qui définissent la solidarité de la famille conjugale. L'action politique fait intervenir, en le modifiant, le même réseau de parenté que celui réglant l'appropriation foncière. Un même ensemble signifiant servira donc aux acteurs à régler la circulation des terres et à articuler les stratégies de pouvoir, le réseau travaillant dans le sens de la fission quand il s'agit des terres, le pouvoir le faisant travailler dans le sens de la fusion.

L'idéologie égalitaire, respectée dans les pratiques foncières, est créée par la pratique du pouvoir, bien que le discours égalitaire efface les différences entre vainqueurs et vaincus, estompant les rapports de subordination et dissimulant à la société globale l'exacte nature des conflits.

Le discours politique, ne détermine pas, par son lexique, un champ social particulier : c'est le code de parenté qui différencie radicalement la société locale de l'ensemble national dont elle est un élément. Instrument du pouvoir latent, il agit au détriment de l'institution muncicpale qui se révèle peu significative.

Kinship and politics are two terms which are not usually associated with each other, especially in a study claiming to describe the everyday life of a Western community. Kinship is a term from the vocabulary of ethnogra-phy, and in spite of differences between different schools it is a word which covers a sociological range which is quite strictly circumscribed (Dumont 1971), while on the other hand politics is a term which is invariably ambiguous. This is true despite the impressive number of works devoted to politics over the years, for the definitions and contents of such a concept have varied in accordance with the theories which formulated the works.

When it is a question of making a synthesis, the scholar is confronted by learned or even brilliant works which, however, leave the ethnologists at a loss in the face of problems which politics sets for society. For example, must politics be regarded as a part of a whole, or as the all-embracing whole upon which all social activities are dependent? Is it necessary to keep alive (in one sense or another) all political thought which, since the time of Machiavelli, has led to making an autonomous theoretical subject of the concept? The question is certainly a big one, and one which it is not easy to resolve. But it has been asked ever since politics became a theoretical field of study, and it recurs whenever an *ad hoc* sociological study examines and attempts to clarify it.

Political life is not restricted to the city or the state. It is found far away from towns, somewhat removed from history, secret, hidden, tucked away in villages, where it pursues its course in the protective and often oppressive shadow of the central government, existing in various and independent forms.

And yet this local politics, this "small politics," has in a similar way been forsaken by modern scholars. It seems to arouse the curiosity of researchers only insofar as its implications have repercussions on national politics. The power structure of a small village is of no interest to political sociology, which demonstrates an *a priori* haughty disdain for such "parochial politics." It prefers the ideological debates of the main national parties, the contests of oratory between their leaders, and voting intentions. It attaches over-importance to the center, while underestimating the periphery: the first is very political because the second is hardly so at all.

Nonetheless, political life is not entirely based on national politics. One has only to spend a few weeks in a small provincial town or village to be convinced of this. Here political life, riddled with "nothings" and agitated by "insignificant" disputes, reveals forces which are so powerful that some people commit their wealth, intelligence, and reputation to it, at the risk of being engulfed in the contempt of their fellow-countrymen.

Is politics limited to the state and ideologies which inspire those serving and opposing it? Are politics and the state two social fields covering the same area? And is there any relationship between these fields? These questions can be reduced to one single query: are the state and politics inseparable? Are they both the scenes upon which the webs of power are woven? Theories appear to be quite divided, if not contradictory, on this question. One concept commonly held claims a parallel between the absence of the state and the absence of politics but, one of the principal contributions of contemporary ethnology has been to prove that the contrary is true (Fortes and Evans-Pritchard 1940).

For a long time European sociology was promoting hypotheses according to which the state and politics were synonymous. However, for some forty years various ethnological investigations have been upsetting this analogy. Apart from certain theoretical divergences which have yet to be cleared up with respect to the extent and functions of politics,[1] it is apparent that there are an impressive number of societies without a state structure, which are marked by the structural and functional importance of links of kinship, but which stand out because of the intensity of the political struggles raging in them.[2]

Thus we are led to record the presence of conflict in all its forms in the process which may lead either the dominant class, or a kinship group, or a religious sect to the use of power. But in speaking of violence, are we not speaking of relationships between human groups, that is to say, alliances and divisions, tactics and strategy? For Marx, politics (and the state) involves violence, coercion, subordination, manipulation, and all practices permitting the existence and maintenance of capitalist power in any form whatsoever. We have verified that politics can exist without a state, but why should this not set similar processes going? Conflict is a part of all human societies, a fact which should not surprise anyone, for it seems obvious that it governs confrontation between human groups and individuals: this assumes the presence of differences which originate and are maintained at all levels of the social milieu, bringing about an imbalance in relationships and the birth of dependency relationships.

Any analysis of power must take into consideration the fact that power involves two participants in unequal relationship with each other, for, as R. Guidieri notes, "on the contrary, it seems to us that even where the relationship is direct and immediate, we must examine its duration, fragility and adaptability. In doing this we must take into account that there is always a winner and a loser in every contract. This is so even if an 'egalitarian' ideology hides this inadequacy between the two participating parties through a strict code such as kinship" (1969:136). Seen from this point of view politics will henceforth be presented as the sum total of means (institutional constraints and ideological values) permitting the existence and exercising of power, here or elsewhere, long ago or recently.

The question may be asked as to whether this body of hypotheses leads us to define every social relationship as political in nature. The reply is affirmative. But here it is a question of discovering whether the specific features of European peasant societies which for centuries have been subjected to the burden of centralism support these hypotheses.

---

[1]   There is certainly quite a large theoretical distance between the supporters of reciprocity (Marcel Mauss, Claude Lévi-Strauss) and those who regard reciprocity as a cover-up for the work of politics within structures where it is expressed: kinship, economic, and so on.

[2]   It is not possible to quote here all the ethnological works which discuss political struggles among acephalous societies. We should remember recent American works concerned with Melanesian and Polynesian societies; also Ettore Blocca's work (1970). This is without forgetting the works of the British school, of which E. E. Evans-Pritchard, Meyer Fortes, John Middleton and Max Gluckman are the most famous representatives. Finally we may stress the French works of Georges Balandier, Françqis Lapierre, Pierre Clastres and R. Guidieri.

PEASANT SOCIETIES

Three theoretical trends divide sociological and ethnological investigations regarding the relationships between peasant communities and the governments which control them. The first regards this relationship as a stable interaction between two poles of a social continuum. This presupposes a common ideological basis in discussions between both partners, whatever the quantitative variations that may affect it (Frankenberg 1966). Nothing is less reliable. The second does not acknowledge this continuity *a priori*, but introduces it *a posteriori*. This permits the restoration of the special nature of certain variables (chosen *a priori* with regard to specific local characteristics). It might be said that this is attempting to characterize a rural community less for itself than for its relationship with the opposite pole, i.e. the state (Jollivet 1965:53). Although this approach to the problem attempts to rediscover the special nature and irreducible extent of microcultures and the peculiar history of each peasant community (Mendras 1965), it does not seek to define analytical variables through the actual qualities of the participants. A third approach to the problem, however, requires a reconsideration of the preceding hypotheses and the empirical bearings they presuppose.

Many of the phenomena present in the rural world appear to bear an originality which should be discerned by and for itself. The village street of Lorraine and the quasi-town of the local market centers of Provence are two cultures strange to one another (Bloch 1964:11; Roubin 1970). Between the forests and pasture land of Brittany and the regions of open fields the native concept of space undergoes irreducible transformations. Moreover, some authors have reversed the continuity hypothesis so as to regard the relationship between the state and peasant communities as a series of discontinuous social groups. This is what we were being invited to believe (without it being clearly formulated) by those working according to the principles of a *continuum a posteriori* when they laid stress on the original features of the history of peasant communities (Mendras 1967). To do this one has to assess the gap between the political life of the state and that of local areas. Wolf (1965) attempted to do this when he wrote: ". . . we must not confuse the theory of state sovereignty with the facts of political life." Thus the state appears to renounce its control of competition between local groups provided that its overall sovereignty is respected. Only those associations cliques, groups, or parties which may endanger the state's integrity by expanding the range of their thoughts and actions to the latter's time and space are strictly subject to the central authorities (Porchnev 1972).

Peasant communities, rather like jigsaw puzzles, with dissimilar parts juxtaposed and ideologically appointed as national territory by the state, define the relationship of individuals in the residential group with special spatial and temporal categories whose structures cooperate with a specific logic (Bailey 1971). Expressed in functionalist terms, the discontinuity hypothesis presents the state as sovereign because it allows internal regulations to function in traditional ways, thereby being highly integrating in its operation. Although the state's final goal is inclined to be toward totalitarian control of its constituent parts, the necessary though contradictory result is to block creativity and therefore productivity in peasant communities (Arend 1966).[3]

The hypothesis of latent discontinuity leads us logically to the establishment of a qualitative disparity between the power networks erected by the state and those worked out by local authorities. The gaps in the nets of the first permit the latter to function and even to pursue their own historical course (Wolf 1965). Consequently we would have two parallel systems which coincide or are ignorant of each other, according to their own dynamics. One would readily agree that mediation and rules are necessary to avoid too many tensions between the two networks. But this does not prohibit local systems from proceeding in their own special, different, and irreducible patterns of behavior with respect to each other and the central authorities.[4] The village, the community, the small region, in short, the local territory, does not constitute a miniaturized form of the central government; on the contrary, autocracy, tyranny, or peasant democracy always represent original forms of local power. How often these human groups have to conform to a single institutional standard, however much we would like to deny it. In fact this is where the special nature of European rural communities resides. And one of the goals of this study is to show how a local community accommodates this fact, while at the same time maintaining the course of its own destiny.

The choosing of discontinuity hypotheses will help us to clarify the preceding analysis from the point of view of the participants alone, though it goes without saying that this is an essential point of view. The limitations and instruments of local power provide these participants with relevant criteria insofar as they are capable of controlling them, in order to use them as effectively as possible. And we may readily imagine the limitations inherent in such an approach, which on occasion may shock those supporting the theory of the omnipotence of state power. This paper is not a rejection of the idea of a comparison between the state and peasant communities based on the *continuum a posteriori*, but is in fact proposing two approaches which are not mutually exclusive. The first is

[3]   The Stalinist attempt to control all aspects of local life resulted above all in the whole of Russian rural society grinding to a halt — becoming immobilized to the point that it functioned only to ensure its own biological survival.

[4]   Such mediations obviously take different forms. They are of an institutional nature, but they may just as easily appear in the most authoritarian guise with the courts and especially the police.

aimed at comparing series of local systems or subsystems, according to the point of reference, in order to be able to sort out the various indigenous forms of local power. The second approach seeks to pin down changes in microsystems which have been induced by the state, according to their form and the instruments used to implement them. The first attitude pursues a line of thought which regards politics as a universal fact, immanent in all manifestations of social life. The second opens the way to research focused on the operations of contemporary power in its relationships with the groups which constitute and are governed by it. It has been decided to develop the first theme here, not because it has any greater scientific value, but simply because of the general orientation of the work. Finally, there is nothing to prevent us from pursuing and considering relationships between the state and peasant communities with respect to the degree of autonomy which reverts to the latter at the expense of the former. However, it is by laying down as premises the absence of the state and the presence of politics that we have gradually been led to establish the concept of "discontinuous removal" of the state.

THE NATION

The example chosen for discussion is located in France. But first a brief description of the actual location and situation of the French village within the total national context would be of help.

When on looks at the modern French political arena it seems to be limited to the capital and to a few towns which encompass the national territory within the web of the urban fabric. However, France is made up of 38,000 communes, which are mainly rural, with many of them very sparsely populated. The creation in 1789 of this new administrative division was most often limited to changing the name of the former administrative division, the parish, without changing its boundaries. Thus the smallest community institutionally organized by the Republic generally conformed to the pattern of the Monarchy, which had itself retained a social position bequeathed since the very dawn of the nation's history (Duby 1962).[5]

The centralization of French administration is not just a figure of speech. France is a state where all decisions concerning the public sphere are subject to the approval of the central authorities or their representatives. One might well wonder whether such powerful control acting for so long a period would allow local peculiarities to continue to exist, except

---

[5] We should note that the modern use of the term *commune* does not mean the same as the term *commune* as used in the Middle Ages, when it served to define a town which had acquired its freedom at the expense of the feudal authority (Petit-Dutaillis 1947).

as folklore. This hypothetical result can be completely rejected by a study of local facts, when they are stripped of the glittering cloak of centralized institutions.

The state and its officials in authority are never very far removed from the village. The prefect, the police, the tax collector, the civil engineer, the justice of the peace, and the director of the military forces exercise a tight control of village life. But are they able to force the peasants to follow rules of conduct which differ too much from the laws of their own class? Furthermore, we know that political regimes which were far more authoritarian have, at their cost, experienced the passive or violent resistance of the peasants when they were not able to adapt to the traditional game of making "innovations" and imposing them by force. True changes only take place with the death of a culture;[6] as long as a culture possesses any vitality, external pressures (even if some of them affect different aspects of social organization) combine with the cultural world of the community without overturning it. And many writers have recorded how peasant communities deviate from, move away from, or completely side-track decisions of the state which do not correspond with their own practices (Mendras 1967). It may also be asserted that it is not really legislative or economic changes which overthrow local social organization; more often it is the demographic changes which result from them.[7] Only then can all the instruments of central government, of force, operate without any opposition — over depopulated villages and reduced populations ready to accept anything, because they have lost everything.

But before slipping or being engulfed in the Jacobean abstraction of urban political practices (reserved for what may conveniently be called "the political class"), peasant communities resist and still demand to retain a power based on former knowledge. How can one fail to see in this final rejection the expression of the different quality of power when it is exercised among human groups where the personal history of each participant is known by all his partners; where an individual's reputation is the achievement of his ancestors; where, in short, the common area appropriated by all also serves as a social definition for existence itself?

In somewhat veiled terms a situation which sociologists usually call "face to face" has just been described, but the expression "back to back" (Bailey 1971:ch. 1) is to be preferred since it accurately translates both the humdrum existence of individual relationships and the conflict underlying all social relationships. After having been *homo faber*, then *homo*

---

[6]   This problem is treated by modern-day ethnology on a more general level; see especially the studies made of American Indian cultures.

[7]   This remark leads us to envisage a qualitative demography where the operative concept of the threshold allows one to determine the limits beyond and below which a social organization can or cannot function.

economicus, will man become simply *homo politicus*? The question has been asked, and it is hoped to give a partial reply to it here.

THE VILLAGE WITHIN THE NATION

One might well ask if the tackling of the study of local power through a description of municipal elections does not represent a clear renunciation of the assumptions on which the hypotheses of this paper are based. Is this not covering up local diversity through national uniformity? However, an opportunity to explain the approach once again arises out of this apparent contradiction. By government decree all the small communes were invited, on a fixed date, to participate in the national "ritual" of democratic voting, a kind of lay communion required by the state on a national scale. Together they elect the authorities of municipal power. At the appointed hour and day rural (and urban) France performs the republican rite. But is this artificial actualization of local conflicts not an additional factor contributing to the standardization of rural communities? Despite the legal obligation which forces peasant communities to play the game of power in concert, all treatises on villages show us the specific features of the local conflict quite clearly when the subject is dealt with.[8] But however oppressive it may be, this constraint does not prevent the participants from retaining control over the rules of the internal game. And everything leads one to believe that this hinders development and therefor the solution to certain conflicts.

Nevertheless, it is the necessities of politics and urban and industrial economy which impel the bourgeois state to become reconciled with the peasant world. This is done, sometimes without its knowledge, in order to obtain the advantages of an alliance against the workers. The constraints of national political practice thus permit peasant communities to preserve the autonomy of their power system, at least in part.

This unchanging policy of French governments since the first third of the nineteenth century has not made relationships easier between a working class and a peasantry which all too often followed two parallel paths. The leaders of the proletarian movement too frequently associated the smallholding peasants (the majority of the rural class) with the leading provincial citizens who spoke in their name in Paris. But what kind of control could be exerted over the obviously abstract policy of the capital by men who for the most part spoke languages and dialects which were far removed from the political rhetoric of Paris? Nevertheless, the

---

[8] It is not possible to quote here all the treatises on villages to which we allude in this text. However, these differences are seen no matter what the authors' theoretical positions are. The difficulties in interpretation arise from the fact that most of the authors discuss the subject implicitly, without devoting any special attention to it.

temporary alliance between the bourgeoisie and the peasantry did not prevent local autonomy from hiding under the formalism of the laws imposed, in order to survive.[9]

"Small politics" is no less affected by waves of violence than "big politics." The superficial peacefulness of the everyday life of many villages is pierced by violent conflicts, the form and expression of which make peasants resemble exotic "savages" more than worldly politicians: in spite of the prescribed institutional machinery, it is more a question for them of who is the strongest. This is because they are under the vigilant observation of their neighbors and relatives.

No one would try to limit local politics to an actual or impending election. The numerical results do not reflect the status of public opinion, as in a city. Instead they represent the parts of a system, a well-known game which has been taking place for many months between individuals and the formal or informal groups which are participating on this occasion.[10] It is the preelectoral period which is most important. This is the time when the partially integrated observer may see revealed the tensions, discussions, and techniques which are normally enveloped in mists of silence. In this sense the absence of phenomena which are characteristic of all electoral preparations will later be shown to have been very relevant.

If one wished to define local politics in a general way one could compare it with an imp — which briefly shows its face and then recedes into the depths of the house, having been only fleetingly seen. Election time is a privileged occasion: it excites, enlivens conversations, arouses passions. It blows up conflicts to extremes — conflicts which on other occasions progress secretly through manipulation and backbiting. Familiar and humdrum, local politics does not belong to any reserved domain. It does not arise from any specialized activity, one restricted to certain people: in other words, it is not a private operation. All or nearly all the inhabitants of a village participate in it by following rules which they have no intention of changing.

Because they are incapable of providing us with effective instruments of analysis, the traditional concepts of political science are useless. The idea of a political party, which is only alive when legislative elections take place, has no meaning at all with regard to municipal power. The ideas of "right" and "left" become blurred and are replaced by parental and family groupings. The public interest becomes confused with quarrels

---

[9]   The fate of the small peasantry under governmental politics in the past ten years allows us to assert that it was a question of a temporary alliance, even though it may have lasted for over a century.

[10]   The municipal council of a village sometimes resembles the leadership of certain political parties, because it reflects temporary combinations between people who have practically daily contact with each other.

whose origin have often become lost in the memories of the participants. Here the concepts of bourgeoisie, proletariat, trained staff, or trade unions prove to be powerless over events. Nevertheless, men and women live in the village without necessarily exercising their professional activities there. Besides the farmers who are the only ones working in the area, we also find factory workers, public service employees, household workers, and a whole range of individuals whose productive work would be defined by sociologists as belonging to the national level. Why should one stand aloof and assume the presence in this village of an unchangeable hiatus with the nation as a whole when concerned with a study of political power? The demographic and sociological history of the village since the end of the nineteenth century suggests a first response to this question. The information provided by this sheds new light on the elections of May 1971.

THE VILLAGE

The commune of Grand-Failly is located in the *arrondissement* of Briey, which occupies the northern end of the *département* of Meurthe et Moselle, near the Belgian and Luxembourgian borders. The village belongs to the region known historically as *Pays-Haut* (literally "the highlands"), which forms an enclave of plateaus and depressions extending from the Ardennes in the east, to the banks of the Moselle in the west. Relatively distant from the industrial centers of the department (Longwy, the Fench basin, the mining basin of Briey), the commune has retained a very distinct rural character. No buildings or secondary residences have been built up to now to upset the spatial layout of Grand-Failly, which still presents the prototype image of the Lorraine village street, with its grey houses, with manure heaps at the front, stretching out the whole length of the only street. Behind the houses the kitchen gardens, which disappear to give place to open fields, form a second row. The monotony of the grey and pale ocher-colored peasant houses is broken here and there by red, violet, green, or yellow shutters from the workers' houses, simple farms newly coated in plaster. At the time of the 1963 census the commune was populated by 309 inhabitants, who occupied almost all of the houses, with 41 percent of the active population being factory workers. Divided between workers and peasants, this village has nevertheless retained its traditional cultural coherence.

This cohesion in the local community appears to be due to the special forms of its slow economic and social evolution. Present-day agricultural holdings are still medium-sized and three-year rotation is still practiced by certain peasants or has only very recently been abandoned. Furthermore, with regard to economic practices the large majority of farmers are trying to escape the monetary channels.[11] Changes affecting communal life occurred in two periods. The first, which started around 1850 and ended after the First World War, was characterized by a mass exodus of agricultural workers (both skilled workers and day-laborers) and the small farmer-artisan group, which caused a serious depletion of the village's population (Lamarche 1969).

The second period, on the other hand, arose out of a change of professional occupation. This period started at the end of the Second World War and was marked by peasants abandoning the working of the land in favor of industrial work, though without thereby leaving the village.[12] In fact they continue to reside on the family farms and to retain ownership of their land. They either continue to spend some time working this land outside their working hours in the factory, or else they rent it to those of their relatives who have remained farmers. Thus the working group does not constitute an element foreign to the local community, as would be the case with imported labor seeking the economic advantages of cheap lodgings. Through the land they own and the family relationships which link them to the peasants, the workers share completely the values and history of the rural society of Lorraine. In spite of a socioprofessional cleavage which might appear upon superficial observation to be based on radically opposed social patterns, the village of Grand-Failly, on the contrary, presents the image of a solid community: "a village which is self-contained."

The accident of regional industrialization and its demographic repercussions on a population marked by the cultural unity derived from its age-long occupation of the land allowed the villages of the *Pays-Haut* to preserve strong peasant traditions when they managed to avoid urbanization. The fact that a powerful industry has only provoked a few changes in a local social organization foreign to the industry's logic cannot but surprise the ethnologist, who is confronted by a paradox which defies all sociological theories of change. After the first visits to the area one might well have thought that the presence in the village of a significant minority of workers from the iron and steel industry would have altered their political behavior. But then the evidence had to be faced: the workers of Grand-Failly had not transposed the class conflicts they had begun to experience in the factory to the peasant farmers.[13] On the contrary, they had brought the village to the factory. With one exception, trade union membership was nonexistent. And in the factory the joint responsibilities

[11]   The common disappeared in 1962.
[12]   The factories of the iron and steel basin of Longwy pick up their workers by a bus service which extends as far as eighty kilometers from the place of work.
[13]   The paradox of the regional position of Grand-Failly allows one to challenge both the American empirical school of social change and Marxist theoretical sociology on the role of productive labor.

of these alleged proletarians are worked out with regard to residential groups, neighborhood relationships, and family relationships experienced in the village (Karnoouh 1972). This is one of the lessons learned from work on the land[14] and from those who live on it. The debt is a big one. How can it be paid?

THE ELECTORAL CAMPAIGN

A chance observer arriving in the village in the course of the two or three weeks preceding municipal elections would be astonished by the absence of evidence indicating the existence of opposing parties. While the towns are covered with a colored maze of contradictory posters, here everything is calm. The only official signboard is a simple wooden plaque attached to the wall of the combined school and town hall, protected by a partly torn-away grill-work. It displays, over the prefect's signature, the official notice proclaiming the date of the forthcoming elections. There are no inscriptions painted on the walls of ruined houses; no public meetings; no handbills on electricity poles; no slogans drawn on the miry asphalt of the streets. And if by chance this visitor should enter the café at the end of an afternoon he would hear animated conversations break off between the few tables of men drinking their evening aperitifs. Daily life would seem dull and almost insignificant to him, apparently unaware of the struggles which are secretly livening it.

However, without penetrating the secrets of the kitchen, the observer who shares the confidences of certain families will gradually see tongues loosening, backbiting being exposed, and disparaging opinions declared. If he has a great deal of patience and his presence does not reduce everyone to silence, then he may be fortunate enough to witness some of the rare disputes which break out in the café.

The villagers' behavior now changes, at least for those who know how to look for this. Certain people who previously used to greet each other now avoid each other, while on the other hand those who never even spoke to each other now visit openly. Some of the regulars at the "bistro" no longer come; they may be seen hastily taking to their cars to go to the next town to buy their cigarettes and petrol. Alliances and divisions crystallize, signified merely by simple gestures, a word, by the drink exchanged after work or before taking the bus to go to the factory. No one greets his neighbor without real reason; every "good day", "good

---

[14] This work is the result of a land inquiry which was developed in the course of numerous visits to the area. Many subjects were tackled there before specifically undertaking the study of local politics during the last two years. On the occasion of the municipal elections of March 1971 a film was made, the purpose of which was to show the indigenous patterns which guide political thought and action (Karnoouh et al. 1971).

evening" and "how are you?" is heavily loaded with meaning. On each occasion the indigenous code must be interpreted, for it has taken on the strangeness of a foreign language: it requires translation.

Such a situation thus prevented us from using a questionnaire which would have condemned us to receiving only a series of stereotyped replies. Certainly one or two residents would have spoken up, but it would have been impossible to tie together the threads of an impassioned conversation without having intimate knowledge of the village, without having established relationships of friendship which only trust will sanction. Accusations (whether they are true or false is not the question) require numerous cross-checks which could be supplied by the few men who are in a position to judge day by day how much credit should be given to them. These natives speak French; no ocean or frontier separates us from their village. To describe and analyze politics in Grand-Failly requires some discretion if one always believes in the value of the spoken word.

Having been filed on the day before the elections (as permitted by law) the two lists side by side represent the results of long bargainings, arduous haggling which has gone on for over a year. For a whole year they will have been assuring themselves of faltering votes, gaining new ones to their cause, estranging those who sympathize with their adversaries, casting doubt on the moral qualities of opponents.

The first list, the "social action list," is made up for the main part of the members of the previous municipal council, except for the mayor and one councillor who are not represented, and a councillor who died as the result of an accident. The second list, "the list for renewal and communal understanding," suggests by its title that it is canvassing for municipal power without wishing thereby to divide the inhabitants of the village. It includes some of those "rejected" from the first list, to which certain marginal elements are added. However, these temporary names do not actually translate the real situation. Each camp brings together interests which a fortiori shatter the unity of the residential group.[15]

Independently of the lists no candidate is allocated any symbol likely to associate him with national politics. It is true that in the course of private conversations some may declare themselves to be on the "left" or "right" when speaking of legislative elections; however, on both lists one finds individuals belonging to both political leanings. Moreover, we were astonished to note that two opposed candidates belonged to a leftist party well known for the strictness of its discipline. This is what aroused our curiosity and led us to seek elsewhere for the solution of this paradox.

---

[15]   The unity of the residential group forms part of the overall ideology of the inhabitants. They are the basis of the residential groups which ritually oppose each other on patronal festivals (Karnoouh 1972).

One must recall the superficial calm of communal life, the absence of posters and slogans and of publicly declared professions of faith. Underground violence and individual encounters are the only instruments of propaganda. Public behavior, greetings, shunning, all these shape the outline and limits which determine allied or opposed groups. Those who do not respect them are making a mistake which is at once subject to sanctions by the group to which they belong. One candidate who is a jovial and very friendly person made a show of demonstrating to everyone that he intended to keep personal friends in both camps. This man, secretary of the local trade union Fédération Nationale des Syndicats d'Exploitants Agricoles), chairman of the hunting club and vice-president of the fishing club, heads institutions grouping either members of a professional group or individuals sharing similar leisure activities in the commune. Through all his activities this candidate thought he would be able to maintain the unity of these groups beyond differences created by the municipal conflict. Thus, in order to put his beliefs into action, during the last weeks before the election he openly visited those of his adversaries with whom he had friendly or institutional relations. Very quickly community vengeance groups accused him of playing a double game. One evening in the café, when the candidates from his own list were gathered together, he was publically treated as a "hypocrite," as a result of which he felt himself obliged to change his tactics, which he did (but not without some hesitation). However, the error was fatal for him; he lost his position in the town hall, and harvested the scorn of adversaries and allies alike. He had not understood that the various offices he held were thankless jobs or honors without power. The villagers understood this, since they had conferred the status of "outsider" on the man, although he had lived in the commune for over fifteen years (Karnoouh 1972). In their eyes he had committed an unforgivable blunder which his position as an "outsider" made irreversible; he was suspected of having made an attempt at reconciliation from which he would have been the sole beneficiary, in defiance of the rules of the game. This was a personal benefit, so thus it was unacceptable to the overall ideology of the residential group since it occurred outside the procedures necessary for the appropriation of power.

Behavior and attitudes are not the only phenomena to reveal the village's division into two hostile groups. Conversations with local residents also express relationships developed by each of the two factions. Once again we find a gap between the facade of a united and peaceful community and the internal, violent, and sectarian conversation. After sketching a brief outline of the attitudes, the methods of articulation between the two sides of local politics will be described.

VILLAGE REPRESENTATION

Like the electoral campaign, native conversation shows alternately its two faces, according to where it is heard: inside or outside the village. Conversation, when it is directed to the outside world or, if one prefers, to society as a whole, undergoes certain changes.

The first concern here is to present an image of peacefulness to the outside world[16] and to avoid, if the occasion should arise, any curious or meddlesome attention directed to the intimacy of the conflict. The ethnologist arriving in Grand-Failly full of good intentions, generous and innocent, is nothing more than a representative of the city, a bigwig, as it were. And if by chance his aversion to neckties should make him prefer a more careless way of dress he may occasion suspicion or surprise in those with whom he talks. He is a person of importance belonging to the world of the state; in that he resembles the subprefect, although more often he is placed in the same category as a tax collector. At the beginning of the investigation it is also not surprising to obtain an incomplete representation of the community: a performance staged so as to affront the state.

This performance, like all performances, has its own setting and its own text. We have observed that the setting is conspicuous by its absence: neither electoral campaign, nor posters, nor slogans. As to the text, it may be divided into three acts which are played simultaneously. The first appeals for unanimity of the inhabitants behind the group of municipal councillors headed by a "leader," the mayor, who never fails to remind the ethnologist: "here we are all comrades." Of course there are also a few black sheep (generally one's opponents), but they prefer to present them as fringe elements and not as opponents. This makes it much easier not to speak of local conflict. Faced with the alleged representative of the world community, the dominant group, the administrators of municipal power, prefer to regard their adversaries as being outside local society. Nevertheless, these outcasts permit the group to accede to power for the time being. Thus it is a question of erasing all signs, obliterating all evidence, which would lead people to suspect the bitterness of struggles: the village is inhabited by "friends" who have dealt with the aberrations of a few thoughtless persons, "madmen" or "jealous people."

The second part of the text stresses the reasons motivating the choice of candidates and the preparation of a list. The arguments invoked refer to the management qualities of those elected: "We've got some good people here," "He has to be capable, otherwise it's not worth the trouble." Every decision appears to be directed by standards stressing technical and administrative efficiency. This habitual and banal talk (which is

---

[16]   On the native definition of the different circles of social membership and the boundaries between the local world and the outside world, see Karnoouh (1972).

similar to that of society as a whole) is easily intelligible to the researcher, who thereby thinks he is facing a "modern" local community. Why should one get excited, when it is so easy to call upon competent people to administer such a small village?

Finally the third theme serves as a conclusion on the style of moral thought. When they define municipal power in a general sense the natives strongly deny any reference to politics, a term they reserve solely for legislative elections. The French term "politics" is not essentially local; municipal elections "are not politics, for where there is politics people are quarreling." This expression seems to be affected by a negative value which is liable to pollute friendly relationships among villagers. Everything leads one to the belief that the idea of politics is rejected insofar as it does not express the essential concerns of one's fellow residents. Thus in its performance local society stresses the pernicious influence of the outside world, which carries with it the germs of evil, the source of all conflicts: it is not the fault of the actors if struggles upset the village; the fault lies in the "politics," whose impurity is gradually invading the community, which previously was untarnished by it. In order to assert their purity in the face of the moral pollution of the outside world, the actors reject the title of "politics" for their internal conflicts (Bailey 1971).[17] The concept and the word do not belong to traditional peasant semantics, though one might have assumed that they were part of it, possessed as they were of republican teaching. But they will not accept it! "Politics" is still on the national level; local conflict operates in other ways. Once again the bid for local autonomy hides behind the institutions of central power. This procedure forces the actors consciously to underrate the intensity of internal struggles, which they reduce to the status of simple "village quarrels." But by doing this they avoid (as far as they can) the meddling of representatives of the central authorities in their own affairs.

However, these "village quarrels" involve hatreds which are more persistent than the divergent opinions of general politics. Local interests offer subjects for disagreement which are more tangible than the abstraction of universal ideas; families bear the weight of conflicts which have passed down from generation to generation. Therefore, why should natives restrict politics by giving a name to it? Why should they close off a particular area of social relationships when power affects every aspect of daily life? Native thought has created a gap between the outside and inside worlds by using two forms of speech. This is the ridiculous situation which the villagers present to the ethnologist. They do this so that he may rightly confuse words and actions of the local community with the way

---

[17] The same meaning of the term politics can be observed in another French region, the Dauphiné.

these are understood by society as a whole. Thanks to this subterfuge the local community retains a high degree of autonomy in its internal conflicts which, at a deeper level, challenge the ritualization of the politics established by the state. Municipal elections in Grand-Failly are political, but villagers prefer to suppress the word and retain the word "action," so that they may act as they think best.

THE VILLAGE SPEAKS TO ITSELF

The attention paid to native speech should be extended to the whole area of the enquiry. In order to obtain internal order it is necessary to return constantly to the same words and recover a coherence of definitions and meaning. At the time of our first visits to the area everyone asserted with persistence that only "good chaps" were elected, that is to say men capable of ensuring good municipal administration. Nevertheless, some years later the same people avowed to us that they supported individuals who no longer possessed that quality. Such contradictions! How is it possible to recover the thread of a conversation which opposes the two parts of its predicate, with so little apparent logic? The problem becomes clearer when one applies oneself to decoding the parts of speech which constitute the instrument of internal communication.

Interpreted according to "standard" French, the idea of "good" signifies a quality of soundness, of efficiency: "one who fulfills the conditions for producing its effect." A second meaning emphasizes the idea of value, of price attached to the thing or person designated (*Dictionnaire Petit Robert*).* These two meanings are not absent from native thought; one may even assume that the very ambiguity of the word permits the participants to use one word to explain the reasons for their political choice, i.e. whether it is directed outside or in. Toward the outside world the group stresses the administrative value of its elected representatives, whereas it denies this quality to itself in the course of its own rhetoric.

The negation of the native concept of "value" (*valeur*) is the source of the means of tackling forms of political conflict. It is necessary to seize upon them when they express themselves most violently, when the proximity of an electoral campaign quickens passions, especially in the year preceding elections. Thus we see alliances being formed and broken up, and this permits accurate definition of the sociological nature of conflicting groups.

Whatever the reporter's opinion may be, the description of adversaries

---

* The French word used is *valable*, which though it means "good" in the sense of "a good chap," literally means "valuable" or "of value." — *Translator*.

is always expressed in moral terms. They form a "gang" of careerists or traitors whose aim is to take over the town hall, to profit from the financial advantages this position may offer. No one is capable of giving exact details on the contents of these prevarications; the accusation of embezzlement may appear somewhat derisory to anyone familiar with the finicky control exerted by the tax collector over the finances of a small commune.[18] All opponents are tainted with faults which reflect a series of relationships between groups or the individuals they represent rather than any reality which could be objectively pinpointed. Every moment of the adversary's "private" life is taken into consideration: his children's education, the running of his house, the purchases he makes in the next village, his ability to drink or not to drink, the quality of the management of his land, if he is a farmer, or the value of his work in the factory. To these variable factors (although they already suffice to build a reputation) must be added the moral qualities of individuals. The latter are inherited through links of consanguinity often based on a past which has been forgotten by the participants. Thus we have a veritable constellation of judgments which will be revealed forthwith according to relationships uniting or opposing future partners.

Two men who are usually described by village opinion as being "able to hold their drink well" find themselves classified as sober by some and the worst of drunkards by others. Sometimes it happens that a quality in one's adversary is recognized: "X is a good chap," but this laudatory opinion is immediately contradicted by the opposite opinion which aims at revealing the pernicious influence of his wife or an influential member of his family. When they propound explicitly on the subject of power, reciprocal accusations appear in the form of psychological opinions. He will be "too personal"; he will want "always to impose his ideas; he is an obstinate person"; or else he will frighten people because he is "too proud." Conversely, each list and each of its members will attribute to themselves alone the ability to defend the community spirit. Thus this becomes the subject of bitter competition whose intended goal is obviously to fall in with the dominant ideology of the residential group: i.e. equality.

Beleaguered from all sides, each participant in the field of politics feels an almost obsessional distrust of his adversaries' designs. This is not only the case with adversaries but it also governs judgments between partners. So-and-so "is a good chap," someone else "must not be trusted, he does just what he pleases." Thus a list with their supporters is more likely to resemble a group or even several opposed groups who might belong to enemy coalitions, if one did not look carefully. By mutually accusing each other of suspicious premeditated acts (Why should one stand at

---

[18]   In 1968 the municipal budget of Grand-Failly was about 100,000 francs.

elections if it is not to appropriate power?), might this not be the most effective way available to the participants to exorcise their own desires? One might well be tempted to believe this, since the peasants of Lorraine consciously reject any idea of personal power. They do this even to the point that some partners mutually denounce each other within the same alliance.

While at the same time concealing them, internal discussion shows the three procedures on, with, or by which politics is built, articulated and works: ideology, its practice, and a translation into moral terms of the relationships between actual groups called into action in power conflicts. This example illustrates what was insisted upon in the introduction to this paper, the fact that power is not a static relationship, but on the contrary a dynamic one of dependency where unequal partners confront each other. This is also what the inhabitants of Grand-Failly are expressing (though with a certain degree of confusion) when they deny any good qualities to their adversaries or to their allies. In fact, how is it possible to combine the equality asserted as the standard of all social relationships and the imbalance of these same relationships when the participants use them for political ends? It is necessary to ask this question at this point, although the answer will not come at once, since it underlies the process of this analysis. Before tackling it, it would seem to be preferable (for purely logical reasons) to examine the idea of "value" in native thought.

Internal speech does not use the term "good" (*valable*) in the sense of a capacity for leadership; however, it may be contained in the concept when one is speaking of certain individuals whose technical competence is acknowledged by everyone, partners and adversaries alike. Generally speaking the word "good" seems to carry a concept of value which undergoes changes (temporarily, let us assume) linked to a certain stage of relationships between the participants. The mobility with which this qualification is applied would convey the idea of a value bound up with the sum total of possibilities which raise a man, and then a social group, to the pinnacle of power, to the detriment of individuals and groups which strictly speaking are identical.

The hypothesis of an exchange value is not therefore to be neglected. It must be added that it assumes the presence of an increase in value at one or the other end of the chain of social partners. Obviously this increase in value is not assessable in terms of money or land, since neither the most well-to-do inhabitants nor those having the largest properties possess political power, so what remains? Power? Perhaps this is the case. It is necessary now to continue by bringing together the sequences of native speech and the political behavior actually produced.

THE FAMILY

Reciprocal mistrust, fear and suspicion carpingly and obsessively manifested by those aspiring to local power and their allies are not just simple assertions. When we invited them to do so, the natives provided us with explanations, working out interpretations for the opinions they held. These exegeses were based on two themes: the family and, to a lesser extent, the neighborhood. The purpose of the present article is to study the first theme. But it is by constantly mistrusting words that one is able to instigate an analysis of social categories which will show both the structures of power and the stakes they represent.

The word "family," *fémïy* or *fémil* in dialect, is the framework for the expression of power. On the other hand, the preponderant role of the "family" manifests itself at every level of everyday life. It serves as a prop for social, economic, and religious relationships, and for the explanations they require. However, the composition of groups which are called "family" varies according to concrete situations. This gives an "accordion" appearance to the native group, expanding and deflating according to the goals pursued. The "family" is reduced to the father, mother, and children when one is describing the consumer and household group.[19] On the other hand it may extend to more than thirty or forty persons gathered together to celebrate a first communion, and exceed a hundred when a marriage takes place.[20]

Between the two poles the "family" can take in the parents and grandparents, the only ones present with the godfather and godmother at a baptism (Karnoouh 1973). There are as many different family groups as there are privileged situations. And finally there is the "family" which, apparently, ensures the election of the candidate, and which is the one which will be treated at this point.

"To be elected it is necessary to have a big family behind one, for other large families are voting against you at the same time." Here, simply stated, is the native explanation for power struggles and the underlying tactics. There are many expressions which reflect the same concept. "Candidates are chosen by families"; or, "the muncipal council is the council of families," as one opponent to the outgoing council said to us. Finally, one pessimistic candidate confided to us: "I have no family; one has to be a superman in Grand-Failly to be elected if one is without a family." All participants agree in acknowledging the intensity of the solidarity of family links whose extent and boundaries fluctuate according to the relative positions of the participants.

[19] This form is not a reduction of a former large family, but the traditional form in Lorraine. It is found again in identical fashion at the beginning of the nineteenth century, but with a much larger number of children.
[20] The "family" category disappears when funerals take place, to make room for the whole residential group.

In other respects we are familiar with the acuteness of family conflicts related to inheritance, a fact which restricts the extension of expressions of solidarity, thereby discouraging the view that relationships of consanguinity form the sole basis for creating a coalition, in spite of the strong integrating power of such relationships.[21] And so one turns to marriage relationships, which form a second basic element of links of solidarity. At times they make up for the lack of blood relations.

The "family" as conceived by local thought cannot be recorded within the framework of a lineage, since in Lorraine we are dealing with a society with an undifferentiated genealogy. Moreover, it is not possible to assign the status of "corporate group" to the "family" category, for in its political dimensions it does not possess the characteristics which define such a group: these are dimensions which are fixed at every moment of life as well as qualities of legal status. An inhabitant of Grand-Failly having to answer for his fickleness of conduct can only do so before the residential group seen as a whole.

Understanding and defining the native category of "family" leads us to use the analytical concept of family (parentèle) which is best translated by the English word "kindred." Kindred is defined as a group of blood relations which is built around a living person. This is not a "corporate group"; its size varies according to the circumstances in which it is engaged, according to the needs of the participants (Wolf 1965; Freeman 1961; Fox 1966, 1967). By declaring that one needs "a large family" to be elected, the speaker was telling us that a strong family must be constituted to assure the success of his political bid. However, experience will prove to us that a family in itself cannot take upon itself the promotion of a candidate or a list; it must seek to join other kindreds (parentèles): in short, the term "families" (familles) also expresses this coalition of kindreds (parentèles). Thus it does not suffice to simply assert point blank the correctness of a translation of a word such as "native" for it to be so, one still has to examine actual practices, i.e. the facts.

Every family has a tendency to extend its size to the maximum limits which are defined by its culture: to encompass all persons for whom any single individual has a term of reference based on blood relationship. The case with which we are concerned already permits us to eliminate relations who do not reside in the village, or more accurately, those among the nonresidents who no longer vote in the commune. This reduces the numbers of certain "families" by half.

Despite opposition and conflicts between blood relations, there are limits within which solidarity can be expressed by the kinship link alone: the father, mother, paternal and maternal grandparents, and children. The nucleus of the family is constituted by the line of direct descent;

---

[21]   For the difference between blood and marriage relationships see Karnoouh (1971).

once the head of the family is free of collateral relationships, the moral obligation no longer operates in such an imperative manner. Whether they are brothers and sisters (i.e. full brothers and sisters), uncle, aunt, nephew and niece, solidarity is not spontaneous: it presupposes the absence of conflicts which may have arisen from inheritances, land sales or land reallocation. It is not unusual to find conflicts between collateral relatives, especially among brothers who are not able to resolve the inheritance of wealth from one generation to another in an amicable manner. As to cousins (the second rank of collateral relationship), they are generally too far removed (Karnoouh 1971), and are linked to closer relatives: father, uncle, brother, nephew. Thus, we are not able to reduce the family of any individual to the sum total of all classes of blood relationships he declares. The boundaries of this unstable group move within this semantic area according to the tempo of conflicts dividing relations. Every aspirant to power has a family which is quite vast, and the purpose of an electoral list is thus to bring together the largest number possible of these divergent groups. When reporters identify the municipal council with a "council of families," they reveal to us the sum total of family connections which control the municipal institution. Thus native thought extends the basic group, and the effect of this is to strengthen the image of force and power represented by the list aspiring to power.

In practice the kindred concept turns out to be the most suitable and operative one to explain the native category of "family" (*famille*), insofar as it allows one to utilize an almost infinite variety of concrete situations, whether of a religious, ceremonial, economic, or political nature. Furthermore, it offers an opportunity to grasp family combinations at the very moment they are forged, in the course of their existence, and when they are transformed to be born anew. At all times the family expresses the partially uncertain nature of groupings formed, the precarious nature of the edifice. But that is not its only advantage, for in spite of the mobility of groups of blood relations, we are able to establish the cultural limits of change, i.e. family size, beyond and within which other forms of social groupings are built which appeal to other relevant features. Finally, the same concept permits us to expand the comparison between human societies, thus revealing the significant differences which underlie the peculiarity of peasant societies of western Europe (Fox 1967).

However, one would not wish to conclude the analysis of the size of the political "family" without pointing out the contradictions which arise from this source of action. In fact the participants find themselves obliged to compensate for a system with a series of impossibilities by rules which control its practice (the selection of candidates). In other words, one needs to consider how strategic requirements can mold decisions and reorganize the system and its formal possibilities.

The site of this contradiction in the family is located precisely in the generation of the parents of a candidate who, in theory, could find himself opposed by a brother on a second list. Such a situation would place parents in an insoluble dilemma: How can they make a choice between two sons? Certainly there are some preferences of a psychological nature between brothers within a family which come to light within such a family without thereby being expressed at the level of social life.

The resolving of the contradiction between possibilities within the system and the choice of a candidate establishes a preference among the brothers which benefits one side. This is explained by the operating of the gerontocratic principle of power in Grand-Failly. Later on the details of this power will be examined; for the moment it is the fact of its operation which is essential: it is the candidate's father who decides. Furthermore, it should be noted that the municipal archives of Grand-Failly do not show evidence of two brothers on opposed lists since at least the elections of 1887.

If from a strictly formal point of view the candidate represents the center of a kindred, the real "heads" of it are the parents (the fathers), · who stand surety for and give official recognition to the candidatures when they themselves do not put together the list. The average ages of the different municipal councils have been relatively low. There are few councillors who seek election beyond the age of 55. Mayors occupy their position at a very young age (between 25 and 29) and never hold the position beyond 60; they leave this post when they are certain of being admitted to the "Council of Elders."[22] Thus the "elders" avoid creating situations which are too contradictory; where having to make a choice between sons would lead to the breaking up of families, and the disastrous effect of this would render the kinship group completely inoperative. This is clearly a particularly crucial decision in which idiosyncratic traits intervene: tactical competency and aptitude, for it is not sufficient to be the son of a "head" to receive the right to represent one's family; it still has to be the son who is most suited to take full charge of the reputation of his "family." The task generally falls upon the eldest sons, who are replaced if they die by the younger sons. These qualities (which are obviously individual) consist of conforming with the ethical aspirations of the residential group: being a good worker, a good neighbor, affirming that one is a faithful defender of the egalitarian spirit of the community — all this while knowing how to handle differences of all kinds which dominate the village.

So because of the gerontocratic principle two brothers may not divide family solidarity between lists. It would not be suitable to the spirit of a "head" to invoke tactical arguments to engage in this type of maneuver,

---

[22]   This council does not exist in any formal manner.

even under the pretext of increasing the election chances of his representatives. The solidarity system and code do not allow this to happen: the unity of families is found in this instance but not elsewhere. If by chance such a decision happened to be taken, it could be described as social suicide; it would require a total upheaval of cultural norms. Today this tactic is not only impracticable, but inconceivable. In Grand-Failly the participants still live under the control of the system of kinship expressed in family discourse.

THE FAMILY IN ACTION

Kinship constraints delineate to the participants the field where power tactics and strategies will be realized. Politics tends to deny the conflicts over land, which force conjugal families to retire within themselves, and to extend the system so as to place first and second cousins on a single list. Political reasons thus develop a centripetal force which impels conjugal families to come together while economic conflicts, on the other hand, deploy centrifugal forces whose effects reduce families to their minimum sizes.

The extension of the kinship system becomes established on a basic system which the natives call "near relations": individuals directly united by "blood" solidarity. In Grand-Failly one does not find any examples suggesting manipulation of blood kinship which would be used by the participants in order to enlarge a network of completely dependent blood relations. The *parentèle* does not offer any such possibility, because it also forms the basis for genealogical conversation. Individuals reconstruct their genealogies by taking living beings as their points of reference, rather than using ancestors whose memory they cannot call upon. Thus relationships of kinship on which are shaped the building of an electoral list and the attempt at extension of blood relationship which this implies, always reflect kinship relationships which are empirically observable.

The tendency to expand families varies from one election to the next. Thus in 1959, for nine municipal councillors representing a homogeneous list, that is [9(9–1)]/2 relationships, we recorded fourteen cousin relationships, or 38.8 percent.[23] In 1966, however, this rate diminished to 19.6 percent. These quantitative variations usually turn out to be rather irrelevant. They can be found scattered among the various councils which have been elected since 1887. They serve mainly to show the difficulties a family experiences in the process of attempts to enlarge itself.

[23] Cousin relationships are defined here as interpreted by native thought and not by the rules of the *Code Civil* or canon law. In fact these are the only ones the participants consciously use. If certain cousin relationships are revealed when conflicts take place, they have not been invented by circumstances: they exist latently.

The force which impels a family to extend its network to the extreme limits available to it through the classification of relations develops the final and ideal goal: to have the maximum number of councillors. But conflicts which cousins inherit and pass on impede the complete realization of this theoretical possibility. So, returning to the evidence of this community, solidarity between brothers and sisters is not eternal; it may disappear at the death of the father, when it is a question of inheriting property or the informal title of family "head." Too much competition between brothers is likely to lead to the breakup of a family. All one needs for this to happen is for one of them not to accept the power supremacy of his brother or for him to feel "left out" of the family inheritance. Then family solidarity disintegrates, and this leads either to new alliances or to a redistribution of bonds between new families.

The ideal model of an expanded family is always partially realized in a list when the kindred's point of departure, like the nucleus of a crystal, develops by its forces in certain privileged directions of the family space where it moves. This kindred-center does not derive its power from any hereditary superiority, but from the number and quality of the bonds which encompass the individuals it controls.

Thus, if its power fails to extend to the point of covering almost all blood relations, the kindred-center will seek allies particularly among relations by marriage: brothers-in-law, sons-in-law, or nephews by marriage. In fact, women are excluded from institutional power. However, they have a great deal of power insofar as they share the inheritance of parents in the same manner as their brothers (Yver 1966). Through a matrimonial alliance kindreds possess a bridge which allows a political alliance to be deployed over a much larger field, thus opening broad tactical possibilities. Kindred "heads" are then called to negotiate political alliances based on the marriages linking their respective blood relations. Vis-à-vis the kindred-center, these allied kindreds are prevailed upon to play two different roles with regard to the power they represent. If one kindred is small in number, it will serve to strengthen the power of the kindred-center, which will seek in this roundabout manner, extra representation within the municipal council. If, on the other hand, the marriage has taken place with a kindred which is large and powerful, the latter will demand one or several representatives, thus expressing its demand to see power shared. In the first example the allied kindred is exercising a simple right of control over the kindred center; while in the second case this right of control is transformed into a more or less balanced sharing of power. When the second situation presents itself, the allied kindred generally claims two or three representatives. These may be either full cousins, or relations by marriage belonging to other small kindreds with whom the second kindred (like the kindred-center) possesses alliances. From the point of view of the kindred-center, this last possibility is not the best, for it implies an almost equal sharing of power, which it is trying at all costs to avoid. In fact the preferences of the kindred-center will be directed to the first option, a solution offering many advantages, while reducing the risks of one day seeing the kindred-center power challenged. The kindred-center retains the essence of power, while continuing to control the small satellite kindreds which in themselves do not have the power necessary to negotiate on terms of equality.

There is also a third possibility, which would have the kindred-center controlled by a union of satellite kindreds. Although this may be envisaged from a strictly logical point of view, it has not been seen to occur in practice. In order not to fear competition from united satellite kindreds, the kindred-center must have more than half the votes with respect to the combined votes of satellite kindreds. This is a necessary condition, but it is not sufficient in itself, because the quantitative aspect may be endangered by clever maneuvering or a proper use of scandal. To avoid such mishaps the kindred-center will have to place itself in a central position in a world of conflict; and it will have to gather together into its own hands the ability to quash attempts at alliance which might be forged against it. Whatever they do the groups on the periphery are condemned to suffer the predominance of the central group unless they wish to become free by going down with it in defeat.

It is now possible to see more clearly the native expressions of local power. When informants compare the municipal council to a "council of families" they are delivering to us (without explicit details) a hint of the kindred fabric which structures the institution. In short, when opponents confirm that the commune is governed by the "large family," they are indicating the road to follow: to seek out the dominant group and the dominated groups within networks of kinship. When "discussing family" (Jolas et al. 1970) the participants conceal the political conflict behind a conversation embracing practically the totality of local practices, not because of any particular taste for mystery, but because of the fact that the kinship system (a subject suggested through conversation about genealogy) provides the various levels of social life with the most effective framework and most economic means of encasing themselves in a coherent world.

VALUE

In the light of the kinship system it is possible once again to take up the expression "good chap" (*gars valable*) and the concept of value which underlies it. It has been noted that this value was no longer that of technical efficiency or financial profitability. If power is no longer to be regarded as the state, the fixed place where a dominant group is located, a sort of empty space which has to be occupied, but rather as the result of a succession of exchanges between groups which are strictly speaking identical but of variable sizes, then the problem of value finds a partial solution. The groups in partnership negotiate power in terms of votes; thus there is a sharing of power according to the weight of the "family" which brings in these votes. The "family" is the means of exchange of participants who are constantly seeking to increase their capital and for whom power constitutes a plus factor. However, this value is not only a matter of quantity. It also includes the concept of quality, which measures the strength of links between members of a family, and which thus ensures a certain permanence to power. This attempt to retain power within the same family group presupposes that it is necessary to reassure oneself from time to time of the quality of the bonds without decreasing their number.

To permit the following generation to strengthen blood links, one wonders whether the best means is not to contract marriage alliances with families which are simply political allies. This is another method of exchange which occurs and its practice must take into account a double strategic requirement: not to reinforce the power of the blood relationship to the detriment of future allies; or, in other words, not to have too many marriages between close blood relatives, in order to avoid a situation where a family may shrink to the point of no longer having allies through marriage with whom to establish political alliances.

If for example one takes the history of marriage alliances which have occurred in the village since the end of the nineteenth century, the gap which exists between political power and land power is shown clearly. To the extent that it may be necessary to own some land to belong by right to the residential group (Karnoouh 1972), power belongs to the family which has known how to settle its internal conflicts, while arranging its marriage alliances with groups which are identical, though smaller in number.

In 1906 the rich peasants[24] lost control of power, having been forced to come to terms with a very powerful family which combined small peasants and artisan-peasants. The transformation in the power relationship was the result of land conflicts within the family of the rich peasants, who, in order to avoid breaking up, engaged in much interbreeding between first and second cousins. This matrimonial strategy prevented (at least in part) too extensive a breaking up of lands; but as a result of it this family began to withdraw into itself, and then went into progressive isolation. After two generations it had to be contented with a minor role.[25]

[24]   The category of landowners having an average of twenty hectares of land. There are no large landowners in Grand-Failly.
[25]   One of its members tried to recover past splendor by profiting from the Vichy regime (1940–1945), but he was not followed by his family. Informants, whatever family they belong to, agree in asserting that he had not followed the rules of the game, because of his having introduced a power whose origin was in world society into the internal struggle.

These few facts tend to show that a strategy of matrimonial alliance based strictly on land appropriation causes families to become isolated at the political level. This practice (which one could call economic strategy) limits bonds of solidarity by restricting matrimonial alliances and ritual kinship to blood relations who, in addition, constitute the potential members of all families (Karnoouh 1973). This narrowing of the family does not take place without strengthening conflicts between brothers, who no longer find groups with whom they may compensate for an internal climate of extreme tension. Families linked by marriage will inevitably break up, as they are henceforth obliged to seek matrimonial alliances outside the residential group.[26] One may also note the political disadvantages which result from these attempts to marry outside the village. If they offer certain economic gains, they sanction, on the other hand, a new loss of local power. For whatever the place of residence of a young couple, the marriage does not bring new political allies. When an individual departs to live in the village of his spouse, his family loses a blood relation. If, on the other hand, the spouse comes to live in the village of the individual, it retains a blood relation, but the marriage-partner (a "stranger in the village") is excluded from political activity, beyond the providing of a vote. In any case a gain of two votes is not an extension of the political alliance: the blood relations of the spouse are always integrated within another residential group.

This argument suggests the regarding of village inbreeding as the means by which a family may extend the full compass of its political activity, by directing its marriages toward families it wishes to integrate. It seems difficult to assert that this is a conscious tactic, insofar as the egalitarian ideology which dominates all local conversation also finds its justification within matrimonial practices. This is seen most strongly when natives condemn family inbreeding which results in concentrating land within a single family. Marriage outside the village is not really favored by the participants, for its result is to transfer land to other villages. Thanks to village inbreeding combined with equal shar-ing between heirs, the participants are assured of seeing their lands circulate from generation to generation among allied members of the residential group. With reciprocity having been deferred, always to be taken up at a later date, the growth of a family also contributes to its breakup.

The ideological role of equality is not only based on marriage alliances, it also invades politics. A form of speech and apparent practice have been established between the kindred-center and satellite kindreds in which each partner will describe himself as the equal of the other and which

---

[26] A quantitative analysis of village inbreeding was carried out at the beginning of the investigation and reported by Lamarche (1969). At this point a qualitative interpretation is being given.

leaves satellite kindreds with the illusion of belonging to the association of equal groups which form the village.

Since the beginning of this century the family made up of small peasants and artisans has pursued a strategy of local inbreeding which has permitted it to remain "in business," while conforming with the dominant ideological norms. Its present head does not refuse to affirm the equality of partners, in spite of the imbalances inherent in the exercising of power: he is the one who possesses it, not the others. On the other hand, this strategy offers compensations in land when matrimonial alliances are undertaken, or by granting a right of control over municipal administration when it gives a seat to its allies. However, when examined over a time-spread of some seventy years, reciprocity between marriage alliances and land exchange is not strictly equal. The chain which starts with one group, to end up in a number of small chains linking more than half the inhabitants, is a network of kinship which works to the political benefit of the kindred-center.

In advancing the concept of a family as a means of exchange whose increase in value would be power, the preceding example was being stated in the form of a general proposition. As we have shown, the "family" value constitutes not only the system, but also the code, the nature of political conversation. There are certainly other expressions capable of replacing the word "family"; both French and the Lorraine dialect have such terms which more or less accurately refer to relationships of kinship (Karnoouh 1971, 1972). But is it not so that for native thought to liken kindreds with the minimal extended forms is to imply that the ideal model of behavior and attitudes within the kindred should derive from an emotional force similar to that which governs relationships within the conjugal family?

The dynamics of politics which impels kindreds to expand is opposed to the secessionist tendencies which originate in the loosening of family ties. The imbalance created by the exercising of power confronts the idea of equality serving as the ideal model for social relationships to the point that the members of a single list (of allied families) verbally exorcise all manifestations of personal appropriation of power. It is by taking into account these doubly antagonistic constraints that we should understand the use of the term "family." It identifies all members of a kindred by sociological marks identical to those which explain the solidarity of the conjugal family.

BY WAY OF CONCLUSION

The kindred formed for political purposes may be interpreted as the result of constraints which appear to be contradictory. Consider them in terms of double opposition, and examine the manner of articulation which allows them to operate simultaneously. Limited by a network of kinship, the kindred experiences structural and normative constraints identical with those of the network as a whole. The classes of relationships are present there, although in a smaller number. Relationships between classes have the same constraints for the kindred, and one can at this point repeat the conclusion of an earlier article:

If one of the goals of European peasant communities is to determine (for each generation) to whom the land belongs and who its custodian will be in the future, it would appear that the essential thing within the framework of this logic is to distinguish (with regard to the rules of succession) the following: groups whose members have prescribed rights, those whose members have preferential rights, and finally those whose members have none. (Karnoouh 1971:48).

Also one should not be surprised to find these tendencies once again within a kindred. Descendants who are excluded from inheritance (cousins) move away from descendants who forthwith ensure their security with regard to land (direct descendants). They do this in order to compete with intermediate descendants (uncles/nephews). Then one may consider that the systematic exclusion of certain descendants constitutes the operation of land distribution among relations. The logical follow-up to such a system leads the local community to be no longer only made up of juxtaposed conjugal families. In fact this is what occurs at the most obvious level: the traditional habitat is that of houses inhabited by a single conjugal family. However, this immediate reality is contradicted at other economic, and especially political, levels.

Strictly speaking, political action, although appreciably altering it, involves the same system of kinship as that which regulates land appropriation. However, this is with a notable difference with respect to the logic of the action, which in the second case is opposed to the first. Here, in order to win and appropriate local power it is necessary to be able to rely on the maximum number of votes supplied by relations. In fact, the thought, expression, and action of the villagers use the semantic field carved out by the terms, the system, the attitude, and the behaviors of kinship in order to create the conditions necessary for the existence of bonds of solidarity. The same linguistic symbol will thus help participants both to govern land circulation and to articulate power strategies. When lands are involved, the system works in the direction of splitting it up, while politics makes it work in the direction of amalgamation.

The powerful kindreds retain their strength by the balance they manage to establish between these antagonistic tendencies. They do this in two ways: either by leaving part of their lands in joint possession for one or two generations, so as to leave to future generations the problem of straightening out land ownership with regard to members who have left or are not farmers; or else (and this applies especially to family "heads") by allowing brothers and sisters to appropriate a larger share of the inheritance, in return for which the latter grant and keep for him a power which is also theirs. When either of these conditions is met, the family which is built around an individual and his brothers may then seek to exercise a power which is guaranteed to it by the number of its members, the form of their bonds, and the importance of the "head."

It is easy to understand the gap between economic and political motives; that is, it is possible to see how the participants use the economy to attain maximum political effectiveness. Thus political power appears to be based on a certain redistribution of wealth which is foreign to any logic of capitalist accumulation. In fact, the kindred-center provides lands by marrying outside the village. Through the "head" it succeeds in assuming its full role by partially renouncing part of the wealth which lawfully it should receive.

Finally, one may wonder why a form of power so foreign to the dominant political form has been maintained in Grand-Failly, in spite of pressures of all kinds which weigh on the village. To understand this it is necessary to give a brief description of the effects of the general economy on the everyday life of the villagers. The influence of changes which have been brought about by modern-day living has not affected the native ideology of equality. Socioprofessional differentiations have not resulted in irreconcilable social differentiations. Fellow residents share the same ethical values, the same concept of collectivization of land. Cultural unity stamps the village with symbols which unite peasants and workers. In fact, how is it possible to gather together conjugal families who are altogether too different, who would indentify their poles of reference by norms and interests which are opposed to each other? With regard to trends in the national economy, peasant farmers have not so much accumulated wealth as the workers (their relations) resident in the village have become identified with the bourgeoisie. The substantial profits realized by the farmers have been absorbed by the purchase of modern farming equipment and investments brought about by the increase in agricultural productivity. Certainly the workers receive slightly higher wages in the Lorraine iron and steel industry;[27] however, they find considerable economic advantages in residing in the village, thanks to the parcels of land cultivated by their wives and the animals or poultry they are able to raise themselves or buy from their farmer neighbors. So the kindreds made up of workers and peasants do not act out their local conflicts as a consequence of these differences. The cultural unity of the residential group, essentially based on the long-time membership of each of the participants

---

[27] A semiskilled worker working three eight-day shifts earns an average of 1100 francs per month (1969–1970).

in the village and on communal equality, has still not been overturned by the state and the political ideologies for which it is the vehicle. Every village perceives the village and its inhabitants as the totality which formulates both their quality as social beings and their persons. In this social context families still fulfill their political role; ideologies which might be in a position to overthrow them do not find in the local community the differences or their manifestations with which to build new conflicts.

One also understands why families which carry out a policy of redistribution of land wealth through matrimonial exchange tend to develop a high degree of inbreeding in the village. Besides the fact that this allows them to extend political alliances, it assures all residents of a visible expression of equality — or at least the possibility of one day seeing the lands of some pass to the hands of others. The system of generalized distribution does not prevent excesses of wealth among the partners. But the chances for an improvement in individual circumstances or a fortunate inheritance cannot stand in the way of either rules for the passing on of possessions in a population which has been peasant for many generations, or the activity of political alliances. The family which experimented with matrimonial alliance for economic purposes lost political power, and later economic power too. Its adversaries and former allies had made daily life very difficult for it by forcing it to engage in many lawsuits to protect itself against various unprovoked assaults. These had been directed against it with general complicity. And it was not able to escape the vengeance of its adversaries by having recourse to judicial measures of the outside world. On the contrary, its political decline was hastened by the silence of witnesses, accomplices of the aggressors. This is what left it helpless and vanquished. The simple fact of having appealed to courts outside the village brought it into disrepute in the eyes of its potential partners; while its adversaries used the representatives of the outside world to reinforce their own strategy. Its return to politics, thanks to the Vichy regime, finally sealed its fate. Because of having broken with the concept of equality, a family was completely ousted from political power, and some of its representatives who were most in the public eye were destroyed. In Grand-Failly the native concept of equality is not an empty word; all its inhabitants are subject to it, and up to now no one has been able to escape it. However, the egalitarian ideology does not have the sole function of justifying family control of politics, or responding to state pressure and the cultural domination which denies it. Locally, egalitarian ideology has a special logic. When a kindred "head," a kindred, an alliance of kindreds, possess power, each of them sets up, at its own level, a difference which is inherent in the very exercising of power. The negation of the concept of equality through the use of power has henceforth to be recorded, a fact which is furthermore emphasized by having this principle respected in land dealings. The gap between those holding power and those subject to it is a fact which cannot be disputed. However, once again egalitarian conversation takes over social practice, when all residents (except for "strangers in the village") are described in the aggregate as equals. Because of this fact all relationships of subordination between conquerors and conquered, between winners and losers, are blurred. Certainly this conversation permits the hiding from the outside world of the exact nature of internal conflicts; but it has an intrinsic value which gives the residential group the means to assert its autonomy with regard to other villages and outside society (Karnoouh 1972).

By permitting small family groups to unite into much larger families, egalitarian ideology reverses the secessionist tendency of the operation of the land economy. In return, and owing to its complete effectiveness, it allows power to operate on the basis of the difference it establishes *de facto*. In one case equality seeks to destroy any attempt at economic stratification among peasant farmers; while in the other it permits the residential group to behave as a single body, despite the family stratification which results from the operation of political power.

The code according to which native thought works out its political conversation does not determine a social field specified by a special vocabulary. The same words are used, sometimes with the same expressions, as are used when speaking of land or economic relations. This aspect of kinship is the basic element which controls social relationships. It is what differentiates local society so radically from the national structure which contains it. From the point of view of the state it operates as an instrument of latent power; but then the municipal institution, which is supposed to be so plain and obvious, turns out to be of little significance, at least when seen from inside. To identify a kindred and its allies with a "large family" is to place on record, beyond the difficult negotiations which establish it, the power of the bonds which lay the foundations of this unity: kinship and marriage.

REFERENCES

ARENDT, HANNAH
   1966   *The origins of totalitarianism*, revised edition. New York: Harcourt Brace Jovanovich. (Originally published 1951 as *The burden of our time*.)
BAILEY, FREDERICK G.
   1971   *Gifts and poisons: the politics of reputation*. Oxford: Blackwell.
BLOCCA, ETTORE
   1970   *Yanoama: récit d'une femme brésilienne enlevée par les Indiens*. Terre Humaine. Paris: Plon.

BLOCH, MARC
1964 *Les caractères originaux de l'histoire rurale française*, volume one. Economies, Sociétés, Civilisations. Paris: Armand Colin. (Originally published 1956.)
DUBY, GEORGES
1962 *L'économie rurale et la vie des campagens dans l'Occident médiéval, France, Angleterre, Empire IXᵉ–XVᵉ siècles.* Collection Historique. Paris: Aubier-Montaigne.
DUMONT, LOUIS
1971 *Introduction à deux theories de l'anthropologie sociale.* Paris: Mouton.
FORTES, MEYER, E. E. EVANS-PRITCHARD
1940 "Introduction," in *African political systems.* Edited by Meyer Fortes and E. E. Evans-Pritchard, 1–23. (Translated 1964 as *Systèmes politiques africains.* Paris: Presses Universitaires de France).
FOX, ROBIN
1966 Kinship and land tenure of Tory Island. *Ulster Folklife* 12:1–17.
1967 *Kinship and marriage.* Pelican Books. Harmondworth: Penguin. (Translated 1972 as *Anthropologie de la parenté* by Tina Jolas and Simone Dreyfus. Les Essais. Paris: Gallimard.)
FRANKENBERG, R.
1966 "British community studies: problems of synthesis," in *The social anthropology of complex societies.* Edited by Michael Banton, 123–154. Conference on New Approaches in Social Anthropology, Cambridge, 1963. London: Tavistock.
FREEMAN, J. D.
1961 On the concept of kindred. *Journal of the Royal Anthropological Institute* 91(2):192–220.
GUIDIERI, R.
1969 Segmentation and political power in Melanesia/Segmentation et pouvoir politique en Mélanésie. *European Sociological Archives/Archives européennes de sociologie* 10:133–145.
JOLAS, TINA, YVONNE VERDIER, FRANÇOISE ZONABEND
1970 Parler famille. *L'Homme* 10(3):5–26.
JOLLIVET, MARCEL
1965 "Methode typologique pour l'étude des sociétés rurales," in *Les transformations des sociétés rurales. Revue Française de Sociologie*, special edition: 33–54.
KARNOOUH, CLAUDE
1971 L'oncle et le cousin. *Études Rurales* 42:7–53.
1972 L'étranger ou le faux inconnu: essai sur la définition spatiale d'autrui dans un village lorrain [The misleading stranger: an essay on the definition of neighbours according to place of residence in North-Eastern France]. *Ethnologie Française* 2(1–2):107–122, 202–203. English summary.
1973 "Parrainage et marrainage: un exemple français; Lorraine rurale," in *Actes: Congrès International d'Ethnologie Européenne, Paris, 24–28 août, 1971.* Edited by Jean Cuisenier. Paris: G.-P. Maisonneuve et Larose.
KARNOOUH, CLAUDE, J. ARLAUD, J. P. LACAM, *directors*
1971 *"Jours tranquilles en Lorraine": essai sur le pouvoir local.* Black-and-white film, 45 minutes.

LAMARCHE, HUGUES
1969 "Grand-Failly en Lorraine." Étude locale 7. Centre National de la Recherche Scientifique/Groupe de Recherches Sociologiques du Centre d'Études Sociologiques/Délégation Générale à la Recherche Scientifique et Technique. Mimeographed paper.

MENDRAS, HENRI
1965 "Études comparées dans les sociétés rurales," in *Les transformations des sociétés rurales*. *Revue Française de Sociologie*, special edition: 16–32.
1967 *La fin des paysans*, chapter one: "Forces et mécanismes du changement." Futuribles. Paris: S.E.D.E.I.S.

PETIT-DUTAILLIS, CHARLES
1947 *Les communes françaises*. L'Évolution de l'Humanité 44. Paris: Albin-Michel.

PORCHNEV, BORIS F.
1972 *Les soulèvements populaires en France au XVIIᵉ siècle*. Sciences. Paris: Flammarion.

ROUBIN, LUCIENNE A.
1970 *Les chambrettes des provençaux*. Civilisation et Mentalités. Paris: Plon.

WOLF, E.
1965 "Kinship, friendship and patron–client relation in complex societies," in *The social anthropology of complex societies*. Edited by Michael Banton, 1–21. Conference on New Approaches in Social Anthropology, Cambridge, 1963. New York: Praeger.

YVER, JEAN
1966 *Essai de géographie coutumière: égalité entre héritiers et exclusion des enfants dotés*. Publications de la Société d'Histoire du Droit. Paris: Sirey.

The Rumanian Household from the Eighteenth to the Early Twentieth Century

PAUL HENRI STAHL

RÉSUMÉ:

Unité sociale fondamentale dès le Moyen-Age, le village voit son rôle subsister encore partiellement de nos jours en Roumanie. Unité sociale vivante, cohérente, il conserve une conscience claire de son homogénéité issue d'une croyance en une origine commune qui amène les villageois à se considérer comme consanguins.

Au cours de l'histoire, la personnalité du village a été reconnue successivement par les différentes formes d'administrations qui se sont succédées. De nos jours, la communauté villageoise perd progressivement ses droits, en grande partie du fait du passage de l'économie patriarcale, où les terres étaient communautaires, à la propriété individuelle.

Parallèlement au village, la ferme constituait une unité sociale spécifique, comprenant le groupe familial et sa propriété, mobilière et immobilière.

Si l'on étudie la répartition des terres entre villages et entre fermes, on s'aperçoit que les principes qui président à cette répartition sont identiques dans les deux cas : il s'agit d'assurer à chaque unité (village ou famille) des conditions égales. Seuls les hommes participent au partage : les fils d'une même famille se partagent le patrimoine au moment de leur mariage, le dernier-né restant dans la maison paternelle et prenant en charge ses vieux parents. Quittant à leur mariage leur maison natale, les filles ne reçoivent en dot que des tissus, des meubles, de l'argent, à l'exclusion des terres.

Dans le cas d'une ferme où il n'y a que des filles, de patrilocal le mariage devient matrilocal et le mari, au lieu de donner à son épouse le nom de sa ferme dans le cas du mariage patrilocal, prend à son tour le nom de la ferme paternelle de sa femme, tout ceci afin d'empêcher la disparition d'une ferme. Dans ce même but, on a recours à l'adoption quand un ménage est sans enfant.

Le passage de la propriété collective à la propriété individuelle ne modifie en rien les modalités du droit de propriété qui diffèrent des règles du droit romain. La terre arable est seulement administrée par le propriétaire et obligatoirement répartie également entre tous les fils. Il n'y a donc point d'héritage au sens moderne du terme. La ferme donne, par sa division, naissance à d'autres fermes.

Dans les villages appliquant l'assolement triennal, chaque ferme reçoit sa part de chacune des trois soles, les parcelles se divisant ainsi à chaque partage jusqu'à devenir minuscules.

Un mariage signifie l'apparition d'une nouvelle ferme, avec construction d'une maison. Lors du mariage, chaque ferme donne respectivement un de ses membres: l'une un garçon, l'autre une fille, les parents du garçon acquérant une position de supériorité par rapport à ceux de la fille. Le rapport de supériorité–infériorité s'étend à tous les membres des deux fermes apparentées et même dépasse ce cadre.

Le système de parrainage accentue encore le rôle de la ferme; un même parrain est transmis selon la lignée masculine, au même titre que la propriété : il assiste au baptême de tous les membres d'une ferme et au mariage de tous ses garçons. La marraine n'a qu'un rôle secondaire. La relation parrain-filleul lie donc en réalité deux fermes et les fermes auxquelles elles donnent naissance, relation qui trouve son reflet dans le langage et les moeurs (interdictions du mariage entre parrain-filleule et marraine–filleul s'étendant sur plusieurs générations).

La relation sage-femme–nouveau-né était calquée, dans le passé, sur celle du parrainage.

La construction d'une ferme neuve est marquée de cérémonies à caractère magique, renforcées par les prières d'un prêtre, afin de protéger la maison et ses dépendances. D'autres éléments magiques, auxquels l'Église s'associe parfois, protègent le village et ses alentours, vignobles et vergers.

S'ajoutant aux relations des fermes entre elles, il faut compter les relations avec l'étranger où la ferme intervient notamment lors de la perception de l'impôt. De même, la position sociale des individus était liée à la ferme et variait, en particulier, lors du mariage, selon que la ferme était asservie ou non. Le déclin de son rôle et de celui du village est lié à l'apparition de la propriété individuelle, puis à la forte émigration vers les villes et vers le Nouveau-Monde, ainsi qu'à l'évolution du statut de la femme qui commence à recevoir des terres en dot. Cependant les anciennes structures étaient encore nettement apparentes après la deuxième guerre mondiale. La collectivisation des terres, en supprimant la propriété, l'héritage et la dot changea jusqu'aux rapports moraux entre les générations, phénomène accentué encore par une intense urbanisation.

The fundamental social unit in the history of Rumania is the village. It has been in existence since the time of the first written documents, and has evolved throughout the centuries; it was established as an important social reality in the Middle Ages and remains as such even in modern times. Some remnants of its former role still subsist today.

Information written on this subject as well as traces left upon the countryside can permit us to see that other, broader, social units existed as well in the past, units called village confederations. These appear to be the result of an even older tribal tradition which, contrary to the tribes of the Albanians or the Montenegrins, died out before the thirteenth century without being documented.[1]

To be sure, the village today is no longer exactly the same, for it has undergone change, but despite these changes some defining features have

---

[1] The question of village confederations was the object of an analysis pursued in the work of Henri H. Stahl (1958–1965: vol. 1, pp. 143–195) and in an older work by the same author (1939:vol. 1, pp. 225–339).

been preserved over the long period between the thirteenth and twentieth centuries. By "village" (*sat*) is meant a human group possessing a particular territory, having a governing body — the village assembly (*obştea*) — which makes decisions in the community, and which develops economic activities and follows a collective pattern of living, accomplishing in association its obligations toward the state, and having a common spiritual life. The village is therefore not a chance assemblage of people living isolated lives but residing near one another; rather it is a living social unit, with strong interior cohesiveness and a clear consciousness of its unity, this consciousness reaffirmed by a belief in a common origin leading them to consider themselves almost as all being blood relatives.[2]

The personality of the village has been recognized by the lords, the princes, and the different administrations that have ruled over the Rumanian region. When the village has not been in conflict with outside interests, its life has gone on peacefully; but, as time has passed, the lords have tended to become more and more troubled by the cohesiveness of the village, for their interest lies in conflict with isolated peasants and not with collectives. Under the influence of these external pressures, and also because of rapid changes in the patriarchical economy as well as the transference of community lands to individuals, various rights have been progressively lost to the village community.

While the Rumanian village is well known to men of science, a second sort of social unit, the household (*gospodăria*), remains largely unknown. A superficial analysis of the traditional village would lead us to believe that it is composed of either individuals or of families. The Rumanian family consists of a single household, husband and wife, their children (before marriage) and — rarely — the grandparents. It is therefore different from the extended family, which may be made up of several married couples, and is common among the neighboring Slavs.

In the present-day language, what is called a household (*gospodăria*) is a whole made up of various parts, including the house, outhouses, grounds, and tools; the accent is thus placed on the economic aspects of life. But the notion of the household has in the past had — and still does have, for the peasants at least — a broader meaning, for it designates the family group (that lives and works together, pays common taxes, and sometimes retains its solidarity before the law) as well as and along with all of its possessions, in terms of both real estate and effects.

In order to provide a better understanding of the place of the household in traditional Rumanian villages, it is necessary to describe briefly a few of its features.

---

[2] Moreover, for the notion of *village*, there is a difference between the current meaning (the habitation and its inhabitants) and the meaning it formerly had for the peasants (which included the territory as well).

PROPERTY

When the common territory of a confederation is divided among its component villages, this division must take the following principle into account: assurance to all of equal conditions.[3] This equality concerns the different lands classed according to their economic utility; each village needs arable land for the cultivation of crops; each needs grazing land for its animals; and each needs woods, forests, and water sources.

This same principle is respected within the village, when the inhabitants of these communities seek their rights. At first glance it would seem that the dividing of community territory is done for the satisfaction of particular individuals, so that for instance the arable land which was the first to become privately owned, appears to belong to individuals. But careful analysis will reveal that the divisions here concern the households. Those who nominally receive a parcel of land receive it in the name of the household they represent. The lands resulting from the division of the village territory are given over exclusively to men; the women only take part if there are no men residing in their household. Moreover, it can be stated that only married men are concerned here, men who already have a household or will necessarily have one soon. Once established, the patrimony of the household is divided among the boys of the family when they marry, when each of them establishes his own household. There will be as many subdivisions in the family household as there are boys in the family.[4]

The youngest son of the family remains even after his marriage in the paternal household. He takes care of his elderly parents and inherits the house and all it contains. Along with this role, he will have a privileged position in peasant oral tradition; he will appear as the most adept, intelligent, and courageous family member, the one who always wins and always saves his brothers.

The daughters receive no land; their dowry consists of clothing, furniture, or money.[5] After their marriage they live in the home newly built by their husband, or else in the home of their in-laws if they marry the youngest son of the family.

The system of transmission of property thus gives rise to new households while at the same time preventing the disappearance of old ones. In order to avoid the disappearance of households, marriages sometimes

[3]   The appearance of inequalities and the struggle to maintain equality of laws is described in the work of Henri H. Stahl (1969:77–108).
[4]   Xenia Costa-Foru (1936) cites several clear examples, drawn from a village studied between the two world wars.
[5]   The bridal cortege would carry the dowry in a carriage, this dowry consisting mainly of clothing in a large box. During certain festivals the young women and their parents would stay under tents in order to await the arrival of the candidates for marriage. The clothing would then be brought out of the box and spread out to be seen by the candidates.

become matrilocal, if there are no sons in a household the daughter remains with her parents and her husband comes to live with her.[6] Usually the woman takes the name of her husband (or rather, that of the paternal household of her husband), but it is quite the contrary when the boy moves in with his wife, for he then takes on the name of his spouse (or rather, that of her paternal household).[7] With the same goal of preventing the disappearance of households, inhabitants may adopt a child if their household has none, preferably choosing a child from a related family that has several offspring.

The right to farm lands which have become "individual" property as well as lands which remain collectively owned[8] is not a personal right of the father, as it might seem at first glance. For, if the arable land is taken into possession only nominally by the father, he is not the proprietor of this land according to the rules of Roman law, for example. He cannot sell the land making up his household for he is only its administrator in name and in the name of his children. He is through this also obliged to give his children a portion of the land upon their marriage, whether he wants to do so or not. Neither can the father divide up the land unequally; each child receives a portion equal to that of his brothers. Disinheritance of a son is a rare occurrence, which must be highly motivated in the eyes of the village collective in terms of grave wrongdoings by the son. Inheritance such as it is today did not exist earlier, for there was never one absolute individual proprietor who left after his death all that he wanted to whomever he wished. On the contrary, the father must leave to each one that which custom has prescribed since the most ancient times. The dividing of property is not carried out at the time of his death, moreover, but when the children marry.

It might be claimed that since the village property belongs to the village, the property of the household belongs to the household. A household does not transmit ownership to individuals but to a group making up another household. The household gives birth to other households then, by division. To be sure, there are exceptions. They vary with the particular historical moment and also with the region in which they occur. We might cite particular situations in which the father plans to sell the goods he has gained through his work, but the difference between goods that are inherited and those that are acquired is obvious.

Children born in the same household have a clear conception of their right over the paternal property. This consciousness is manifested not

[6] The parallels with the extended family notion of the southern Slavs are numerous and greatly interesting, both in the similarities and the differences they present. Among the Slavs as well, in order to prevent the disappearance of a particular household, marriage may become matrilocal in certain circumstances.
[7] See the analysis made by Henri H. Stahl (1958–1965:vol. 2, pp. 109–151).
[8] It is the grazing-lands, the mountain areas, and the forests, that remain for the longest time as collective property.

only among the peasants, but also among the lords and the former inhabitants of cities. Examples provided by ancient documents are extremely rich.

In villages that practice three-crop rotation, each farm must have one parcel of land within each of the three planting areas. At the time of the division of the land each son receives a portion of each parcel; property is thus divided up more quickly than would otherwise be the case and this gives rise to the existence of many small parcels.[9] But even in villages in which this system is not practiced, the parcels are each divided among the sons, especially if the value of the various parcels is not the same. Obviously this relates to the same concern for equality.

KINSHIP

It has been seen that marriage signifies the appearance of a new household. The husband and wife will henceforth have the same name, that of the father's household. They will transmit this name to other households at the time of their sons' marriages.

The marriage is preceded by the construction of a house. In popular parlance the term house (*casa*) often designates the entire household. The situation is comparable to that of the Slavic populations of the Balkan peninsula: the name *kăšta* (among the Bulgarians) and *kuča* (among the Serbo-Croations) designates both the house and the household.[10] In ancient Rumanian documents the household is often designated by the name for the house.

At the time of the marriage two households each give up one of their members; one gives up a boy, and the other a girl. The parents of the boy are called "the great-in-laws" (*socrii mari*) and they acquire a position of superiority in relation to the parents of the girl, called "the lesser in-laws" (*socrii mici*).[11] This is a normal situation for a system in which men have a dominant role. It also brings with it certain relationships of superiority and inferiority among all of the members of the two households that have become related through the marriage; the family of the boy has a superior position even if the girl is wealthier. Sometimes these relationships extend beyond the framework of the two households and touch on related households; being related to the husband assures one of a position of superiority regarding the family of the wife.

[9]   Three-crop rotation was imposed upon the Rumanians by the Austrian administration of Transylvania. In 1941, in the department of Făgăraş for example, there was an average of 16.5 parcels of land for each of the three different crops, the average dimensions of the parcels being around 0.4 hectares (Cresin 1945:103).
[10]   The classical description remains that of Bogišić (1884).
[11]   For the use and diffusion of these names, see the work of Scurtu (1966).

The role of the household becomes even clearer when we analyze the system of godfathers in this society. The church requires that every child have a godfather at the time of his baptism. But this requirement is not such a simple one, for there are complex relations characteristic of the Balkan region to be considered here,[12] and the choice of a godfather must take into account several rules that are more precise than just those mentioned above. The godfather of the child at the time of his baptism is the same one who cared for his father and who also was his godfather at the time of his marriage. When the child marries, he will be aided by this same godfather, and this last affirmation is true only for those boys who, through this process, will continue the tradition of the paternal household. On the other hand, the daughters, who at their baptism will have the godfather of their father, will have the godfather of their husband after they are married. The children of the new couple will in turn have the same godfather as their father and as all of the members of their father's household.

We might therefore conclude that godfathership is transmitted according to the male's lineage, just as are property, names, or marks of property placed upon objects belonging to a particular household. A single godfather will assist at the baptism of all of the members of a household that might be called a filial household, and at the marriages of all of the sons in this household as well. He will later act as the godfather of the members of the households resulting from the subdivision of the godsons' households.

If the godfather dies or if his advanced age prevents him from performing his assigned duty, one of his sons is chosen, preferably the one who has remained to live in the paternal household. The godmother has a secondary role in the system; she is usually the wife of the godfather and exercises some function from the fact that she is part of the household of her husband.

It is therefore clear at this point that the relationship between godfather and godson which apparently links two people to one another actually links two households and the households to which they give birth. The peasants emphasize this situation through their language; all of the members of the godson's household (sometimes even the most distant relatives) will call by the name of "godfather" the godfather of only one among them, and even the other people living in the godfather's household will call this person by that name. A relationship of superiority–inferiority is formed, the godfather-household holding a superior position. The godson's household can in turn develop relation-

[12] A good study in this regard is that of Eugene A. Hammel (1968) who, while being mainly interested in the Serbo-Croatians, also prints data and descriptions of this custom among the Rumanians of Timoc (called *Vlakhs* in his work, after the name given them by the Slavs).

ships of godfathership with other households, thus becoming a godfather-household itself and having its own position of superiority. All of the households in a particular village are thus related to one another, two by two.

The church prohibits the marriage of a godson and his godmother or that of a goddaughter and her godfather. This prohibition is extended by the peasants, who apply it to several generations removed from the godfather or godson.

The relationship between the midwife and the newborn baby is less well understood. In the contemporary village, the midwife is the one who can ensure a hastened delivery according to health laws. In the past, the same midwife was traditionally chosen within a household community for all of the newborns of a second household. This practice was sufficiently well entrenched that young girls who knew nothing about delivery were often called upon to act as midwives, simply because they were members of the household whose job it was to provide such women and there were none available who were old enough.

The relationship between two households is reminiscent here of that established when godfathers are selected; similarities between the phenomena are evident, but lack of any more significant information prevents us from insisting upon a parallelism.[13]

MAGIC

Among the village's different magical practices, we can draw a distinction between those that concern the entire village and those which have to do with just a portion of the village. Yet another category of magic might include those practices aimed at influencing the life of the household.[14] This paper will not enter into a detailed description of these different forms of magic, but instead will merely enumerate the principal features of each.

The home is inhabited by the nuclear family living within a household. As it is, it may house a single married couple and the children thereof.[15] From the moment of its construction, rules are respected that will ensure the well-being of the people and the prosperity of the household. The site is selected with care so as to avoid haunted areas. Work is begun with the sacrifice of an animal, a ritual supper, and offerings. The completion of

---

[13] Interesting data have been gathered in the villages of Oltenia (Lorinţ 1967).

[14] Ştefania Cristescu-Golopenţia (1944) devotes a volume to the study of this subject in the village of Drăguş. The study of the calendar of the peasants' festivals provides an identification of a whole series of these practices (Marian 1898–1901).

[15] Most of the time the peasant houses possessed only a single living room (Stahl 1958).

this work is marked by the placing of a green tree on the roof of the house, and, once again, by a ritual supper with the sacrifice of — most often — a bird. Finally, in order to enter the house, one must observe the rules drawn up by tradition.

It is obvious that these ceremonies concern neither isolated individuals nor the village as a whole, but precisely the members of the household community. In addition to these somewhat pagan practices, the prayers of a priest are also of importance, officiating over the place where the house is to be built and blessing it. The priest returns to the area periodically, his visits always having the same goal of protecting the household.

Special ceremonies can involve the courtyard, the surrounding lands, the animals, and the crops. The whole household (except for lands situated beyond the village) is fenced off and there is a main gateway. Upon the door is placed the design that is supposed to protect the people within and all of their goods.[16]

The lands, vineyards, and orchards of the households are protected by other magical devices. Let us note the two that are most important because of their frequency of occurrence; one is the skull of a horse fixed on a post, and the other a pillar planted in the earth with a head on top surrounded by straw and cloth (*potča*).[17] A whole series of magical operations, with which the Church is sometimes associated, is supposed to protect the harvest of the entire village.

EXTERNAL RELATIONSHIPS

It has been seen that an important part of the social relationships of these people occurs between different households. The household also intervenes sometimes in affairs involving occurrences outside the village proper, such as in the field of taxation. In the past taxes were not levied on individuals, but rather on households. The state administration often fixed taxes by village; the villages then met in assemblies and levied taxes on households instead, being certain to take into account the ability of each household to pay. One of the taxes that was most often contested in the past was the tax on smoke (*fumărit*). The state demanded for each unit of smoke produced, and therefore for each smoke-producing chimney, a fixed sum of money. What was at issue was thus not a tax on smoke but a tax on the home. In order to comprehend this fully, we must remember

[16]   Found only in some areas, main entrances made of monuments also included motifs having a protective function as well as others having a purely decorative one (Stahl 1960).
[17]   The skull of the horse guarded over the cultivation of vegetables, vineyards, and fruit trees; it also appeared in wood constructions as a decorative element with a magic function (Stahl, P. H. 1969).

that the traditional peasant home had only a single hearth;[18] the family prepared its meals, warmed itself, and slept around a single fire and in a single room of a house. Nowadays the home signifies the *gospodăria* and thus indirectly refers to the entire household.

Numerous examples could be cited here from old documents in which state authorities call peasants by their proper names; these names often hide those of the households. Even the social position of someone could be determined by his belonging to a particular household; thus, the peasants were or were not serfs according to their parents' position. But the case did arise where one of the two pairs of parents were serfs and the other pair not. In order to resolve these problems it had to be remembered that marriage was patrilocal, and the wife left her own home to reside with her husband, adopted his name, his economic position, his position in the village, and his place in church during the office.[19] If the wife were born into a free family and married a man with the status of a serf, adopting the status of her husband's household, she would consequently adopt his status as well. Their children, born into a household bound in serfdom would in turn be serfs themselves.

The weakening of the role of the household follows a long path of evolution parallel to that of the village; it touches in an unequal fashion its different functions. The increase in the amount of individual property as well as the appearance of important differences in wealth can accompany the woman's change of status. She might begin to receive as her dowry not only money, clothes, and furniture, but also land.[20] The property of the household, once unitary and belonging only to the male members of the group, can then become the individual property of the two spouses, who may then do with it what seems to both of them to be in their best interests.

Emigration to cities or to the New World upset the system of distribution and transmission of property. Some of the children left their homelands, and disputes between those who left the village and those who remained increased. The old system of having the last-born son live in the paternal household also presupposed that none of the last-born would leave either the home or the village, a situation which was to be contradicted by reality.

[18] The rooms in a house did not all have some form of heating and, even if they have, they could only be used occasionally; this was the case, for example, in "parlor" rooms (Stahl 1963, 1967).

[19] To attend mass or to participate in organized festivities near the church in memory of the dead, each person would sit in a place reserved for his family. Changes occur for women who, after marriage, go to sit next to their husbands. Other systems are even more complicated, however; studying them will reveal hierarchies, kinship relations, and deep-seated beliefs, whether it is a case of peasant churches, the aristocracy's churches, or even royal churches.

[20] This process appears to happen first among the aristocracy and the inhabitants of cities.

Each person tended to become the absolute proprietor of his parcels of land; he could abandon them, sell them, rent them, without anyone's being able to oppose these actions, since the new codes of law permitted his doing so. The entire social system is thus regulated.

Despite that, however, in many Rumanian villages there remained even after the Second World War some elements characteristic of the former system of households. Collective ownership of the land was to interrupt these traditions; property became state owned, dowries of land were no longer apparent, and inheritance of land also became inconceivable. Urbanization brought about a rush of migration of an intensity hitherto unknown. The moral relationships between generations also began to change, and parents no longer had the same means at their disposal to impose regulations upon their children. We should add that the home, whose evolution has been quite slow throughout history, is now changing rapidly; newlyweds now very rarely accept the idea of living with their parents in old and outdated households.

REFERENCES

BOGIŠIĆ, VALTAZAR
   1884   *De la forme dite inokosna de la famille rurale chez les Serbes et les Croates*. Paris: Thorin.
COSTA-FORU, XENIA
   1936   Quelques aspects de la vie familiale en Roumanie. *Archives pour la Science et la Réforme Sociale* 13(1):113–118. Bucharest.
CRESIN, ROMAN
   1945   *Recensământul agricol al României din 1941* [The 1941 agricultural census of Rumania]. Bucharest: Institut Central de Statistică.
CRISTESCU-GOLOPENȚIA, ȘTEFANIA
   1944   *Drăguş un sat din Țara Oltului (Făgăraş): manifestări spirituale, credințe şi rituri magice* [Drăguş, a village of the Olt area (Făgăraş): spiritual demonstrations, beliefs and magic rituals]. Bucharest: Institutul de Ştiinţe Sociale al României.
HAMMEL, EUGENE A.
   1968   *Alternative social structures and ritual relations in the Balkans*. Englewood Cliffs, N.J.: Prentice-Hall.
LORINȚ, FLORICA
   1967   Tradiția "moaşei de neam" în Gorj [The "wise woman of the lineage" tradition in Gorj]. *Revista de Etnografie şi Folclor* 12(2):127–132.
LORINȚ, FLORICA, C. ERETESCU
   1967   "Moşii" în obiceiurile vieţii familiale [The "old people" in the customs of family life]. *Revista de Etnografie şi Folclor* 12(4):299–307.
MARIAN, SIMION FLOREA
   1898–1901   *Sărbătorile la Români: studiu etnografic* [Festivals among the Rumanians: an ethnographic study], three volumes. Bucharest: Carol Göbl.

SCURTU, VASILE
1966   *Termenii de înrudire în limba română* [Rumanian kinship terminology].
       Bucharest: Editura Academiei Republicii Socialiste România.
STAHL, HENRI H.
1939   *Néréj, un village d'une région archaïque*, three volumes. Bucharest:
       Institut de Sciences Sociales de Roumanie.
1958–1965 *Contributii la studiul satelor devălmaşe româneşti* [Contributions to
       the study of the Rumanian cooperative village], three volumes. Buchar-
       est: Editura Academei Republicii Populare Romîne.
1969   *Les anciennes communautés villageoises roumaines*. Bucharest/Paris:
       Editura Academiei Republicii Socialiste România/Centre National de
       la Recherche Scientifique.
STAHL, PAUL H.
1958   *Planurile caselor românesti ţărăneşti* [Plans of Rumanian peasant
       houses]. Sibiu: Muzeul Brukenthal.
1960   Porţile ţărăneşti la Români [Rumanian peasant doorways]. *Studii şi
       Cercetări de Istoria Artei : Seria Arta Plastica* 7(2):81–106.
1963   "Casa ţărănească la Români în secolul al XIX-lea" [The Rumanian
       peasant house in the nineteenth century], in *Anuarul Muzeului Etno-
       grafic al Transylvaniei pe anii 1959–1961* [Transylvanian Ethno-
       graphic Museum Annual, 1959–1961]. Cluj.
1967   Interioare ţărăneşti din România (secolul al XIX-lea şi începutul
       secolului al XX-lea) [Peasant interiors in Rumania (nineteenth and
       early twentieth centuries)]. *Studii şi Comunicari* 13:85–104. Sibiu:
       Muzeul Brukenthal.
1969   *Romanian folklore and folk art*. Bucharest: Meridiane.

Situational Signs and Social Attentiveness: The Conception of Reality Among a Group of Sicilian Illiterates

MATILDE CALLARI GALLI and GUALTIERO HARRISON

RÉSUMÉ: CONCEPTION DE LA RÉALITÉ DANS UN GROUPE D'ILLETTRÉS SICILIENS

Caractérisée par une culture populaire avant tout orale coexistant avec les problèmes du monde industrialisé, l'île de Lampedusa se trouve placée dans une situation de "ghetto," où la bureaucratie est investie d'une mission particulière: médiateur entre deux mondes, elle doit faire passer les messages de la communauté vers la société et inversement.

A l'intérieur de ce monde clos, les relations de parenté, d'amitié, de travail sont réglées selon une étiquette stricte. Issue de deux types de population, l'une agricole, l'autre vivant de la pêche en mer, la société de l'île connaissait deux modes de production correspondant à deux structures familiales et sociales différentes. Avec le temps, le second type social a prévalu. Dans le contexte social actuel, le manque d'instruction passé de ces insulaires est, pour les tenants de la culture moderne, ce qui conditionne leur vie présente, ce présent qui demain sera devenu passé et qui détermine le futur.

Inconscients de leur état passé de subordination, ils attribuent leur situation à leur propre faute, inversant les relations causales. En conséquence, les deux modèles historiques et temporels propres aux deux cultures coexistant actuelle-

The research, under the direction of Professor Paolo Brezzi, received for the three years in question a grant of 4,500,000 lire from the Consiglio Nazionale delle Ricerche (Comitato di Scienze Storiche, Filosofiche e Filologiche). The anthropological part was done by Professors Matilde Callari Galli and Gualtiero Harrison, who hold the chairs of cultural anthropology at the Universities of Bologna and Padua respectively.

At many points in this paper we have tried to render into Italian, and thence into English, the construction of sentences as we have recorded them from the voices of our informants. Communicating our experience through the written medium unavoidably entails the distortion of translating.

We have extensively revised and reorganized the paper we presented at the Pre-Congress Wingspread Conference and the IXth International Congress of Anthropological and Ethnological Sciences in Chicago. In this effort, we gratefully acknowledge the considerable editorial assistance of Dr. James Silverberg, although we must accept complete responsibility for the final product.

ment — celle des insulaires et celle de la bureaucratie — fonctionnent jusque dans les moindres détails de la vie courante comme les vecteurs d'une idéologie, où le "Destin" immanent, intemporel, sert de justification à leur conception inversée de l'histoire et des relations causales.

Lampedusa, where we carried out our research for three years ending September 1972, is the largest of the Pelagian islands. Its distance from Marina di Palma — the nearest locality on the Sicilian coast — is 113.5 miles. The distance from Mahdiyya, on the African coast, is 75 miles.

The choice of the community was the object of preliminary research and many detailed discussions. The authors of the present study agreed that, in order to go deeply into some hypotheses derived from research carried out for three years (1966–1969) in four Sicilian municipalities, it was indispensable to select a place enjoying the advantages of a "small community." Examining the classical parameters stated by Robert Redfield (1955), and comparing them with the situations present in many municipalities of the southern Italian area, Lampedusa appeared to be the ideal spot.

Its geographical makeup and its history make it identifiable and at the same time typical. The activity prevailing on the island for about a century now is fishing. This uniformity, which involves about 80 percent of the population and influences the whole life of the group, makes the island community highly *homogeneous*. At the same time, although drawn in the last dozen years into the capitalist system and, at an elementary subsistence level, into the consumers' economy typical of the European geographical area, the community is still *self-sufficient*, thanks to its sea abounding in fish. Difficulties of communication forced the community into an isolation that was practically total in the winter months. Being circumscribed in time and space because of historical and geographical conditions, there is a possibility of reconstructing the dynamics of its social organization and tracing the evolution of traits constituting collective life from their genesis.

It is the purpose of the present paper to describe the concept of reality in Lampedusa and to explain it in terms of the conceptual conflicts present in an illiterate culture. Some of the premises present in Lampedusa thinking derive from the earlier preliterate period of an exclusively oral tradition; others derive from the literate culture of the broader nation-state if not from the industrialized world in general. Most of the material described herein concerns the preliterate concept of reality.

In the preliterate oral tradition of Lampedusa, behavior seems to respond (i.e. to be explainable by reference) to two sets of premises: *situational signs* and *the ethics/etiquette of social attentiveness*. The situational premises comprise an inventory of perceived "signs" — some unconscious or, at least not verbally specified and perhaps not even susceptible to verbal formulation by their native users. These signs inter-pret events and lead to understanding, to an ability to relate to events, even if they are not used to predict and control events. The premises of social attentiveness comprise a continuum of ethical and etiquette stan-dards which heighten the sensitivity of social interrelations and which, among other consequences, inhibit any violent display of hostility in the community. An understanding of both sets of premises, and of the fact that Lampedusans are enculturated to them both, makes it possible to understand the conclusions that they frequently reach — and the behavior they frequently display — when particular events take place. There is a constant contradiction between these premises of their oral tradition and those of the literate culture that characterizes the dominant nation-state (and world) of which they are a part. And this contradiction in their premises, in their conception of reality, reinforces their split dependency on two different channels of communication — one among illiterates and the other between illiterates and literates — which weakens their capacities for expression and exacerbates their social exclusion, their ghetto situation.

RESEARCH TECHNIQUES IN AN ILLITERATE CULTURE

Lampedusa's demographic size (during the years of our research actual inhabitants of the island numbered about 2,500) permitted deep and repeated contacts with a sample highly representative of the whole com-munity: 250 persons (i.e. 10 percent of the real population). The number of persons examined indirectly (sons under age, old people living with the family, wives, daughters married or under age) through information gathered from family heads, is quite high: a total of 1,000 persons. We two anthropologists mostly stayed on the island by turns, except for a month every year, when we stayed there together to establish in agree-ment the lines of successive researches.

   We carried out our study of Lampedusa using a wide array of anthro-pological research techniques. Our greatest effort was that of adapting different techniques to different problems, always trying to identify the most appropriate ones. The experience we had acquired previously in Sicily was invaluable from this point of view. Among the field techniques we used were: participating observation; overheard conversations about childhood and problems concerning work; "life histories," partial or total; interviews focused on particular topics; group interactions; stimu-lation of "cultural happenings"; use of key (steady) informants; photo-graphs of culturally relevant situations, taken by us and interpreted by the "natives." For bureaucratic go-betweens, *curricula vitae* were obtained from their life histories; within these narratives each protagonist related the intertwining of his "career" with that of other go-betweens; they all belonged to the same age grade and had come together during their formative years, outside the island, and then almost daily on the island. The materials have been ordered according to the methodological plan suggested by Oscar Lewis (1961) when several persons who have been associated with a certain event speak about it. Particular care was taken to record the occupation of space and proxemic behavior, using particular procedures worked out by the authors (Galli and Harrison 1973), partly adapting those formulated by Edward T. Hall (1963).

Lampedusa was known in ancient times under many names — Lopadusa (Strabo and Ptolemy), Lampidusa (Mercator), Lapadusa (Scillace), Lipadusa (Ariosto) — and was inhabited by various permanent settlements: Greek, Carthaginian, Roman, Arab, and Maltese. Apparently, the island was uninhabited, except by hermits who were dwelling in caves, at the time of some famous duels between the paladins of Charlemagne. It is said that one hermit built a chapel with two fronts: mosque on one side and Christian church on the other, closing the appropriate entrance as soon as he saw the Christian or Mohammedan flag on the mast of an approaching ship.

In 1463 Alfonso of Aragon granted the practically deserted island in emphyteusis to Giovanni Caro of the barons of Montechiaro. In the seventeenth century it passed to the Tomasi, together with the Barony of Montechiaro, through the marriage of the last descendant of the De Caro to Ferdinando Tomasi. Like the De Caro, the Tomasi variously tried to fortify it against the incursions of pirates, mostly from Africa, who were seeking a base for raids on Sicily as well as a source of water and game and a refuge from storms. In June 1800, a small number of Maltese settlers were given the island in emphyteusis by the Tomasi princes. In 1843 Ferdinand II bought the island from the Tomasi for 12,000 ducats, and in that same year published an edict inviting the subjects of the Kingdom of the Two Sicilies to settle in Lampedusa. These mid-nineteenth-century colonists were mostly illiterate peasant families to whom the new, unknown territory appeared more desirable than their poverty-stricken homeland.

The first migration was guided by Bernardo Sanvinsente and comprised 120 persons; among the few nonilliterates were a medical man, a judicial officer, and a secretary, A. Conti. The latter was the author of a history of Lampedusa, published in 1909 in Palermo and entitled *L'Isola di Lampedusa*, which book has been lost; there are a few handwritten copies of the original, which we have consulted to write the present notes. All the settlers received stipends: three *salme* of land and the choice of a dwelling site in the planned town. The expedition, on three boats — *La Rondine, Il Giglio dell'Onde*, and *L'Antilope* — left Sicily on September 18, 1843, and landed in Lampedusa on September 22. The judicial officer notified the few Maltese inhabitants that their emphyteusis grant had lapsed and was dissolved because they had not paid the ground rent. All the Maltese but two (De Battista and Caruana) left Lampedusa. The first settlers came from the provinces of Palermo and Agrigento, mostly from Misilmeri, Recalmuto, and Monreale; they were laborers and masons. In the following years other immigrations took place from Pantelleria, Utica, Lipari, and Isola delle Femmine, mostly consisting of fishermen. In 1847 the inhabitants numbered 700.

When the Kingdom of the Two Sicilies was annexed to Italy, following Garibaldi's victorious campaign which conquered it from one tyrant to confer it on another, the island of Lampedusa became part of the new national territory. Being much nearer to Africa than to Europe, the government in Rome always considered it more as an overseas territory than as a municipality of its national territory. In 1872, a short time after the unification of Italy, the national government decided to place on the island a colony of convicts, which stayed there until the beginning of World War II in 1940. The officials directing the penal colony used the convicts to cut down the timber on the island. Earth and water disappeared with the woods and the environmental conditions were so radically changed that the original peasants were obliged to become fishermen.

Since the remote and mythical epochs, when a sailor could navigate the Mediterranean on a boat dug out of a tree trunk, using as a sail a picture of the Virgin of Porto Salvo (today the island's patron), other means of communication have connected Lampedusa to the European continent: first a weekly postal steamer, later daily air service; and since then radio, magazines, cinema, and television. After half a century of development in virtual isolation, the island has been experiencing new accumulations of objects and information throughout the most recent half century. At the end of the sixties, hotel speculation and anthropological speculation arrived at Lampedusa. The former has inevitably doomed the island to transform itself, casting members of the community into the roles of "noble savages" for future tourists from a society of leisure. But the community is also playing a role for the anthropologists. Torn from the poverty of their original territory and brutally transplanted on a virtually uninhabited island; deprived of trees, water, and arable earth on the windswept island they were colonizing; bombed in World War II by the bearers of democracy, freedom, and progress; confused by messages from the consumers' society; and today in many respects deprived of the produce from a sea on which drifts of oil are floating while their island becomes a "tourists' paradise," the Lampedusans at first mistook us anthropologists for enthusiastic submarine fishermen. The misunderstanding having been cleared up, they tried to understand how they could adjust to our needs, how to exaggerate certain aspects of their daily life, how to become sufficiently exotic.

We were already familiar with "... the strange Sicilian urge to tell strangers hair-raising stories ..." (Lampedusa 1970:116), in literature and from our own earlier research experiences. We once arranged a meeting between a group of our informants from a town ill-famed as "the heart of the Mafia" and a renowned American sociologist who had come there to learn about the "Mafiosi," to interview on the subject of murders that had taken place in the district. Our own objective data recorded hundreds of murders, mostly unpunished, and links between the uncon-victed presumed murderers and a large part of the community's families through relations of kinship and *comparatico* (co-godparenthood). The sociologist had expected the men to keep silent in accordance with a stereotype about *omertá*, which the police see as complicity with criminals and the natives as "manliness" (*omo* = man). Despite his expectations, he obtained extremely exhaustive answers to his questions. In fact, the hundreds of murders became thousands; the slaughter of animals became infanticide; gory rites of initiation were invented, in the style of the Grand Guignol. And, on taking leave, the most brilliant informant asked us, as the hosts of the occasion, *"Risponnemmo giusto?"* ("Did we give the right answers?", i.e. Did we answer correctly, exactly as you expected?)

Our need to control for errors introduced by this pattern of exaggerat-ing the exotic made our full participation in the daily life of the com-munity and our knowledge of the local dialect all the more necessary. We played some informal but recognizable roles in the community; for example, to observe the learning situation of schoolchildren we both taught for some weeks in the *dopo-scuola* (the two-hour afternoon ses-sion when pupils do homework at school under the supervision of some teacher other than the one they have in morning classes).

We also had access to written records, of course. The documents we consulted in the archives of Naples and Palermo allowed us to reconstruct the island's official history. There is also, in Lampedusa itself, an archive of the registers that the Catholic church began to keep at the arrival of the first colonizers in 1843 and still keeps up to date today: marriage certifi-cates, records of baptisms and deaths. In his ecclesiastical Latin the *curatus vicarius*, noting down these births, deaths, and marriages, tells the story of humble subjects, who, trusting to fortune, had left their ter-ritories with beautiful Greek and Arab names, poor in hopes and resources: Misilmeri and Recalmuto, Monreale, Pantelleria, Ustuca, and Lipari.

In brief, we had at our disposal two ways in which to reconstruct Lampedusa's history: (1) on the one hand the written documents which, covering three hundred years, identified some conspicuous events of social life, and which therefore enable us to make the past present again, to connect yesterday with today; (2) on the other, the mythical tales of today's inhabitants that connect the present, in its problematic reality, with the past.

Writing makes the past contemporary, as oral tradition predates the present. The distinction between history and myth appears arbitrary, and the judgment which assigns to written history, as compared with oral history, a greater objectivity, also appears arbitrary and unjustified. Not all men have had an equal possibility of contributing to the making of written history, and those who have done the writing have been very few. And these few have written it exactly in order to justify before future generations the privilege (bound to class origin) that they claimed, of being the only ones who had made history.

But the historiographical lines on which our research moved are only apparently parallel tracks. They differ not only and exclusively in their reciprocal perspective: from the past to the present — so as to make the past present — the perspective of written history; from the present to the past — to predate the present — the perspective of oral history. The two histories differ because the first is the history of victors, and the second the history of the vanquished. It is difficult for anthropologists — at least for us — to take sides, openly and finally, for one or the other of them. We can be against the social-evolutionist position of interpreting human history according to a pattern of unilinear progress; at the same time, we can be for "progress," we can want to struggle in order to obtain a transformation of the world, greater social justice, the improvement of man, and the development of his potentials. We can reject, at an epistemological level, a unidirectional conception of progress, while at the same time accepting it at the ideological level, in order to plan for the future.

The distinction between the victors' written history and the oral history of the vanquished is part of two more general orientations in time, which are different: the first, at its limit, tends to nullify the present, reducing all time to the past or to the future; the second hypertrophizes the present to the point of denying any one time (past, future) outside it.

LAMPEDUSA'S ILLITERATE CULTURE

These two temporal orientations seem to predominate, respectively, in *preliterate* and *literate* cultures. Lampedusa's culture ought to be a preliterate culture, because all social communication within the community is oral. Every moment of collective life, from the organization of working relations and ways of production to ties with family and friends, from the exercise of political power to the part taken in religious events, is structured by face-to-face relations, coherently established by verbal interaction. Lampedusa's culture should be a literate culture because the island, a component part of the national territory, comes under the state law which prescribes compulsory education for all citizens of the Italian republic.

But Lampedusa is neither the one nor the other, and exactly because of this, paradoxically, having to be the one and the other at the same time, it is in reality what we have defined as "an *illiterate* culture" (Harrison and Galli 1970, 1973). In our writing we have adopted the offical definition given by UNESCO to the term *illiterate:* anyone is illiterate if he is unable to write and read a simple account of his daily life. In the official statistics of the Italian republic, however, national pride includes among literates those who, at least once in their lifetime, have been inscribed in a school class. In Sicily, for example, the official 1961 census listed as "total illiterates" 15 percent of those of school and postschool age; adding those who had not completed the compulsory school, the percentage of "functional illiterates" rose to 38 percent and the reality that we found during our research in the region's cities (Palermo, Bagheria, Corleone, Trappeto) was much more serious (Harrison and Galli 1973).

According to the definition of "total illiterate" as a person who has never attended any scholastic class, the percentage in Lampedusa is lower than the corresponding percentage in the Sicilian region (official accounts speak of 10 percent). But in a sample representing the social strata and age grades of the island, containing one hundred individuals who had attended elementary schools, only four might be defined as literate according to the UNESCO formula. The entire school organization, indeed, appears casual and accidental: a class in the school sometimes has as many as thirteen teacher changes during the seven-month school year; the pupils go to school irregularly and rarely finish the whole yearly course, because in April they go to sea, and the younger ones work in seasonal factories, canning mackerel. Even those who complete the school cycle in this irregular and partial manner, by the time it is over, make less and less use of the written medium, and very soon pass on to increase the number of half-illiterates. Anyhow, writing would be of very little use to them, for they communicate with relatives at a distance through a friend or relation who, by chance or purpose goes to see them. In the island there is no municipal library and no bookseller; only copies of some newspapers get there, with delays of days and weeks.

In an "illiterate culture" such as Lampedusa, therefore, as long as one is inside the community, one does not need to be literate. But in external relations with the rest of the nation, with "the Continent," the community is "literate" according to what is presumed by the law and required for the consumption of goods produced by the industrial system. Illiterates are not only unable to communicate through the medium of writing, but above all and in the first place, they evade and break the law on compulsory education and, potentially, all other laws, which are always written laws: the citizen is obliged not only to observe them, but also to be acquainted with them. The term *illiterate culture* thus means a situation of conflict, conflict that is present in every social aspect, in every moment of the individual's existence. It is a "ghetto situation," unfair to those who have to submit to it. The community is internally ruled by preliterate patterns, while in its external relations it must adapt to official and institutionalized patterns that belong to a culture based on literate education.

The community is politically managed by a local elite of public administrators, parish priests, political and union officials, defenders of police law and order, schoolteachers, physicians, pharmacists, and bank clerks. These persons are always the illiterate culture — and, when the state's law does not prevent it, from the community itself — but they have been brought up according to the official rules of the dominant system, namely of the educated-people's culture. From a juridical-formal point of view they represent the central institutionalized power in a delegated and decentralized form. In Lampedusa they have received most of their training outside the community (the only education beyond the compulsory schools on the island is an attempt at a vocational school connected with fishing activities which has had very limited success). They leave the island, choosing as the city for their scholastic emigration the capital of the province from which their family originated: Trapani, Palermo, or Agrigento. But these persons have been chosen by the dominant central system according to selective standards which consider above all the degree to which they belong to the community. How much they have progressed in their socialization within the educated culture matters much less. Their curricula mention more failures than successes; hence they have not left the community and become outsiders through individual promotion. The most successful individuals do not return to the community, they become outsiders, and to that extent the community itself becomes socially impoverished.

Essentially the social function of the local elite is determined by their roles as bureaucratic mediators much more than by their status specialties (e.g. as public administrator, parish priest, etc.). As bureaucratic mediators they translate the messages of ideology, politics, techniques, and values from the national and international into the local field, and vice versa; from society to community and from community to society.

Their social positions are perceivable at different levels. For the literate society they are marginal officials, with a low grade of professional training, performing functions that are barely relevant to the global system due to the scant importance attributed to the community. The juridical status ascribed to them is superficially equal to similar statuses at the center of the system, but perspectives of a developing career and of social mobility, pursued like mirages, are lacking. Their social mobility is noticeably compressed and can develop only within the boundaries of the local community. But by examining their social "image" within the community, it is possible to perceive a new dimension. Within the community, the bureaucratic mediator is perceived as the official of a delegated and decentralized power, but his social status is not placed correctly within the hierarchy according to which the central institution is structured. For the community, the *parrino* is not the parish priest, hierarchically subject to the ecclesiastic authority of the Archbishop, the Curia, the Pope. Rather he is the Church, while the Pope — a five-hour flight away — belongs to another world and is perceived as the parish priest of Rome, the curate of "those others," the curate of "the gentlefolk." The sergeant major of the carabinieri (military police) has, in the community, powers superior to those of his general in the national field. The sergeant major's power in Lampedusa, from a juridical point of view, is within the limits of the law, just as is his general's; but from a sociological point of view, i.e. from the community's point of view, it is a power allocated by the community, to be renewed day by day, which may be absolute to the point of arbitrariness or may be reduced to the formal action of accompanying the funeral of one of the citizens.

Also from the point of view of an illiterate community, its relations with the central powers of the state are always predetermined by a protective attitude, like a "Magna Mater's," assumed by the community. Any lack of interest shown by the state authorities is considered aggravating: they are blamed in a tone resembling that of a mother who resents her child's conduct "after all my sacrifices for his good." But if a cabinet minister takes to heart the conditions of economic underdevelopment and applies funds from the state budget to public works in Lampedusa, or if he solves individual problems — arranges a desired transfer or a pension — the community "adopts" that minister as one of its citizens. Such protection and affection must get their reward and this relation will last forever, or rather it will last until betrayed. In sum, the function of the local elite, the bureaucratic mediators, is like that of the servants in the Commedia dell'Arte; their role is to bring in contact the two main characters, who, due to the machination of the plot, could only appear together on the stage at the end of the performance, as the whole play centered on difficulties that prevented their communication.

The grossest form of alienation through illiteracy, however, derives from the social selection process of the educational system, based yesterday on classroom questioning and marking and today on the psychological test and the IQ. Teaching in schools, today as yesterday, declares itself a promoter of equality and spreader of the light of reason, while in reality it produces a barrier between the "deserving" and the "undeserving". Through its standards of assessment, with their semblance of increasing objectivity, it succeeds in persuading the "unde-serving" that their present subordinate position in social, economic, and political life is caused by an objective and natural condition: their real lack of merit. In consequence, illiterates always attribute their present position to their own fault. They do not see themselves as persons disadvantaged today precisely because yesterday they were rejected by society; rather, they consider their rejection of yesterday to be a result of their condition of inferiority. Educated people say that the illiterates have gained consciousness of their inferiority, as it applies both to today and yesterday: "they had no use for schooling."

The two historical and temporal models of culture (literate and illit-erate) function like carrier structures of ideology, of political judgment, on the disadvantaged "ghetto" position of the illiterates. For the edu-cated culture, the illiterate's past nonattendance in school is what con-ditions his present; this present, which tomorrow will have become a past, conditions the future. The illiterate culture thus receives the harshest judgment from the society of the educated, a denigrated world that is motionless because it is without a past and without a future. For the illiterate culture, the present state of inferiority of its members is not ascribed to an initial exclusion, when school rejected them because they were the children of illiterate parents. Predating and making retroactive their present condition, yesterday's exclusion is explained by today's inferiority. And this apparent chronological absurdity is justified and obviated by recourse to Fate, which said "no" to the illiterate, yesterday as tomorrow; because Fate is imminent in every moment, it is outside time, it determines time.

That folklore anthropologists should speak of oral tradition only in folk culture, and sociologists of social problems only in the literate indus-trial world, was an acceptable strategy in the development of science. But the reality of the world — not only the reality of a small island lost in the Mediterranean — comprises precisely the simultaneous existence of the two patterns, oral and literate, in the "ghetto" situation of illiterate culture. As the "ghettos" of illiterate culture continue to expand, it will be increasingly difficult to find that folk creativity which is so greatly prized by the admirers of preliterate folk society, and it will be increasingly difficult to sustain the delusion that the police can successfully block the "ghetto" rebellion until the time when peaceful integration has come to pass. Anthropologists have given surprisingly little attention to the influ-ence of writing on the social life of humanity (cf. Goody 1968), even though, as ethnographers dealing with preliterate populations and archaeologists studying prehistory, they could well be designated as "specialists on preliterate society." The sociological imagination of the Western world has lessened concerning the problems of illiteracy and with an unjustified air of triumph it is noted that the percentages are diminishing, forgetting the population explosion that is taking place. Yet, according to official data, the number of those now living in the world without being able to read and write is on the increase. Everything becomes even more strange when we consider that attention to the differences represented by societies with an oral tradition really has emerged just when, according to the hypothesis of the illiterate culture, the preliterate societies are disappearing from the world, i.e. just when the nation-states formed in the Third World have accepted the principle of compulsory education, thus transforming their preliterate citizens into illiterates.

Today the anthropological view of traditions as such seems anachronistic, because to the oral tradition have been added the officialism of a written national language and the influence of electrical and electronic communication media. Today anthropologists are repeating, in the fields of communication and tradition, the myopic error of those who earlier in the field of political organization used to speak of segmentary and acephalous societies, neglecting the existence of a colonial administration which had destroyed the aboriginal political organization and created "a body without a head" (Crowder 1968). But today a great deal has changed in the ideology and practice of the Western neocapitalist system: folk traditions have been resuscitated and transformed into consumer goods, while at the same time an ecological ideology has been created. Nature is being rediscovered; city consumers are being convinced that they need a weekend, summer holiday, winter holiday, a second and a third house. Hence, a touristic value has been conferred on the very same areas that have become depopulated by convincing their aborigines (the primitives of the Third World and the peasants of Western society) to become urbanized through the mirage of a fuller life that is richer because it is loaded with industrial objects. The gospel of alphabetic instruction was spread among these "savages" so as to make them more available for their exodus out of "the country" and toward "the city." The illiterates continue to be considered guilty and to be rejected because they do not yet possess the traditional use of writing, even though today education has produced, with its science and its technology, new communication tools, which transform the uses and meanings of writing.

Far removed from the rural regions where their patterns of oral culture were created, the illiterates are today being crowded into city areas, precisely the cities that educated people are now abandoning (Galli and Harrison 1972). What is no longer good enough for the ruling class can and must be good enough for the subordinate classes. Between yesterday and today cities have exploded, the aborigines — southerners in Milan and blacks in Chicago — with their subeducation and their illiterate culture, are making cities unfit for nice, prosperous, and educated middle-class people.

OTHER ASPECTS OF LAMPEDUSA'S SOCIAL ORGANIZATION

Today, not much land is fit for cultivation. While Sanvinsente mentions abundant rains and lightning (1869 [1849]:35), today precipitation is extremely scanty: in winter nobody remembers it ever to have snowed, and in the whole year 1969 there were sixty-one rainy days. There are no springs and wells are rare and formed by infiltrations of sea water, favored by the calcareous soil. The level of water in the wells increases and diminishes with the tide, and its degree of salinity varies with the wells' distance from the sea and the more or less filtrating quality of the soil. The temperature ranges between a minimum of 7.2°C(44.9°F)and a maximum of 30.6°C (87.1°F); the minimum mean temperature is 13.8°C (56.8°F), the maximum mean 23.4°C (74.1°F).

The flora of Lampedusa is Afro-Sicilian, differing more from Sicily than from Africa. Today, fruit trees are rare: fig, pomegranate, locust-tree, peach, and olive prevail; prickly pear trees are very common. Tall trees are lacking, except for a few palms. Some shrubs of *periploca*, commonly called *la macchia di seta*, grow among the rocks; a century ago this plant covered the whole island and was used for filling mattresses and pillows. We collected much evidence concerning the extensive timber cover that existed before the convicts cut it down. It is mentioned by Pietro Calcara (1846:32), Sanvinsente (1869), and Giovanni Gussone (1832:86). Old people talk about it, tell stories about hunting and wild beasts, and legends of children lost in the thick undergrowth and miraculously saved by generous animals. It is attested to also by nicknames derived from now-extinct fauna, still borne by some local families. Old people's tales and legends, circulating in the community, often mention surprising fauna: deer, lions, tropical serpents; they are all fantasies going back to the times when the island was all covered with shrubs and peopled by animals. Today Lampedusa has rabbits, mice, rats, two kinds of snake (*Coelopeltis lacertina* and *Macroprotodon cucullatus*); there are no lizards, while *Gongyli ocellati*, usually called *tiri*, abound. Flocks of migrant birds land seasonally on the island: turtle doves, quails, cranes, wild pigeons. The sea abounds in shellfish, crabs, sponges, coral, and fishes: mackerel, African sardines, anchovies, ricciole, perches, mullets, moray eels, bass, and bream.

In the last half century the community underwent an accelerated process of modernization. At the same time, it entered into contemporary history, with Winston Churchill recording in his Nobel-Prize-winning history how the island surrendered to the Allied armies. Lampedusa was, as war bulletins used to say in those days, attacked "from the sky and from the sea" and two thirds of the island was destroyed while its population took shelter in its caves. The inhabitants recall that the number of soldiers was double that of the population, but the Nobel laureate, then prime minister, writes that as a matter of fact the island surrendered on June 13, 1943, "to the pilot of an aircraft who had been compelled to land there by lack of fuel" (Churchill 1952:30–31).

Even during the three years of our research we have noticed increasingly rapid transformations. Capitalist speculation has decreed that the island is soon to become a center for tourism and sea bathing, a "paradise for nautical sports," as the travel agency publicity puts it. Industrial and urban civilization needs its dreams and idyllic refuges in order to escape from smog, ecological decay, pollution, and noise. The fishing families, with whom we have been acquainted during our research, will become tourist and hotel personnel, and the whole island will become an artificial natural reserve. The island's fate is decided. Its population will adjust to their new social role. To "invent" natural innocence is a job that pays quite well. Their history is no different from that of all "colonized" populations: they are our product, differing from us because we want them to differ; they are a product of colonialism and they have accepted being different as their role.

Today Lampedusa has 4,311 registered "residents," divided into 1,142 families; about 80 percent of the active population's activities are concerned with the sea. There are few peasants, about one hundred; goatherds are very few, only eight. The only inhabited center is the village of Lampedusa, built around the port. The port itself is shaped like a shamrock leaf. On its eastern tip stand the oldest houses of the fishermen. In the summer some of the little bays (Cala Guitigia, Cala Pisana, Cala Francese, Cala Madonna, Vallone dello Scoglio) are inhabited to attract tourists who wish to live as much as possible on the sea.

The social organization was at one time characterized by the intersection of two social categories: peasants and fishermen. The first settlers mostly worked the fields that they received from the Bourbon king as a reward for colonizing. Later a second wave of settlers, from Isola delle Femmine, brought the sea element. For most of the nineteenth century, through endogamous marriages, these two productive activities and two family aggregates persisted as two parallel social structures. Then the woods were cut down, the rains diminished almost to extinction, the earth was swept off by the wind and carried to the sea, and with the earth the wind also carried off the peasants, all of whom became fishermen. At this point the island became unproductive and, even more important, the two social aggregates began to mix through marriages between former peasant families and the original fishing families. The earlier double structure was given a new form. The land practically became female property, even if from a formal juridical point of view it could continue to belong to men and women equally. It was brought into marriages by the women as dowry or inherited by them at their parents' death, while males, during their parents' lifetime, received an advance on the estate for the purpose of buying boats, nets, and other fishing implements. Until the advent of tourism and land speculation, the land itself had mainly a symbolic value; even its sentimental value was small. In fact it represented primarily a point of reference in marriage exchanges, giving land tenure a function in the control of incest.

In the many myths dealing with marriages, marriage always joins a man and a woman who were greatly separated, belonging to groups of differing habits and customs, whether by a difference in social extraction or by the arrival of one mate from a remote country. Even concerning the first marriage, celebrated five years after the arrival of the colonizing subjects, the oral myth mentions the nuptials as the happy outcome of a difficult love affair between a noblewoman and a plebeian. In other narratives about marriage at least one party must be an outsider whose arrival was due to atmospheric causes, a favorable wind blowing toward the island or a storm that wrecked a ship on the rocks. The most meaningful aspect of these myths is the different racial and social origin of husband and wife, meant to deny since the beginning what is denied now in everyday life; that the two are blood relations. Since a common family name might, due to its objective nature, give the lie to such a denial, the community uses surnames only for official written deeds; and between themselves Lampedusans are known and addressed by nicknames. A nickname, *'nciuria*, is given both to men and women, to real estate (cultivated fields, houses), and to boats. It has been possible to establish a correlation man–boat, woman–real estate. The boat takes its owner's or its builder's nickname, as the house or land takes a woman's nickname; reciprocally a man's nickname is nearly always connected with his work at sea, and a woman's with her activity on land.

In Lampedusa, the most complicated system of interpersonal relations is *comparatico* (co-godparenthood) — a controversial theme in anthropological interpretation. There is a marriage *comparatico* as well as the ones established on the occasions of baptism and of confirmation (*cresima*). At one time there was also a *comparatico di San Giovanni*. *"Semo cumpari fino a Natali; soccu avemu ni spartemu, fino all'acqua ca vivemu"* (we are *cumpari* until Christmas, whatever we have we share, down to the water on which we live). These words were uttered on June 24 (Saint John's day) by groups that collected for a trip to the country. These groups could be intersexual, but usually they were unisexual age groups. Of all the *comparatici*, the most important — according to our informants — is the one by baptism. The terms of reference that define this relationship are three : *figlioccio; padrino (madrina); compare (commare)*. *Figliocci (o/a)-padrino (madrina)* signify the relation between the newborn child and the two adults (the godfather and his wife), who guarantee his or her future spiritual life; *compare (commare)–compare (commare)* signify the relation between the parents of the child receiving baptism and the godparents. The closeness of the *padrino–figlioccio* relation is evident in the proverb, widespread on the island, *"da parrini si pigghia a vina"* (from the godfather one gets his temperament), and in the actual behavior of looking for a physical resemblance between godson and godfather.

Alongside the system of kinship on Lampedusa another structure exists: that of the fishing group. It is more difficult to reconstruct because written documents are lacking, and above all because it is informal, operating on an unconscious level, and now in process of dissolution.

At sunset or at dawn the boats come out of the port in a compactly united group which then "explodes," each boat going in a different direction. On their return — next morning or after three or four days, according to the type of fishing — some boats and motorboats are overloaded with fish, others loaded, and others half full. Why did the men of the boat that comes back half empty not go to fish on the richer bank? We would get the answer, "Because the others were already there"; to our next question "Why don't they go there beforehand?" the fishermen would respond concisely: "Because they know the others go there later." Even without walls, without mortar, the sea can be divided, like the land, in many fields. From a juridical point of view one cannot speak of ownership, hence the state's defense of private property is lacking, but while the state's law is more remote than the continent and may eventually settle a controversy, it is local social control in Lampedusa that acts as a regulator, inhibiting controversy. We experienced one case where some fishermen tried to fish in an area belonging to another boat, but later they were "persuaded" to give back the mackerel they had caught.

Possession of a bank is hereditary: the right of exploiting belongs always to the same fishing group and that group remains the same even if, with the passage of years, its individual members change. For months we were given the impression that the crews of boats and motorboats were formed on the spur of the moment, almost accidentally (fishermen who were relatives or friends or simply those who were available on the market). The justification was always commonplace: "He is capable," or "he has nets," or "he has a boat." However, in each boat there were capable men, who sometimes were close relatives and sometimes not and, in spite of some variations, the groups tended to remain constant.

In every boat group three generations exist: while the old men become older and then die, adults are getting old, the young become adults, and new young men become part of the crew. These youths are always relatives of someone in the group, on the father's or on the mother's side. But in a population of 4,000 this is inevitable: even in cases where kinship was denied by a Lampedusan, the parish documents would confirm it. Well, but how are the new young men chosen? Once again the verbalized explanation pointed to the obvious: among those who are available, the fishing group tries to get hold of the best young man. Only after we had been in Lampedusa for a while did it become apparent that it is the relation between godfather and godson that acts as a link between the structure of kinship and the structure of fishing groups. Thus it is explained how two brothers may belong to two different fishing groups. The godfather of the new adept is a member of the fishing group that owns a particular bank whether he be the boat owner, the boat chief, the fishing-chief, the owner of the nets, or in brief, any other member of that group. To be a member of that fishing group, the godfather is related by a series of godparental links to the first discoverer of the bank. No one in the community thinks that he belongs to the fishing group because of these links to the first discoverer of the bank, but just because he is the godson of a member. The banks of fishes, natural and artificial (for instance a sunk steamer), are usually called *secche*, with the addition of a specific name that they received from their discoverer: *secca bongiorno e dammi u pani'*; *secca sperone*; *secca immiruteddu*. Some are directly named after their discoverer and his surname or nickname. Going back with the aid of our informants to the approximate date on which the bank was given its name, it has been possible, by consulting the parish records, to identify the discoverer's godchildren, and receive confirmation from the informants that they later on came into the fishing group of their godfather. When the organization of work was shifted toward the uni-production of fishing activity, godfathers were chosen, with increasing frequency, among fishermen and still more specifically among the descendants of settlers from Isola delle Femmine.

Lampedusans go in family groups to public events on the island, e.g. the theater, but during the performance the family groups get smaller, or rather are "widowed" of some men, who form groups according to the social structure that is most determinant for them, the fishing group. That group, which has no contractual force, is apparently informal, unstruc-tured, and changing all the time through the introduction of new mem-bers and the loss of the older ones, but it is in fact unchangeable because of the link with the fishing area. The group on the right occasions and in the right places — i.e. in relevant social situations — reconfirms its unity, soliciting the attention of other groups, proving to itself (to its members) and to the whole community the priority of the sacral link of the fishing group, above the sacramentality and the juridical recognition of the kinship group. Even the women of the crew have a link binding them to each other which is stronger than ties with other relatives and affines. This is expressed particularly when they are anxious concerning the safety at sea of the group's boat.

We have noticed a proxemic expression of the two principal social structures, family groups and fishing groups. The members of the family group, when they walk about in the street or sit at table, always tend to occupy space side by side. The fishing group, which on the boat is in a circle due to the functionality of work, is always arranged in a circle on land also, and repeats in its microcosm the pattern of a culture where space is circular, where time is circular.

LAMPEDUSAN USE OF SITUATIONAL SIGNS

On Lampedusa we became aware of many acts which were explainable only in terms of situational "signals" or "signs." Some of these premonitory signs are common to the whole group; there are others which only work within a family circle, almost variations on the themes of shared signs; others, still more special, belong to the individual. This was not new to us; in fact, for several years we had been recording signs of danger as utilized in illiterate culture.

At the beginning of our earlier research activity, we were in a part of Sicily where some villages were destroyed by an earthquake and there, as in Lampedusa, dogs had barked, domestic animals had been restless, the sky was red, the air was "heavy" — exactly "an air of earthquake" — and so on. Already eight years ago we noticed that recourse to the use of these signs increased in situations of crisis and fear, becoming the fundamental system of reference in disastrous situations. In normal situations the illiterates tended on the contrary to accept — i.e. to submit — to the system of signs belonging to the educated society. This same situational feature of the use of "signs" occurs in Lampedusa.

We have stated above that in Lampedusa the signs of accidents may be individual, familiar, or collective. This is a classification for practical purposes, built on the recurrence of the signs themselves: most of the population refer to some of them, others belong only to certain individuals. But this classification has merely heuristic value. For one thing, it is obvious that even the most individual signs are, in a certain sense, collective, because they are produced by the community's culture. Moreover, the social value attributed to foreboding — and every man, be he educated, preliterate, or illiterate, has what we may call forebodings — is not absolute for any society or any individual, but is always relative to the situation. When several persons who are involved in the same situation all have signs, even if their signs are individual in expression, these signs are seized by the collectivity, they acquire a meaning and a direction, they become signs for the other individuals.

One evening in Lampedusa a boat was late coming back; the women of five families had begun, an hour before, to spy on one another. Then Rosa, the wife of zu Raffaele, decided to come out and look at the sea. This should really have been done by Maria — it was due to her by the rules of etiquette because she was the wife of zu Turi, the chief of the boat — but Maria was away from the island. For Rosa this had been a difficult decision; Maria would have been more sure of herself in timing and gestures. To come out on the quay too early would have shown a baseless anxiety had the boat subsequently come back to port. On the other hand, to have come out too late, if an accident had really happened, would have been interpreted as a dishonorable lack of interest.

Women learn through experience to manage their fear: to hide it when the delay is still brief and to increase it if help can be given only by strangers, in case relatives and friends are still at sea. When the men are at sea they know that they can count on such "fears" on the part of their wives arousing the community and obliging the others to interfere. Anxiety is not judged on the basis of whether it is shown quietly or hysterically. Judgment is always given in situational terms, i.e. they judge whether it explodes at the right moment, not earlier or later.

The women say they came out of their houses because at that moment they "felt" their dear ones to be in danger. One might almost say they "feel" something because otherwise their behavior would seem absolutely unintelligible. On other occasions, with a longer delay and in worse weather conditions, no women are to be seen on the quay and the alarm therefore does not strike. But on those occasions there has not been any sign of an accident. The women speak of a system of "signs" which they have learned to interpret since childhood. An illiterate who became anxious for the safety of his dear ones without having perceived signs of an accident would be like an educated person who entered into an anxious condition, fearing for his dear ones' safety, an hour before the time fixed for their return.

Rosa, faced with some delay on the part of the boat, has had her signs, so-called individual ones, and she attributes value to them because the other women of the crew's members have also had signs. She would be the first to reject the close correlation between the oil spilled by Concetta and the hitch of the boat's engine, nor have these and other signs, hers or belonging to other persons, happened recently. Therefore Rosa came out and the women of the other men on the boat followed her.

On Lampedusa, some "signs" were used by the islanders that we ethnographers could not perceive and which did not seem to lend themselves to verbal expression in terms of sensory perception by the Lampedusans. For example, there is Antonino's story, the least mysterious among many others. Perhaps Antonino is sensitive and able to show his qualities to a degree superior to others; at any rate, in the village there is none with Antonino's "gift." In the months when the fish called *serre* pass, it is difficult to meet him; he spends his days on the rocks, looking at the sea day and night, because up to half a mile's distance he is able to see the shoal of *serre*, at a depth of several feet (*braccia*). When we asked him how he could see the fishes, he at first said abruptly, "I know it, I feel it." And this had seemed to us an attempt to change the subject, to keep a professional secret. A few days later he explained he could see where the fishes were by the color of the sea, and he said so apparently using an analogy which might be understood "by an educated person like you." He used to say that the sea changes color, both at night and in the daytime, although neither of us anthropologists, standing alongside him by turns for a whole week, succeeded in perceiving these chromatic variations of the sea when small shoals passed.

All the island's inhabitants, as compared with us anthropologists, possess exceptional abilities of coming into harmony with natural phenomena, and their conception of fate, either positive or negative, is closely connected with this relation of theirs with nature. On this point they differ not only from educated city people but also from illiterate peasants, nor could it be otherwise: in the island attention to atmospheric signs is necessary to avoid accidents, and the weather on the sea is always a risk, changing rapidly and, according to them, being different from one fishing area to another. They wondered not only that one of us anthropologists should use a sailboat for sport and amusement, but even more that we should trust the meteorological forecasts of the radio and of the port authorities. To them there is not a single weather: many weathers coexist, and even the migrations of fishes and birds cooperate in the balance of alternating seasons. It often happens that the sky over Lampedusa is suddenly covered with clouds rent by lightning, and then suddenly becomes clear, while not a drop of rain has fallen. They say that there has been no rain because of a certain situation (for instance the passage of a flight of birds). The illiterates are not so "savage" as to think that the beating of wings can magically put clouds to flight. What they mean is that if the birds fly it will not rain. They make use, so to speak, of an animal science, the one known to animals who know when and where to migrate.

Certain "signs" are particularly malevolent. In an earlier period, there was more envy in the village, people could "take you by the eye." Such a *malocchio* would be followed by misfortune if you did not recite the *razione* for taking it away. At first we ethnographers regarded these *razioni* as simple warding-off devices, ways of avoiding future harm. But the true function of the *razione* is that it serves to explain an event; it is a way of placing oneself in syntony with the situation, of acquiring the capacity of hearing nature's message. A *razione* that literally seems meant to change weather conditions is really used to interpret them, to understand their meaning. Men also fear *malocchio* if the boat of a fishing party that has always been fruitful comes back without any fish. But they never recite the *razione* directly, they always call other men to recite it for them, differently from the women who recite theirs personally and directly. If, by mistake, you cut off your son's *trizzi'e donna* — tangled locks of hair, which are formed on children's heads and which do not get cut but are allowed to fall as the hair grows — and if subsequently your son falls ill, it is because the *lochi 'e casa*, the spirits of your home, had taken a liking to your son but have now taken offense at what you have done and are angry.

The *razione* is taught to a woman on Christmas by her "husband's aunt." "The husband's aunt" who has this function may be the sister of the husband's father or the wife of the brother of the husband's father. In the case of Rosa, and in the other cases in which the aunt who had taught the *razione* was the wife of the father's brother, they were all also relatives of the women to whom they were teaching the ritual formula, independently from her marriage: her mother's sister or the sisters of the wife of one of the mother's brothers. Anyhow all have referred to the depository of the *razione* as "the husband's aunt."

LAMPEDUSAN SOCIAL ATTENTIVENESS

On the island interpersonal relations of kinship, *comparatico*, friendship, and work are always characterized by extreme attentiveness to one another's sensitivity. Attentiveness is their "etiquette," regulating relations within the community, while with strangers they make an effort to apply at the same time the other people's patterns, namely those "good manners" which they think should regulate relations on "the Continent," in the big cities. In general it is as if the Lampedusan did not ask himself "What will he think of me if I behave in such a manner?" but rather, "What can he think that I am thinking of him?" Hence they are not touchy in the common meaning of this term, rather they are always careful not to hurt other people's sensitivity.

But, of course, attentiveness is not simply the commandment "love your enemy." On the island there are tensions, rivalries, and hatreds. Attentiveness does not abolish rivalry, but avoids crime, and on the island no blood has ever been shed. "*L'Appassoluto*" is rather disliked by the community; he passes for one who "is afraid of work," and also his honesty is doubted. He was at the head of the only attempt at founding a cooperative on the island, which would free the fishermen from exploitation by the *rigattieri*, who buy a crate of mullet for 10,000 lire and sell the fish at 3,000–4,000 lire a kilo on the "Continent," making — their expenses subtracted — a gain of about fifty to one hundred percent. The cooperative failed and no new initiative has been taken, for it is said while somebody gained everybody else lost by it. On a later occasion, when Appassoluto had equipped the largest and handsomest motor fishing boat on the island, everybody, including his relatives, followed with joy the ever deepening failure of his enterprise. But nobody attacked him openly or showed satisfaction, not even those whom the community considered his enemies. All were careful not to hurt the feelings of Appassoluto's brothers, and above all of his mother. Toward the man himself they took pains to show great interest and compassion, which he decoded correctly as "rotting his guts," and he showed in turn attentiveness to his family by not getting into a fight over the affair to avoid implicating the family.

Attentiveness was, of course, all-important in provoking the appearance at the harbor of Rosa and the other women. This attention was intended more for the community's sake than for their dear ones, far off at sea. It was necessary to inform relatives and friends that an accident was impending, and also to occupy the socially correct space: the harbor. From other points of the island grieving eyes might hover on the horizon, to anticipate the possibility of the boat's return. From the quay at the edge of the port the women would be the last able to see the arrival of any boat, but they themselves could be seen from every window looking out on the sea from above. Meanwhile other men and women came out from their doorways to occupy their space as comforters, whether later events would provoke smiles or tears.

When there is an accident, it is everybody's accident: the relatives have to retire into the house of the boat's chief, while all other houses remain empty; everybody is collected at the port, no longer waiting, but expressing their grief over the others and over themselves. Mourning lasts for months and years, involving, with different periods and degrees, even the remotest relatives. The dead man's family has the role of the mourning hero, while the community is the second main character rather than a choir. The so-called strict mourning imposes very hard restrictions, whose harshness is perceived even by those who wear it, but there is never a refusal to bear its weight. Mourning is much less a sign of personal grief, and much more a way, for the relatives, of reciprocating the grief shown by the community.

The rescue of zu Turi's boat also entailed clear examples of attentiveness. The rescue party met zu Turi's lost boat half way, as it was being hauled by a motor fishing boat of Greek *spugnari*. The axle of the boat's propeller had been broken, and could only be repaired by drawing the boat up on land. All day long they had been waiting for help, certain that it would arrive, and also knowing which boats would come. If the Greeks had not offered their aid, it should not have been sought, because the relatives, who had set off to rescue them, would have taken offense, as a mark of distrust in their readiness to come. But it was not possible to reject the help of the Greeks, for the foreigners would have taken it as an indication that the islanders are not willing to reciprocate help and hospitality.

Attentiveness was much in evidence when we were interviewing to learn about the structure of the fishing group. Did one select his relatives as crewmates? Then why did Pino M. not take Simone G., who was his cousin? Perhaps because he was not capable? Attentiveness broke in with ample praises for Simone's capability. Perhaps it was a relative's unluckiness — the good or poor catch he made according to the shoals and banks where he went to fish? Again attentiveness broke in, and on the subject of good fortune it became even more strict, because it is even more impolite to say to somebody that he is unlucky than to say he is less capable.

Another occasion on which to observe many instances of attentiveness is that of the festivities in honor of the Virgin of Porto Salvo. A few days after his rescue, we were invited by Zu Turi — our best friend among our informants — to join his group for these festivities.

Devotion to the Virgin of Lampedusa is scattered throughout the world and she is represented in paintings and statues and worshiped in shrines and churches. The most remote is the one of Rio de Janeiro, where the title due to the Señora de Lampedusa, since 1747, has been Patroness of Slaves. On the island, her shrine is at Cala Madonna, about two kilometers' distance from the inhabited area, in the church that was up to 1843 cut in two by a little gate behind which was "the room of the stone seats," used by the Muslim cult. In 1843 Sanvinsente found the statue on the ground, mutilated, and got it repaired, that it might become the symbol of the new colonization. Anglo-American bombing razed the church — a rare architectonic specimen of religious syncretism — to the ground, but this time the statue remained untouched, the sign of a miracle.

The festivities begin with a pilgrimage to the shrine and continue alternating religious rites and "civil" celebrations, closing each night with a show in the public square. Two Sundays before September 22 the whole population goes to Cala Madonna, to take the statue and bring it to the village church and then in a procession through the village streets. From the highest point of the rocks, the pageant looks like a colored serpent, but on mixing with the people one perceives it to be subdivided into groups, between which there are intervals of space. The impression of a compact body is not only due to perspective, for between the different groups members are continually detached as they hasten on or fall back according to convenience and respect — i.e. according to attentiveness. They exchange courtesy visits, with compliments and greetings.

It is during such visits that even today, though in a lesser proportion than in the past, young people become acquainted and marriages are arranged. It is clear that on a tiny island everybody is acquainted with everybody else since birth, and the young people who would be introduced to one another on this occasion have already been courting for some time, or at least have "looked at one another," while both of them ask, and receive an answer from the age group of their own sex: "Did he look at me?" "He looked at you." But the road to the shrine is the most suitable social space for the community to find out what it knows already.

Some go back and forth, from one group to the other, but always with an excuse: a shoe has got unlaced or a cigarette has to be lit in a contrary wind. There are the occasional "peacemakers" between two men or two families. Their observance of attentiveness is extremely difficult: each must be careful not to be the one who inserts himself into one of the two groups, in which case he would be considered by the other as part of the adverse group; also each must be careful as to the right time for mixing the two groups by coming and going between them. If a peacemaker knows times, spaces, and ways, he will be able to utter the cry: *"E che ne scordammo della Madonna?"* [Are we then forgetting the Virgin?]. The answering cry: *"Viva la Madonna di Porto Salvo, viva, viva!"* implicating both groups, makes them a single group.

Meanwhile other groups have observed the scene, without looking, and as soon as they hear that peace is made, freed from the weight of attentiveness to avoid taking sides with one or the other — to prevent "the quarrel," as they acutely say, from becoming incurable — they feel that now they can approach, and they begin to touch now one, now another, embracing them, kissing them, holding them by the hand or arm in arm.

The peacemaker's task is really a social drama; months ago the community has given him this task and for months he has been carrying it out. But the drama is critical for the marriageable girl and for the peacemaker, because an error of form in the last act might destroy months of patient preparation; such cases have happened. But it is not a final formal act, as is, for instance, the signing of an international treaty, even if its ritualistic solemnity is not to be undervalued. For the parties to "the quarrel" or to the love game, all the actions performed during the preparatory phases are projected (in a psychoanalytical sense) into the festival procession and hence all preceding approaches are formal. But it is then that the community becomes formally conscious of them. Substantially the agreement is considered to be dated as of the occasion of the festival. The two young people may *imparolarsi* [exchange the word, the promise of betrothal] on any day of the succeeding months; that the economic motives for "the quarrel" may be solved much later, continuing to drag on for weeks and months, is also a formal fact. In view of the arrangements that the families make, the official engagement may take place in any day of the year, but it also will be predated by the community to the day of the procession to the shrine.

To make peace after an oath of eternal hatred, and to exchange vows of eternal love in a nonrelevant place, would be a lack of attentiveness in respect to the community. Assent by the community has greater value than the sacrament or the laws of the state. In Lampedusa, the betrothed often do the *fuitina*, they pretend an elopement, or even an abduction, spending the night and a few following days in a relative's house and only later through a restricted and inexpensive ceremony, they make their peace with church and state.

On each of the three evenings, about 8 P.M., every family comes out of its house, carrying chairs upside down on their heads, and makes for the theater. In the center of the village a piece of accidental and apparently chaotic town planning has repeated the shamrock-leaf pattern of the port, with two squares, the church, and the municipal building, and with a broad space which, in the three days' festival, becomes an open-air theater. The actors are usually "poor devils" of the theatrical world, but that other poor devil, the organizer, introduces them as stars of national, even of international fame. Sometimes a comic actor or a singer who once had his moments of success and popularity turns up. But the public prefers child actors, who repeat the songs and imitate the gestures of well-known stars in cinema and television, or — if it has been a good year for fishing — a famous TV personality, who, however, bleeds to death the resources of the committee for civil festivities. Only the television star and the child star succeed in gaining applause; other performances end in silence.

The spectators sit on their chairs, after having contributed to the expenses, each according to his ability. They form groups of relatives, every year at the same place, excepting the first rows which are left to the youngest and most enthusiastic. The women keep their seats through the whole spectacle; the men, at every interval between items, stand up and exchange places as a courtesy. Not that the seat offered is necessarily better for seeing the stage, which has been mounted, the first day, on metal drums, poles and stones; the men in changing places tend to reconstruct, on the structure of each family nucleus, the structure of the fishing party.

THE CONFLICT OF TRADITIONS IN LAMPEDUSA: THE CONCEPTION OF REALITY IN AN ILLITERATE CULTURE

The process of modernization has been making its disruptive force felt on the island, as cited earlier. Modernization modifies the island, attacking it contemporarily on two sides: young men prefer to embark for fishing in the Atlantic, attracted not so much by high profits as by the system of social insurance, and thus discovering at the same time a citizen's rights in a modern state and a temporal dimension in conflict with their traditional orientation. They begin to think of the future, but still in terms of the ever-present: the future is the present of old people. They tell their children that they will have them get more schooling, in hopes of their gaining a diploma, a "piece of paper," which guarantees them a "permanent job," felt by old people as a predated pension.

On the other side, modernization attacks the island through speculation on land for the use of tourism, and the female element suddenly finds itself in possession of riches in the form of real estate.

Lampedusa is already prepared for mass tourism, and the old fishermen look at it in astonishment. Their children, on the other hand, have invented the image of a fish pierced by the underwater fisherman's trident; the precious image is printed on cheap sweaters and causes them to be sold at very high prices; in August the whole island overflows with them, and in megalomaniac dreams the image spreads the island all over "the Continent," throughout the world.

In the presence of these changes, we began to think of ourselves as the archaeologists of an oral culture and tradition, over which had been added, by successive layers, the written tradition, then the electric, then the electronic. And we thought that the illiterate tradition might fit somewhere in this stratification. Archaeologists, yes, but in a cataclysm where the waves of an earthquake constantly upset the layers — causing what is newest to sink to the bottom and the old to emerge — while a second earthquake might turn it upside down once more. After some months we came to understand that the illiterate culture is precisely in this cataclysmic situation. In the space of a little less than ten years, reality has become transformed in our presence; today, compared to such a near yesterday, the gestures, actions, and words of the oral tradition are often only a memory. Today we are confronted with a situation of conflict under which lives a community of illiterates, who must follow the weather to reduce the risks of their work, and must also follow the chronological time that is dictated by the dominant society of educated people.

There is an old fisherman, for example, who takes tourists around the island. His own experience in educated society was very brief: he left the island only once, in 1915, when he went by steamer to Sicily, by train to a city where he became a "war sailor" and, falling ill after only a few weeks, back to his island by steamer. Today, he fits himself and his boat into modernization and goes around and around the island, the whole day long, during the two tourist months of July and August. He cannot understand why tourists, making the journey he undertook in 1915, should pay him several thousand lire in order to photograph, from the sea, the coast, the creeks, the grotto. "And," says he, "they do not look at anything."

The old fisherman knows the coasts and the bottom of the sea as a scholar knows how books are arranged on the shelves of his library. But he knows them, one might say, globally — sea, land, and sky — and perceives them globally with his whole body, sight and smell, hearing and touch. When the sirocco or the east wind is blowing, the old sailor says that the sirocco has a smell that is not always the same. One smell is given to the wind by a grotto, while another smell comes from a beach. According to him, the smell — not the sirocco — determines the opportunity to go fishing, determines the boat's route, because the smell is perceived not only by the fisherman, the fish also perceive it. Apparently, in an earlier period, there were more names for the winds; these names corresponded perhaps to the different smells that the sea had, perhaps to the different "tastes" of the sea, because the fish tasted different. Today the winds bear names chosen by the educated people; today with a motor one can go fishing with any wind, but for the fisherman it is not only the fishing technique which has changed, not only man and his ability to perceive smells: the sea, the sky, and the fish have also changed. An entire world is lost, beyond repair, to a future world which may be or may not be. In the meantime, today, for the illiterate the different planes of reality are intermixed, confused.

A similar example of the conflict in traditions that confronts the members of an illiterate community is present in the case of Zu Sparagghiuni, manager of the local restaurant. Here is his complaint based on the imposition of the dominant educated society's chronology: during two months in the year he has to work all day long and part of the night to feed underwater-fishing tourists and sailors; in the remaining ten months the restaurant is transformed into a private dwelling, whose only clients are the pilots of the line plane and we anthropologists. Zu Sparagghiuni wonders why "those gentlemen," the summer tourists, are ready, being on a holiday, to eat badly and be served worse. He says that if they came from March to June, or in September and October, they would find the same sea, the same sunlight, and they might be treated like gentlemen. "But no; they come at the top of the heat, when the island is already full of tourists; they snatch chairs and forks from one another and corrupt my sons and grandchildren by tipping them hundreds and thousands of lire to steal from other gentlemen a dish of spaghetti or a bed on which to fling themselves. And they complain that prices are high, that there is not enough water for washing, and that the food is bad." And even among the islanders themselves, it is apparent that as traditional interpersonal ties are getting slacker "attentiveness" is diminishing.

The conception of reality for Lampedusa women and young people similarly entails a conflict between the oral and literate traditions of their illiterate culture. Airplanes and television have reached Lampedusa, so that Trapani has become nearer than before and Milan or Naples come into the houses of the population every day through the television screen. Historical progress has caused the island *fattucchiere* (sorcerers) to disappear, but that same progress makes it possible to go by air to Trapani where, it seems, there are good *fattucchiere* capable of freeing people from the *fattura* and of placing it on others. At night, when silence is absolute, the women recite: "Glorious Saint Monica/I am overwhelmed by you/Come from Naples and Milan/And give us news." This is followed seven times by Pater, Ave, and Gloria. After this the noises of the night attest to the working of sorcery: the noises of cocks, dogs, and bells become favorable signs; those of cats and children, unfavorable. And even a mother who declared that she did not believe in the "superstitions" about the *trizzi'e donna*, avoided cutting her son's hair because she feared hurting the feelings of the *lochi 'e casa*, which, another informant explained, "Punish us by appearing, if we tell what they do."

If your child falls ill you call a doctor, book a seat in the plane, use medicines, and make vows of alms and pilgrimages; you pray and hope, you act, you take trouble. If the doctor tells you that you must give your son sugar with his medicine, you must give it to him, and at the same time, you must not be embittered, if the child "turns sour," as your milk does. If, due to your sorrow, you forgot to throw the milk on the floor and to wash your breast with oil simultaneously, the fact that the same sorrow was also for your son is shown by the fact that he "became crooked." Later, when grown up, his appearance would cause others to cross themselves, to make the "sign" themselves, because his misfortune might become a misfortune for them as well. If, on the other hand, the child recovers, you carry it in the procession, the child wearing its *abitino* (ecclesiastical habit) as a friar if a boy and as a nun if a girl, to show that for that year the child belongs to the divinity that saved it. And, in gratitude, even if it is the last lobster left in the sea, the doctor will be the first to have it. The miracle has been performed by all, Virgin and doctor, medicine and vows. You must help yourself and everybody must help you.

When a fishing party forms in response to old Antonino's advice that "tomorrow morning they [fish] will pass at Cala Uccello," the youngest men of the crew, in those last hours of the night, act as if they are playing rather than working. The atmosphere of play is increased by the wary manner of their preparations that night: the fish must not hear the noise of their preparations. These young fishermen have, on their motorboats, an echo-sounding machine. To go fishing in rowboats, led by the voice of Antonino, who says he "feels" the fishes as he directs the boats from the rocks, actually does not seem like work to them. But they would never be so rude as to miss Antonino's fishing party; also experience should have taught them that he deserves to be trusted, for the boats come back with such heavy loads that they barely escape sinking.

It might be tempting to interpret these examples from Lampedusa as documenting a historical sequence that begins with superstitions and ends with a triumph of rational thought. We feel that such a sequence may not be "true" for all social strata and all ethnic categories; rather that the historical condition of subordinate strata and categories has resulted in a split and conflict-laden conception of reality, one that is characteristic of illiterate culture.

REFERENCES

CALCARA, PIETRO
1846 *Descrizione dell'isola di Lampedusa*. Palermo: R. Palgano.
CONTI, A.
1909 "L'isola di Lampedusa." Manuscript.
CHURCHILL, SIR WINSTON L. S.
1952 *The Second World War*, volume five: *Closing the ring*. London: Cassell.
CROWDER, MICHAEL
1968 *West Africa under colonial rule*. London: Hutchinson.
GALLI, MATILDE CALLARI, GUALTIERO HARRISON
1972 Partecipazione sul processo di formazione dell'ambiente urbano. *Parametro* 11:22–27.
1973 Tane e vermi: la cultura degli esclusi nel degrado urbano di Palermo. *Parametro* 16:22–29.
GOODY, JACK
1968 "Introduction," in *Literacy in traditional societies*. Cambridge: Cambridge University Press.
GUSSONE, GIOVANNI
1832 *Notizie sulle isole Linosa, e Lampione Lampedusa, e descrizione di una nuova specie di Stapelia che Trovasi in questa ultima*. Naples: n.p.
HALL, EDWARD T.
1963 A system for the notation of proxemic behavior. *American Anthropologist* 65(5):1003–1026.
HARRISON, GUALTIERO, MATILDE CALLARI GALLI
1970 La cultura analfabeta. *Le Scienze — Edizione Italiana di Scientific American* 22:11–21.
1973 *Né leggere né scrivere*, third edition. Milan: Feltrinelli.
LAMPEDUSA, GIUSEPPE TOMASI DI
1970 *Il Gattopardo*, sixteenth edition. Milan: Feltrinelli.
LEWIS, OSCAR
1961 *The children of Sanchez*. New York: Random House.
REDFIELD, ROBERT
1955 *The little community: viewpoints for the study of a human whole*. Chicago: University of Chicago Press.
SANVINSENTE, BERNARDO
1869 *L'isola di Lampedusa eretta a colonia dal munificentissimo nostro sovevano Ferdinando II*, second edition. Naples: Militare. (Originally published 1849.)

Business Structure in a Turkish City

MÜBECCEL B. KIRAY

RÉSUMÉ: STRUCTURE DU TRAVAIL DANS UNE VILLE TURQUE

Le but de cette communication est d'envisager les types d'organisation du travail et leur application en tant que révélateurs du changement social. Si l'on considère que le changement social associé à l'urbanisation et à l'industrialisation se reflète dans la structure de l'emploi, qui à son tour se réfléchit dans celle de l'organisation, l'auteur analysera dans cette perspective les caractéristiques du travail dans la ville d'Izmir. Celles-ci sont liées à un urbanisme à structure pré-industrielle et à un commerce organisé selon les modèles typiques du XIXᵉ siècle. La différenciation et l'organisation des affaires se situent actuellement sur trois niveaux : (1) les colporteurs, en nombre indéterminé, sans organisation ni spécialisation; (2) les petits artisans et commerçants, au nombre de 6000, cantonnés dans certains quartiers commerçants et connaissant un début d'organisation; (3) enfin les quelques 500 enterprises commerciales et industrielles, plus différenciées, plus spécialisées et organisées, nanties de capitaux, de sources d'énergie et de personnel. Elles sont enregistrées à la Chambre de Commerce d'Izmir et à la Chambre d'Industrie de la Région égéenne.

L'étude comparative de ces trois groupes en termes de quantité, de différenciation, de spécialisation et d'organisation révèle lá structure sociale du travail dans la ville d'Izmir où l'on peut affirmer, statistiques et tableaux comparatifs à l'appui, que l'activité de colportage est la plus largement représentée et regroupe le plus grand pourcentage de population tout en étant la moins organisée. Le petit artisanat, bien que dix fois plus important numériquement que les entreprises inscrites à la Chambre de Commerce, ne peut constituer un groupe defini par la spécialisation ni par l'autonomie du travail.

Enfin les études statistiques montrent que dans le monde des affaires proprement dit, le volume croissant du commerce ne va pas de pair avec la modernisation et l'expansion et que, par rapport au grand commerce, les entreprises de taille

Material for this study was collected in 1967–1968 in Izmir by various techniques, including a probability sample survey applied to the enterprises registered at the Chamber of Commerce or of Industry.

moyenne sont mieux organisées, plus actives et comportent un personnel plus qualifié.

The twentieth century may well be recognized as the age of organizations for modern industrial societies. In society at large, in industry and commerce, in government and politics, in philanthropy and entertainment, in communication and social service, organized activity is the common and dominant form. Modern industrial society exists with the readiness to organize itself and social development involves and implies organizational development. Social structural growth, by its nature, involves increasing complexity. One of the most important changes that occurs as organizations become larger and more complex is the development of administrative apparatus and the increase of specialization in division of labor. Given the conditions of modern mass society, in which specialization and interdependence are basic characteristics, no function could be performed properly except through the mechanism of large-scale organizations.

Max Weber felt this and wrote extensively on "bureaucracy," dealing basically with the inner dynamics of complex organizations (Weber 1946, 1947). He also indicated that preindustrial societies lack to a great extent such organizations. He treated the subject as a dichotomy between those societies which have complex organizations and those that do not. For a fast changing and developing society, however, it is important to know how such organizations grow and what role they play in general in the process of social change and development.

Recent literature on development has given considerable attention to change technology, to its economic relations as well as to its cultural and social psychological aspects such as valuations of and attitudes toward socioeconomic change. But very little has been written on the change and development of formal business organizations, which constitute the basic "social" aspect of development in societies as yet not industrialized. Most studies of complex organizations and work organizations have been restricted to modern industrial society, and very few analyses of social and economic development have focused specifically on the role of different types of organizations in the development process (see Udy 1971; Blau and Scott 1963; Stinchcombe 1964). It is proposed in this paper to investigate the possibility that types of organizations and the way such organizations develop may be an indicator of social development.

In a society undergoing urbanization and industrialization the trend is toward increasing emphasis on expertise, which stimulates organizational complexity. In other words social change associated with urbanization and industrialization reflects in occupational structure, which in turn reflects in organizational structure. Using material collected from Ismir, a metropolitan city on the coast of the Aegean Sea, with a population of about one million, on such social structural characteristics of business life, trends of specialization and organization as indicators of development in the socioeconomic life of a developing country will be discussed.

Today's business structure of Izmir has its origins in the preindustrial city structure and the intensive outer-directed commercial structure of the nineteenth century. The growth of business differentiation and organization out of that structure today manifests itself in three stages of evolution. First of all, there are *peddlers* of an unknown number, unorganized and with no specialization, concentrating their activities on the streets. They do not have a definite location. They are engaged in sales and repairs of various forms. Although most of them are in the commercial sector, some could be considered to be in the production and service sectors as well.

The second group is again not organized, but its activities have differentiated within its own domain, and a division of labor has set in. They are settled in certain shopping areas, and are labeled small traders and artisans (*esnaf*). This group handles small-scale trade and small-scale manufacturing. Even though single businesses do not involve any organization, within each trade and for each artifact there have been attempts at organization of "small proprietors associations." The number of these *esnaf* is estimated to be around sixty thousand.

Over these two groups are the commercial, industrial, and service enterprises, almost five thousand in number. This group is more differentiated, specialized, and organized, and has known quantities of capital, energy and power, wage workers, and administrative personnel. They are registered at the Izmir Chamber of Commerce and at the Aegean Region Chamber of Industry. The analysis of these three different groups of businesses in terms of number, differentiation, specialization, and organization will give us meaningful data for comparison of the social structure of business in Izmir.

PEDDLERS

The number of itinerant small traders — peddlers — has shown an incredible increase — in proportion to the increasing numbers of people, no longer tied to the land, which have migrated to the city. In fact these peddlers mainly serve this population, which has very low purchasing power. This group has neither specialization nor organization, and even though as a rule they have to obtain a sales permit from the municipality, it is not known how many have this document. Registrations at the municipal offices are very disorderly, as a result of the nature of the peddling. Through the years some of the registered peddlers have changed locality, some have changed their trade, some have left the city, and some have become janitors or factory workers without notifying the authorities. It is not possible to determine where and when each newspaper seller or fruit or vegetable peddler works.

In Izmir's business structure it is possible to differentiate peddlers into two types: mobile and stationary. Stationary peddlers (*işportacı*) sell lower quality goods than those of stores for lower prices, but without any control of profit and without paying any rent. Thus they further lower their costs to a minimum, maximize their accessibility to customers, and increase their profits. The goods they sell are mostly those that can be carried easily. These peddlers operate in the central shopping streets of the city, sometimes quietly, sometimes shouting, bringing together the functions of advertising and shop window display in one action. The term that indicates the stationary peddler (*işportacı*) is not used for those walking on the residential streets selling vegetables and similar goods, although the functioning of both types is the same. Peddlers increase their activities, especially during official or religious holidays, when stores are closed but the working population is free. Another advantage for the peddlers comes from the fact that, in the spatial structure of the shopping areas, retail shopping, in terms of the customer's purchasing power, is not differentiated at all, so that newly migrated people, unaccustomed to shopping in large cities, looking for cheap goods, can find them in the main retail sales area but without entering the stores if they do not wish to.

There are generally two ways of becoming a peddler. The first one involves starting the business with one's own capital, which may range from fifty to three thousand liras.[1] The second one involves borrowing goods from a shopkeeper and sharing the profit after selling them. Almost always the unemployed, even university students, try this kind of trading as a supplementary job. Some peddlers make attempts at selling in a certain place by registering with the shopkeepers' association. This is one step forward in terms of organizational development. Another movement in the 1960's involved attempts at gathering together all peddlers into an organization. This involved especially the peddlers of Anafartalar Caddesi, the most important retail sales area in Izmir. The attempt at organization came from administrative authorities. Salepçioğlu Hanı, one of the commercial buildings built at the beginning of the nineteenth century on the main retail shopping street, was rented from a trust, and the municipality, together with the peddlers built around five hundred small shops in the large courtyard of this building. The municipality then rented these shops to the peddlers for a nominal fee of two liras per month. However, as time went on, the peddlers again went out to the

---

[1]   In 1973 one American dollar was approximately fourteen Turkish liras.

streets, claiming the customers did not come to the courtyard. In 1968 almost ninety percent of these shops were used as storage areas by the peddlers. This case illustrates beautifully how the peddlers are forced to walk around to maximize their accessibility in the business district in order to make a profit.

Basically the things they sell and do are so diverse and disorderly that it is impossible to classify them. There are some types of peddling and some services that cannot be included in a certain division of labor or profession. Such "nondefinable" jobs exist not only in Izmir, and Turkey, but in all societies with the same socioeconomic structure. Peddling, with its very low contribution to production, in addition to being an involution, has really, in urban centers of underdeveloped societies, to be accepted as hidden unemployment due to migration from rural areas (Geertz 1968).

SMALL TRADERS AND ARTISANS

An extremely large part of trade and manufacturing in Izmir today is taken care of by what could be called small traders and manufacturers. The official name given them is *esnaf*, which is the same as that given to the premodern feudal trader. The term, *esnaf*, indicates the person dealing with trade in the business life of a preindustrial society. He is classified along with the craftsman who produces nonagricultural goods. However, nowadays the meaning of the term *esnaf* indicates only the small scale of the business. There is no relation between today's shopkeeper and, for example, the shopkeeper of the eighteenth century, in terms of division of labor, behavior and values, and type of organization — such as guilds. In fact, while the law uses the feudal term, *esnaf*, the shopkeepers use the term *occupation* for their activities, which reflects the type of division of labor of a modern industrial urban society. Artisans also are mostly concerned with activities of a modern order, such as electrical and radio repair, shirtmaking, driving or car repairing, and so on. These traders and artisans are organized as associations by law. There are forty-four registered associations in the municipality. It is estimated that their membership numbers around 60,000 which shows the large place small trading occupies in Izmir's business life.

The majority of today's manufacturing shopkeepers are tied to the established larger trader who does the marketing. This dependence increases when the same organization also supplies the raw materials. For example, when the members of the shirtmakers' association were against the price policy of the shirt wholesalers, they manifested their opposition by talking about resistance by striking, using the wage earners' terms for resistance. Even though small-scale services and manufacturers are organized through their associations, and manufacture with their own tools and sell their products themselves, they sometimes refer to themselves as employees, sometimes as employers. Because of this they form an in-between group and actually are very much aware of it.[2] Since the activities of shopkeepers are dispersed and not much differentiated, it is neither possible to attempt standardized, high-quality, high-volume production, nor to protect the handicraft nature of the high-quality craftsman production of older times. Therefore, although always struggling to become large-scale traders or manufacturers, this group still manifests the phenomenon of demanding their rights by striking. Another contrast is evidenced in the continual clash of this group's interests and demands with the interests of the more organized, more specialized traders and manufacturing factory-owners. If the latter group is to grow it is likely to be at the expense of the former. Much thought needs to be given to the encouragement of manufacturing shopkeepers if poor quality mass production is not wanted. It is still true today that the dominant manufacturing circle in Izmir comprises such businesses, which have their own newspapers and banks (Halk Bankası). These businesses receive special support from the government and are a source of obvious waste in resource utilization. For example, according to the figures of the regional planning office, seventy percent of the total value added in Izmir during 1965 was created in large-scale, organized industry, thirty percent in small manufacturing. Small manufacturing, however, employs sixty percent of the total number of employees (Bölge Plânlama Dairesi 1971). They also hinder the growth of impersonal business-to-business inter-relationships, as well as blocking any trend toward specialization and organization.

ORGANIZATIONS REGISTERED WITH THE CHAMBER OF COMMERCE AND INDUSTRY

At present in Izmir there are more than 5000 enterprises registered with the Chamber of Commerce or of Industry. These exhibit great heterogeneity in scope and nature. At least one quarter of all commercial enterprises and close to half of all manufacturers listed can in fact also be categorized as small trade and craft manufacturing organizations. They often work with the most primitive technology and organizational set-up, and their sales are confined to the local neighborhood market. Most of these are registered with the Chamber of Commerce or of Industry, not because their present scope merits it, but because by misrepresenting the value of their capital investment and gaining access to the chamber they

---

[2]   For a discussion of traditional "jobs" and modern "occupations" see Udy (1971) and Dahrendorf (1964).

hope to be eligible for better credit facilities and enhance their future prospects. There are numerous enterprises of a similar scope which have not registered with the chamber and hence remain in the small trade category.

Of those registered with the Chamber of Commerce or of Industry, that is, the enterprises which hypothetically occupy the highest echelons in the Izmir business and entrepreneurial hierarchy, 2.58 percent have no administrative personnel. An additional 50.5 percent mention a single employee working in an administrative capacity. One can easily surmise that this individual is in most cases a part-time accountant employed to ensure accuracy in bookkeeping and hence obviate any complications with the tax authorities. Thus when the size of the administrative component, including those working in a clerical capacity, is taken as a rough indicator of structural differentiation and organizational complexity, 53 percent of all the enterprises registered with the Chamber of Commerce or of Industry in Izmir, fall into the lowest two categories (see Table 1). As can be observed, 23 percent of the total number of enterprises employ two individuals in an administrative capacity; sixteen percent employ three to five and finally, seven percent employ six or more individuals who can be classified as administrative personnel. The proportion of enterprises which list twenty-five or more administrative personnel is only two percent. This panorama reveals that the complex and differentiated administrative structure associated with large enterprises in Western industrial societies cannot be observed in Izmir.

The internal differentiation and complexity of large-scale commerce in Izmir today does not appear to be very different from what it was at the end of the nineteenth century. The financial and industrial orga-

Table 1. Number of administrative personnel by type of enterprise

Enterprise		None	1	2	3–5	6–25	>25	Total
Small trader	n	5	32	2	1	–	–	40
	%	12.5	80.0	5.0	2.5	–	–	100.0
Merchant	n	3	60	18	5	–	–	86
	%	3.8	69.7	20.8	5.7	–	–	100.0
Wholesaler	n	–	7	5	3	1	–	16
	%	–	43.7	31.3	18.7	6.3	–	100.0
Import–export	n	–	7	9	4	–	–	20
	%	–	35.0	45.0	20.0	–	–	100.0
Manufacturing	n	–	30	27	23	10	6	96
	%	–	31.3	28.1	23.9	10.4	6.3	100.0
Service	n	–	18	6	6	4	–	34
	%	–	53.1	17.6	17.6	11.7	–	100.0
Contractors	n	–	2	6	9	1	–	18
	%	–	11.1	33.4	50.0	5.5	–	100.0
Total	n	8	156	73	51	16	6	310
	%	2.5	50.5	23.6	16.4	5.1	1.9	100.0

nizations on the other hand, appear to be more developed in this respect. The financial organizations, especially the banks, have become more differentiated structurally, as indicated by the growing size of the administrative component. They have also sought to establish branches in the various parts of the city and hence exhibit a progressively increasing degree of complexity. The big industrial organizations again often feel the need for large numbers of administrative personnel in organizing both production and sales.

The establishment of branches seems to be another important indicator of organizational complexity. It often reflects the differentiation of such structural components as sales and production. Eighteen percent of the enterprises in Izmir have branch sections. As far as the larger factories are concerned, such as chemicals, paint or textiles, a clear pattern is observable. First the administrative offices tend to become relocated in the central business district of the city, in the area densely populated by offices of various other firms, then a separate retail store is established. The process is thus a vertical hierarchical differentiation of functional divisions. Horizontal expansion in the form of increasing numbers of branches which perform identical functions, can be observed in the case of banks and transportation firms, which comprise 19.4 percent of the enterprises in our sample. No other type of enterprise has yet achieved a level of organizational complexity symbolized by the "chain stores" in the industrialized societies.

When the existing branch sections in Izmir are taken into consideration, it can be observed that in 68.6 percent of the cases the headquarters are also located in the city (see Table 2). For 26 percent the headquarters are located in other cities of Turkey. The import companies do not appear as branch sections of any particular firm abroad since they operate in an

Table 2.   Location of branch sections

	A branch section itself		Branch is in Izmir		Branch is in Aegean region		Branch is in other large city		Branch is in Anatolia		
	n	%	n	%	n	%	n	%	n	%	Total
Trader	1	20.00	4	80.00	–	–	–	–	–	–	5
Merchant	3	30.00	3	30.00	3	30.00	1	10.00	–	–	10
Wholesaler	2	28.57	4	57.15	1	14.28	–	–	–	–	7
Manufacturer	2	8.69	7	30.43	5	21.74	9	39.14	–	–	23
Import–export	1	25.00	1	25.00	1	25.00	–	–	1	25.00	4
Service	5	33.34	2	13.33	1	6.66	2	13.33	5	33.34	15
Construction and architecture	1	33.33	–	–	2	66.67	–	–	–	–	3
Total	15		21		13		12		6		67

independent representational capacity. Some of the foreign export companies are not "branches" since, although established by foreigners, they are based in Izmir.

Regardless of how one evaluates it, the scope of organizational activity is too low for expansion in the form of new branches. Only about 13 percent of the establishments in our sample have attempted to increase the size of their administrative component in recent years. When production, number of workers, and machine renovation are taken into consideration, then the proportion of enterprises which have expanded goes up to 25 percent.

Distribution of the labor force in terms of skills, excluding the administrative component, could be taken as a second important criterion of assessment and reveals an additional dimension of modernization in business life from a sociological point of view. In line with the general tendency observed in nonindustrialized societies, the majority of enterprises in Izmir are one-man establishments and the overall concentration in terms of numbers is in the unskilled category. When we keep in mind that cleaning and allied service workers are included in the "unskilled" category, the number of establishments which do not even utilize this sort of help is a surprisingly high 31 percent, as can be observed in Table 3. The number of workers employed by commercial enterprises such as traders, merchants, importers, wholesalers, and so on, never exceeds ten. Manufacturing enterprises are more heterogeneous in this respect but still, the proportion of establishments that employ ten or fewer workers constitutes more than 40 percent of the enterprises. Thus the concentration is again in the lower categories.

Table 3. Number of unskilled workers by type of enterprise

Enterprise		None	1–10	11–100	100	Total
Trade	n	18	22	–	–	40
	%	45.0	55.0	–	–	100.0
Commerce	n	45	41	–	–	86
	%	52.4	47.6	–	–	100.0
Wholesale	n	9	7	–	–	16
	%	56.3	43.7	–	–	100.0
Import–export	n	8	12	–	–	20
	%	40.0	60.0	–	–	100.0
Manufacturing	n	7	45	28	16	96
	%	7.3	46.8	29.2	16.7	100.0
Service	n	11	20	3	–	34
	%	32.3	59.0	8.7	–	100.0
Construction	n	–	7	10	1	18
	%	–	39.0	55.5	5.5	100.0
Total	n	98	154	41	17	310
	%	31.6	49.7	13.2	5.5	100.0

Forty percent of the establishments do not employ any workers who may be classified in the skilled category. As can be observed in Table 4 below, those which utilize up to five skilled workers constitute another 42 percent. Apart from these two groupings, which make up 60 percent of all enterprises, the number of skilled workers employed varies considerably, but never exceeds thirty in number (see Table 4).

Table 4.   Number of skilled workers by type of enterprise

| Enterprise | Number of skilled workers | | | | | | | | | |
| | None | | 1–5 | | 6–10 | | 10 or more | | Total | |
	n	%	n	%	n	%	n	%	n	%
Trader	24	60.00	16	40.0	–	–	–	–	40	100.0
Merchant	53	61.7	31	36.0	–	–	2	2.3	86	100.0
Wholesaler	6	37.5	7	43.8	–	–	3	18.7	16	100.0
Import–export	8	40.0	10	50.0	2	10.0	–	–	20	100.0
Manufacturing	24	25.0	39	40.7	11	11.4	22	22.9	96	100.0
Services	9	26.5	17	50.1	2	5.8	6	17.6	34	100.0
Construction	1	5.5	10	55.6	4	22.2	3	16.7	18	100.0
Total	125	40.3	130	42.0	19	6.1	36	11.6	310	100.0

The graduates of vocational-technical schools, trained as skilled workers of superior capacity and qualified to work as foremen, are employed in conspicuously limited numbers. It can be observed in Table 5 that only 13 percent of the enterprises employ graduates of vocational-technical schools, and half of these are confined to one worker. The explanation for this could be twofold. On the one hand, the training received by vocational-technical school graduates prepares them for work in small establishments rather than large enterprises. Regardless of how small or unproductive it may be, the graduates also prefer to work in small shops of their own, instead of joining the lower-middle ranks of a large enter-

Table 5.   Number of vocational-technical school graduates employed by type of enterprise

| Enterprise | Number of vocational-technical school graduates employed | | | | | | | |
| | None | | 1–5 | | 6 or more | | Total | |
	n	%	n	%	n	%	n	%
Trader	39	97.5	1	2.5	–	–	40	100.0
Merchant	85	98.9	1	1.1	–	–	86	100.0
Wholesaler	14	87.5	2	12.5	–	–	16	100.0
Import–export	19	95.0	1	5.0	–	–	20	100.0
Manufacturing	70	73.0	22	22.9	4	4.1	96	100.0
Service	31	91.4	2	5.8	1	2.8	34	100.0
Construction	12	66.7	6	33.3	–	–	18	100.0
Total	270	87.1	35	11.2	5	1.6	310	100.0

prise. The entrepreneurs on the other hand often fail to recognize the superior training of vocational-technical school graduates and are reluctant to employ them in responsible positions at higher wages. Thus the lack of specialization and differentiation in organizational life as a characteristic of social structure is once again reflected in the training and employment of vocational-technical school graduates.

As far as the university graduates, the top of the hierarchy of specialization, are concerned, in 75 percent of the enterprises, there are none employed (see Table 6). As can be observed, the main concentration of university graduates is in construction and finance institutions. When we keep in mind that establishments which do not employ any university graduates and those where only one, often the owner himself, is a university graduate, constitute 90 percent of the organizations in our sample, the paucity of specialization and differentiation in the employment structure of business is once again revealed.

Table 6. Number of university graduates by type of enterprise

| Enterprise | Number of university graduates employed | | | | | | | |
| | None | | 1–5 | | 6 or more | | Total | |
	n	%	n	%	n	%	n	%
Trader	39	97.5	1	2.5	–	–	40	100.0
Merchant	71	82.6	15	17.4	–	–	86	100.0
Wholesaler	7	43.8	8	50.0	1	6.2	16	100.0
Import–export	17	85.0	3	15.0	–	–	20	100.0
Manufacturing	64	66.7	28	29.2	4	4.1	96	100.0
Service	23	67.8	5	14.6	6	17.6	34	100.0
Construction	3	16.6	13	72.3	2	11.1	18	100.0
Total	224	72.6	73	23.2	13	4.2	310	100.0

Communication Patterns Developed in Organizational Interaction

If one of the dimensions of complexity of the organization as a social development shows itself in the number and type of specialized people they employ, and the subunits into which they have been organized, another one consists of the intensity of the interactions the unit organization has with its environment for its interdependent relations. As a representative aspect of such interactions the communication patterns of business establishments in Izmir have been examined in order to see social development in a perspective of intensity of interactions, which should also be parallel to organizational development. The pattern of communication, in form and intensity, seems to differentiate according to the organizational development of the business establishment. The communication patterns of the 60,000 and more small traders and artisans (*esnaf ve zanaatkar*) of Izmir who were not registered with the Chamber of Commerce or of Industry seem to vary. Since in the sample contact could not be established with a group representing the unregistered small traders, it was attempted to investigate their communications through observations by participation. According to the findings, in addition to ordinary channels of communication, such as letters and telephone, both small hotels in Izmir and the coffeehouses established within the central business district seem to play an important role in the intracity and intraregion communications of these establishments.

Small hotels have other functions in the flow of people and communications between the city and the region than that of providing shelter to the transient population in the city. First of all, the majority of the small hotels receive customers from one particular part of the region, in fact often from a certain settlement in that region. A hotel specializing in this way in the course of events assumes some of the communication functions. The hotelkeeper or the clerk provides the connection between the city and the village the customers come from. The region can naturally utilize telephones, letters and cables; but people often resort to the hotel to send small parcels or to forward messages. An additional feature complementing this process is the arrangement of daily buses leaving from the hotel and operating between Izmir and the settlement from which the hotel gets most of its customers. Written or oral messages are left at the hotel, the hotel gives them to the bus driver, who delivers them to the village or town.

Since transportation also is not completely organized, most of the buses leave from the municipal stations but also stop in front of these hotels before leaving the city. The number of passengers the buses get from the stations is greater, so it is not for the sake of passengers that buses change route but for the sake of the importance of the messages they carry from the hotels to the villages. It is not possible to detect the intensity of this flow, but it can be inferred to be quite strong if we keep in mind that 50 percent of hotels in Izmir have specialized in attracting customers from single settlements, and forty percent of these hotels provide such "convenience" for communication, according to another probability sample survey applied to hotels.

As far as coffeehouses are concerned, they have a well-defined role in the intracity communication. Business people who do not have a specific location (such as construction foremen and repairmen), or transport people who do not belong to an organization, have certain coffeehouses as their base. Contact with such people is accomplished by telephone, by sending a messenger, or by coming in person to that certain coffeehouse. The best example of this type of communication is a coffeehouse located in the middle of the business center. Since the 1880's this place has been a coffeehouse where coachmen wait to be called to work. If a coachman is not there when he gets a call, the owner of the coffeehouse, or his helper, delivers the message when he comes. The only aspect that has shown a change over time has been the addition of truck drivers to the coachmen, and the changing of the ratio between these two groups. Such a communication, which is unorganized and has no impersonal relationship pattern or specialization, corresponds to a social structure which is in transition to a more rational and efficient one.

For the business enterprises registered in Chamber of Commerce or of Industry, and thereby in our sample, the dominant communication channel seems to be the telephone. Letter and cable follow it (see Table 7). From such a dominance one could infer that there is not much concern about keeping records in business establishments. If telephone communications were recorded, this would have been reflected in the number of letters or cables. The type of communication that was closest to face-to-face communication seems to be the one preferred most. Another interpretation might be that businesses were aware that the more advanced technology yields higher effectiveness and satisfaction, and makes up for what is lost by lack of organization. If this is accepted then the fact is that even in such an underdeveloped and underdifferentiated business structure the most rational technology is the one most advanced.

Table 7. Communication type and amount by enterprises

	Letter		Telegram		Telephone		Total	
	n	%	n	%	n	%	n	%
None	63	20.3	169	54.5	40	12.9	272	29.2
Less than one per day	64	20.7	79	25.5	–	–	143	15.4
1–10 per day	143	46.1	49	15.8	146	47.1	338	36.4
11–20 per day	17	5.5	4	1.3	48	15.5	69	7.4
More than 20 per day	18	5.8	2	0.6	73	23.6	93	10.0
Did not state	5	1.6	7	2.3	3	0.9	15	1.6
Total	310	100.0	310	100.0	310	100.0	930	100.0

The differences of intensity between all kinds of commercial and all kinds of manufacturing activities show interesting variations. While the average number of communications per area of business per day was forty-four for import–export firms, for middle-scale manufacturing it was sixty, in large-scale manufacturing it was almost ninety-five, in factory production it was one hundred and twenty-seven. Thus the communications made by large industrial enterprises are triple those of the largest trade activities such as importing and exporting, an activity which arranges buying and selling over a large region and involves many foreign countries (see Table 8).

Table 8.   Number of communications per day per enterprise

Enterprise	Letter	Telegram	Telephone	Total
Trader	0.90	0.01	3.72	4.63
Merchant	1.99	0.22	8.69	10.90
Wholesaler	4.09	1.27	10.20	15.56
Import-export	4.20	4.54	35.36	44.10
Construction	4.55	0.25	27.60	32.40
Service	9.90	4.34	42.30	56.54
Small manufacturing	3.52	0.24	8.88	12.64
Medium manufacturing	9.60	1.95	49.95	61.50
Large manufacturing	20.43	1.18	72.85	94.46
Factory manufac- turing	23.00	3.50	108.15	134.65

CONCLUSIONS

Our discussion up to here shows that in Izmir peddling, with its most diverse and disorderly activities, constitutes a major part of business life and serves the largest clientele but lacks any organizations. In fact the very nature of this type of business, as we have seen, thwarts even the best intentions to give it some organization or order. The small traders and craftsmen, although altogether modern in their context, with their small business characteristics, are still a section of business life ten times larger than the relatively organized Chamber of Commerce or of Industry members, but they both organizationally as well as in their relations with other businesses display characteristics that could not be considered either as specialized "occupations" or independent "jobs." Among the relatively organized business the data here has shown that growth in the volume of commerce does not entail concomitant modernization and expansion in terms of specialization or new modes of organization. Apart from large industry and large service organizations such as banks the potential for growing specialization and increasing organizational complexity appears to be very limited. In comparison with large-scale commerce even medium-sized industry is a more efficient type of work organization, as revealed in our discussion of numbers of administrative personnel, numbers and skills of workers, and the intensity of communications.

REFERENCES

BLAU, P., W. R. SCOTT
  1963 *Formal organizations*. London: Routledge and Kegan Paul.
BÖLGE PLÂNLAMA DAIRESI
  1971 *Ege bölgesi* [The Aegean region]. Ankara: Plânlama.
DAHRENDORF, RALF
  1964 Recent changes in the class structure of European societies. *Dædalus* 93(1):224–270. (Partially reprinted 1969 as "The service class," in *Industrial man*. Edited by Tom Burns, 140–150. Harmondsworth: Penguin).
GEERTZ, C.
  1968 *Agricultural involution*. Berkeley: University of California Press.
STINCHCOMBE, A. L.
  1969 "Social structure and the invention of organizational forms," in *Industrial man*. Edited by Tom Burns, 153–195. Harmondsworth: Penguin.
UDY, S. H.
  1971 *Work in traditional and modern society*. Englewood Cliffs, N. J.: Prentice-Hall.
WEBER, MAX
  1946 *Essays in sociology*. Translated by H. Gerth and C. Wright Mills. New York: Oxford University Press.
  1947 *The theory of social and economic organization*. Translated by A. M. Henderson and Talcott Parsons. New York: Oxford University Press.

Biographical Notes

BRANIMIR BRATANIĆ (1910–   ) was born in Jastrebarsko, Croatia, Yugoslavia, and educated at the University of Zagreb where he earned diplomas in Slavic Studies and Ethnology and later a Ph.D. Presently he is a Professor in and Chairman of the Department of Ethnology and Director of its Ethnological Institute, Faculty of Philosophy, University of Zagreb. His research has been in the area of European ethnology, especially on the history of plowing implements, and on ethnological methodology, with particular emphasis on ethnological cartography as an instrument of research. He was a founding member and vice-president of the Ethnological Society of Yugoslavia and is Chairman of the Committee for the Ethnological Atlas of Yugoslavia. On an international level, he has been a member of the Permanent International Committee on Research on the History of Agricultural Implements, President of the Standing International Atlas Commission and Chairman of the Organizing Committee of the Ethnological Atlas of Europe and Its Bordering Countries. He also has served on the editorial board of international scientific journals such as *Current Anthropology*, *Ethnologia Europaea*, and *Ethnologia Slavica*.

MATILDE CALLARI GALLI (1934–   ) is currently Professor of Cultural Anthropology at the Università di Bologna (Italy). She has conducted extensive research on educational problems among the illiterate communities of southern Italy (Sicily, Lampedusa). Her primary interest is the use of space and the problems of communication in urban settings. Mrs. Matilde Callari Galli is the author of several publications on the relationship between education and culture and communication and culture.

JEAN CUISENIER (1927–   ) was born in Paris. He attended university in Paris, where he took a degree in Philosophy and, later, a Ph.D. in Literature and Human Sciences. His first research was done in Tunis, where he spent five years. This research resulted in publications in the areas of economic anthropology and Arabic and Turkish kinship systems. His appointment as Vice-Director of the Centre de Sociologie européenne resulted in research on Turkey, Yugoslavia, and Spain. Since 1968 he has been Director of the Centre d'Ethnologie Française at the Centre National de la Recherche Scientifique as well as Director of the Musée National des Arts et Traditions Populaires. He also teaches at the Ecole des Hautes Etudes en Sciences Sociales and edits several publications, notably the journal *Ethnologie Française*. His current interest is in French anthropology.

BARBARA K. HALPERN (1931–   ) received a B.A. in Geography and Geology from Barnard College, and an M.A. in Linguistics and a Ph.D. in Anthropology from the University of Massachusetts, Amherst. She has been a research associate at the University of Massachusetts and is presently devoting full time to writing. During the past twenty-five years she has conducted extensive field research in southeastern Europe and Southeast Asia and has coauthored several books. Her articles have appeared in diverse journals and anthologies and reflect a growing interest in women's roles, aspects of oral traditional behavior, and symbolic anthropology. Current work on an ethnography of communication in rural Serbia draws on fourteen field trips to that region as well as on comparative work with Serbian immigrants to North America.

JOEL M. HALPERN (1929–   ) was born in New York City. He received his B.A. from the University of Michigan in 1950 and his Ph.D. in Anthropology from Columbia University in 1956. He has been Professor of Anthropology at the University of Massachusetts, Amherst since 1967. He has done fieldwork in Yugoslavia, Laos, and the Arctic. His publications include *The changing village community* (1967), *A Serbian village in historical perspective* (with Barbara K. Halpern, 1972) as well as articles and monographs dealing with Southeast Asia, urbanization, and peasant societies. His current research interests concern historical demography and social structure.

GUALTIERO HARRISON (1936–   ) is currently Professor of Cultural Anthropology at the Università di Padova (Italy). His main research interests are focused on illiterate culture (he has done fieldwork for several years in four Sicilian communities and in Lampedusa) and on bilingualism and biculturalism (fieldwork in Italo-Albanian communities in southern Italy). He has published essays and books on these subjects.

CLAUDE KARNOOUH (1940–   ) was born in Paris. He received a degree in Chemistry from the Sorbonne and in Ethnology from the University of Paris X–Nanterre. For some time he taught anthropology at the latter university. Currently he is a chargé de recherches at the Centre National de la Recherche Scientifique (Groupe de Recherches Sociologiques Paris X–Nanterre). After conducting field studies in French rural communities, he is now engaged in field research in northern Rumania with special emphasis on the social hierarchy and the ritual life among those peasants who are not part of collectivistic organizations.

MÜBECCEL B. KIRAY. No biographical data available.

WILLIAM H. McNEILL (1917–   ) was born in Vancouver, Canada. He received a B.A. and M.A. from the University of Chicago and a Ph.D. in History from Cornell. After service in the U.S. Army during World War II he joined the faculty of the University of Chicago in 1947 and has remained there since. He has written about fifteen books on European and world history and is a member of the Philosophical Society, the American Academy of Arts and Sciences, and the British Academy.

MIHAI POP (1907–   ) was born in Maramureş, Rumania, studied Slavistics and Ethnology at the universities of Bucharest, Prague, Warsaw, Krakow, and Bonn, and received a Ph.D. from Bratislava University. He is an Honoured Professor at Bucharest University and has conducted research on oral literature, and on social structures, norms and rites in communities in Rumania and other parts of central and southeastern Europe which have oral cultural traditions. He is Editor of the *Revue of Ethnography and Folklore*, President of the International Society for Ethnology and Folklore, and an Honorary Fellow of the American Society of Semiotics and of the International Association for Semiotic Studies.

MARTINE SEGALEN (1940–   ) earned a Doctorat du 3e cycle in Sociology. At present she is a chargée de recherches at the Centre National de la Recherche Scientifique (Centre d'Ethnologie Française) and attachée to the Departement Coutumes, Rituels et Symbols (Musée National des Arts et Traditions Populaires). She has studied — through fieldwork and the use of demographical, historical, and anthropological methods — the family, marriage, and social relationships in French rural communities and is now shifting her attention to urban ethnology through the study of some popular celebrations in the Paris area.

PAUL HENRI STAHL (1925–   ) graduated in Sociology and received his Ph.D. at the University of Bucharest and is now Directeur d'études associé (Professor) at the Ecole des Hautes Etudes en Sciences Sociales (Sorbonne) and a member of the Laboratory of Social Anthropology. His specialization is in the study of the social life of southeastern Europe, and his publications concern social organization, housing and settlement, and folk arts.

Index of Names

Index of Subjects